WAR
&
PEACE

D1365424

Recent Titles in the
Children's and Young Adult Literature Reference Series
Catherine Barr, Series Editor

Popular Series Fiction for Middle School and Teen Readers:
A Reading and Selection Guide
Rebecca L. Thomas and Catherine Barr

Fantasy Literature for Children and Young Adults:
A Comprehensive Guide. Fifth Edition
Ruth Nadelman Lynn

The Children's and Young Adult Literature Handbook:
A Research and Reference Guide
John T. Gillespie

A to Zoo: Subject Access to Children's Picture Books. Seventh Edition
Carolyn W. Lima and John A. Lima

Best Books for Children: Preschool Through Grade 6. Eighth Edition
Catherine Barr and John T. Gillespie

The Newbery/Printz Companion:
Booktalk and Related Materials for Award Winners and Honor Books
John T. Gillespie and Corinne J. Naden

Books Kids Will Sit Still For 3: A Read-Aloud Guide
Judy Freeman

Classic Teenplots: A Booktalk Guide to Use with Readers Ages 12–18
John T. Gillespie and Corinne J. Naden

Best Books for Middle School and Junior High Readers: Grades 6–9.
Supplement to the First Edition
John T. Gillespie and Catherine Barr

Best Books for High School Readers: Grades 9–12.
Supplement to the First Edition
John T. Gillespie and Catherine Barr

WAR
&
PEACE

**A GUIDE TO LITERATURE
AND NEW MEDIA**
GRADES 4–8

Virginia A. Walter

A Member of the Greenwood Publishing Group

Westport, Connecticut ◆ London

Library of Congress Cataloging-in-Publication Data

Walter, Virginia A.
  War & peace : a guide to literature and new media : grades 4–8 / By Virginia
A. Walter.
      p. cm. — (Children's and young adult literature reference)
  Distinctive title: War and peace
  Includes bibliographical references and indexes.
  ISBN 1-59158-271-7 (pbk : alk. paper)
  1. War. 2. Peace. 3. Children and war. 4. War—Bibliography. 5. Peace—
Bibliography. 6. Children and war—Bibliography. I. Title. II. Title: War and
peace.
  U21.2.W3446 2007
  016.3036'6   2006030671

British Library Cataloguing in Publication Data is available.

Library of Congress Catalog Card Number: 2006030671
ISBN: 1-59158-271-7

Libraries Unlimited, 88 Post Road West, Westport, CT 06881
A Member of the Greenwood Publishing Group, Inc.
www.lu.com

Printed in the United States of America

The paper used in this book complies with the
Permanent Paper Standard issued by the National
Information Standards Organization (Z39.48–1984).

10 9 8 7 6 5 4 3 2 1

TABLE OF CONTENTS

PART III: RESOURCES FOR ADULTS

APPENDIX AND INDEXES

INTRODUCTION

IN 1991, WHEN AMERICAN SOLDIERS WERE FIGHTING a war in a desert that many of us had trouble finding on a map, I wrote a book about war and peace in children's literature. That book, *War and Peace Literature for Children and Young Adults: A Resource Guide to Significant Issues* (1993) is now out of print but available in many libraries. It aimed to be comprehensive in its coverage of books published through 1991 for children from the preschool years through early adolescence.

By the time that book was published in 1993, the first Gulf War had ended; and the United States was at least temporarily at peace. However, even then one could see the seeds of the next war in the events of the last. President George H. W. Bush had talked about going back to Iraq and "finishing the job," presumably by eliminating Saddam Hussein. Now his son has taken on that challenge himself, and we are most decidedly at war. This is a strange war we are fighting. It is being played out primarily in the country of Iraq, but the enemy is a stateless and amorphous "terrorism." It is hard to understand how we will win this war or how we will even know that we have won.

When I wrote the introduction to the 1993 book, I observed that the urgency of the nuclear threat seemed to have eased with the end of the Cold War. Now we are again worrying about what it means if two "rogue states," Iran and North Korea, develop nuclear weapons.

This is a book for adults who care about children living in the frightening, complex, and uncertain world of the 21st century. It is an increasingly interdependent world in which events in Kabul or Pyongyang can suddenly make a difference in Los Angeles or Minneapolis. This book presents literature and information as vehicles for creating frames of reference, shared meanings, and scaffolds of knowledge. It urges adults to use books and information as starting points for dialogues with children about war and peace.

Adults often find it difficult to talk to children in their care about issues and events that are important in the adult world, about things that really matter. We feel awkward about communicating the facts of life and uncertain about how best to talk about death, religion, violence, injustice, racism, evil, and war. What these subjects have in common is a high level of abstraction and an ideological burden. How do we tell a 10-year-old that her father has died or that "nigger" and "kike" are bad words? How do we explain the September 11, 2001, attacks on the World Trade Center without indicting all Islamic people? How do we tell a 12-year-old that some men hate our country enough that they are willing to kill themselves if it will do us harm? What is the child capable of understanding? How much truth should one tell? Sometimes books can provide the language and the frame of reference to get us started on these difficult conversations. Books can extend a child's experiences beyond his or her own everyday world and make abstract or historical concepts more concrete and comprehensible.

HOW THIS BOOK IS ORGANIZED

Part I provides background material for the adult who plans to share books and information about war and peace with children in grades four through eight. Chapters here discuss children and war, some issues relating to children's information needs and rights, and techniques for sharing books with children. Part II is the heart of the book, containing thematic resource lists: War as History, Hope and Glory, The Consequences of War, The Horrors of War, The American Home Front, Peace and Alternatives to War, and two case studies that pull together many thematic strands—The Trojan War and September 11, 2001. Each resource list has an introduction that helps to contextualize the books and new media contained in it. The resources included here have primarily been published or created since 1991, picking up where my earlier book left off. A few classics from earlier times have been repeated here, however. The cut-off date for resources is 2004. Part III contains two resource lists of adult materials: Children and War, Children and Peace; and Children's Literature About War and Peace. Finally, a number of indexes provide multiple points of access to the resources.

PART I

THE RIGHT BOOK FOR THE RIGHT CHILD AT THE RIGHT TIME

CHILDREN AND WAR

WHY CONNECT CHILDREN WITH BOOKS ABOUT war and peace? The answers to this question vary, depending on one's perspectives on childhood and one's political opinions. Here is a multi-faceted rationale for leading children to books that will give them a framework and foundation for forming their own opinions.

WAR IS A FACT OF 21ST-CENTURY LIFE.

War, or the threat of war, has been in the news for as long as I can remember. Here are the stories on the front page of the national edition of the *New York Times* on Saturday, July 8, 2006: the ongoing military response to the killing of 24 Iraqi civilians by Marines in November 2005; the arrest of suspects in a failed plot to bomb train tunnels in New York; the resurgence of Taliban forces in Afghanistan; and the use of the Internet by military families as a way to stay in touch. The two remaining stories deal with letters of complaint to mayors of New York that have been saved in the municipal archives and a possible scandal involving an American music producer who was arrested in Dubai and various influential Americans, including Senator Orrin Hatch.

The *Los Angeles Times* headlines the same story about the New York tunnel plot. It also has a piece about the Lebanese female attorney who is defending Saddam Hussein in his war crimes trial and another about the death of a local Marine who had proposed to his girlfriend last year at home plate in Angel Stadium. Non-war-related articles deal with the Mexican presidential election, the trial of a Chinese businessman on charges of corruption, and a human-interest story about a 30-year high school reunion.

Most of the 9- to 14-year-olds whose interests and information needs we are addressing in this book are probably not avid newspaper readers. Sports, entertainment, and popular culture may hold more interest for many of them. However, it cannot escape their attention that they live in a world at war. If past history is any indicator, they will also grow up to inherit a world at war. American boys will register for the draft when they turn 18. Boys and girls alike will consider the possibility of military service as a career, a patriotic duty, or a means of acquiring educational and occupational benefits. They will be called upon to make political choices based on their knowledge of world events as well as their own values and opinions. They will need to understand where they stand on the subjects of war and peace.

WARS ARE SIGNIFICANT HISTORICAL AND SOCIOLOGICAL EVENTS.

If war were to be miraculously ended for all time tomorrow, children of today would still need to know about past wars. Wars have shaped the world they live in today. Northern Ireland, the former Yugoslavia, Uganda, Palestine, and Israel are just a few regions of the world in which conflicts have continued for decades with roots far in the past and the cycle of violence being passed on to each succeeding generation.

One cannot understand American history without understanding the wars that have dominated it. Historians Fred Anderson and Andrew Cayton (2005) assert that Americans like to think of themselves as a peace-loving people. This belief leads us to think that we fight wars only to make the world a better, safer, freer place. We give pride of place on the Mall in Washington, D.C., as well as in our national memory to our own Revolution, the Civil War, and World War II—wars for freedom that are the central defining moments in American history. However, Anderson and Cayton (p. xiii) point out that we have also fought wars for no other reason than to extend our power and our empire—the War of 1812, the Mexican-American war, the Spanish-American War, and our many wars against the Native Americans. These wars are also part of our history and must be accounted for.

These are complicated issues, and most of us will take a lifetime to sort them out and to form our own opinions about them. We do our children a great service by helping them to construct the foundation of information on which they can build a scaffold of knowledge and understanding.

WAR AFFECTS CHILDREN AS WELL AS ADULTS.

In some parts of the world, children take up arms against their perceived enemies. Whether they do so voluntarily or through coercion, they are active combatants. Children are also victims of wars fought in their own backyards.

The United States does not release data about civilian casualties in the Iraq War. However, the British anti-war group Iraq Body Count estimates the number to be between 38,960 and 43,397 ("Iraq Body Count," 2006). Almost every day brings heartrending stories of children wounded, killed, or orphaned through sectarian violence or as collateral damage by U.S. troops. Suat Mohammed, an Iraqi psychologist, spoke as well of the emotional toll being exacted on the children who witness these acts of violence day after day and on the parents who don't know how to protect them or comfort them. "Children are growing afraid to interact with other children. They are afraid of relationships. This generation, when it grows up, will create an unstable, weak society. They will curse us for what we have wrought in Iraq" (Levey, 2005, p. A7).

Here in the United States, both fathers and mothers have been called up for service overseas. American children have lost parents in this war. The Pentagon offers a number of programs—including puppet shows—designed to help children develop resilience as they cope with a parent called up for active duty ("War's Trauma . . . ," 2005). The nonprofit National Military Family Association also recognizes that many soldiers serving abroad have children at home. Their Web site offers many useful links to resources that can help when one or more parent is deployed overseas (National Military Family Association, 2006).

Young people have not been enlisted as combatants on the American home front nor have they been specifically targeted with propaganda in our more recent wars, as they were in World War II. However, some young people have written letters to men and women serving in Iraq and Afghanistan, usually as part of a group effort organized by a teacher or youth group leader. They have joined their parents in marches and demonstrations in support of or opposition to the war in Iraq.

Civil wars and political unrest in many parts of the world not only involve children directly in violence; they also produce refugees and the phenomenon of unaccompanied children seeking safe havens. Some of those refugee children will eventually come to the United States and sit in American classrooms, bringing their wartime memories with them. This may be reason enough for a book that links children to information about war and peace.

Recently we have been stunned by stories from the Darfur region of southern Sudan. An exhibition of drawings by children in Darfur reflected their experiences in stark visual images. Dr. Annie Sparrow, the Human Rights Watch worker who collected the drawings, discussed them in an interview on the PBS "News Hour." Of one, she said, "It actually looks as if it's a picture of men dancing with women. But the men in the green are Sudanese soldiers taking the women to be raped." Sparrow asked a 9-year-old girl to explain her drawing. "She pointed to the man at the bottom of the picture and she said, 'That's a Janjaweed. He's running after us. They're all running after us. And we're holding on to each other and running and screaming'" ("Darfur's Smallest Witnesses," 2005).

The use of terrorist tactics in sectarian and other civil disturbances has increased the possibility that children will be harmed accidentally or even targeted by violence. The mass killing of school children in Beslan, Russia, on the first day of school in 2004 was a particularly haunting example. When soldiers stormed the building in an attempt to rescue the children and parents held hostage by terrorists inside, 331 people died, including 186 children ("Beslan School Siege," 2004). In fact, children in Chechnya had lived with the reality of this kind of violence for many years. One reporter described life in Grozny, Chechnya, as "an unending low-level siege in which everyone is a hostage" (Mydans, 2004).

It is important that children living in the relative safety and security of their American homes develop compassion, tolerance, and understanding of the violence that threatens children elsewhere in the world. They are citizens of the world, not just the United States.

CHILDREN HAVE A RIGHT TO THE KNOWLEDGE
AND INFORMATION THAT IS CRITICAL TO THEIR
PRESENT AND FUTURE WELL-BEING.

This rationale will be developed more fully in the next chapter. However, the notion that children have a right to information that affects their lives is a significant justification for the existence of this book. Children often need assistance from adults before they can exercise their rights. This book can serve as a guidebook for adults who act as information advocates for young people.

Children's Information Needs and Rights

IN SAN DIEGO, CALIFORNIA, A 9-YEAR-OLD BOY
hugs his Marine father who is being deployed to Iraq. In Brooklyn,
New York, a 10-year-old girl cries when a classmate tells her that his
father told him the attack on the World Trade Center was a Jewish plot.
In Minneapolis, Minnesota, two middle school girls talk about a classmate, a Somali immigrant who wears the traditional Muslim head cov-
ering. They wonder if her older brothers are terrorists. In Seattle,
Washington, a 13-year-old boy tells the reference librarian that he needs
to do a report for social studies about the 2001 attacks on New York
and Washington, D.C. All of these children have information needs.

The concept of information needs underlies much theory,
research, and practice in library and information science. Librarians
tacitly assume that people ask questions to satisfy information needs.
The most commonly accepted scholarly approach to information needs
sees them as the products of a complex interrelationship between a
person's emotional and cognitive state and a particular situation. People
need information in order to make sense of that situation (Dervin and
Nilan, 1986). If you define information very broadly as ". . . all knowledge, ideas, facts, data, and imaginative works of mine which are communicated formally and/or informally in any format," you can see that
an information need occurs whenever people are in situations that

require information for resolution or closure or progress of any kind (Chen and Hernon, 1982, p. 5).

Brenda Dervin asks us to think of an information need as a kind of impediment or obstacle that keeps a person from moving forward in cognitive space and time. The individual must bridge the information gap by "asking questions, creating ideas, and/or obtaining resources" (Dervin, 1989, p. 77). If we think of information needs in this way, they seem less abstract, arising as they do out of concrete circumstances.

Obviously, many information needs are left unmet or partially unmet, and people still go on with their lives. They move around the gap or impediment, making the best choices they can under the circumstances or retreating from the situation. In fact, some information needs may actually go unnoticed or unarticulated by the people who have them. Andrew Green (1990) finds that people are frequently unaware of their information needs, focusing more often on their information wants.

These concepts of information wants and needs are helpful in focusing our thinking about children's access to information. I have argued elsewhere (Walter, 1994) that children's information needs are often defined by adults such as teachers with homework assignments, after-school care providers with a need to control or entertain their charges, and parents with implicit or explicit intentions to socialize their offspring. This often results in the phenomenon of the imposed query, as Melissa Gross (1995, 2006) has defined it. We see children coming to libraries with information needs that they have not defined themselves. Rather, a teacher has told them to write a report on a Civil War battle or a current event. These are queries with identifiable goals. The child's information needs will be satisfied when they find appropriate materials on a battle or a current event. The boy with the homework assignment dealing with 9/11 has an imposed query.

On the other hand, children are also active agents in their own information domains, generating their own needs. The child with the Civil War battle query imposed by his teacher may have his own self-generated need for information about *manga* drawing techniques or medieval weapons. These queries are just as goal-oriented as those needed to meet school requirements. They simply bridge other cognitive gaps—perhaps satisfying the child's curiosity or enabling him to pursue a hobby or perfect a skill.

More elusive are the unvoiced questions of childhood. Because of their more limited experiences and frames of reference, children often just don't know what they don't know. It may take a sensitive adult to help them articulate these unspoken questions. The boy whose father is leaving for active duty in the Marines, the child who has heard an unsubstantiated rumor about 9/11, and the girls with the Somali classmate all have unspoken information needs. Caring, sensitive adults might recognize those unspoken needs and respond to them. The boy's mother might recognize that the father's leave-taking is raising questions about the war and its risks. The teacher of the teenage girls with the Muslim classmate or the parent of the sobbing child in New York might see opportunities to correct misinformation. The existing theory and research on information needs, however, does not fully account for the unspoken questions and untold stories that characterize some of the most significant information gaps in the lives of children, particularly when the topic is sensitive or obfuscated by layers of adult confusion and ideological baggage.

Melissa Gross and I have teased out a model of children's information needs in the sensitive area of HIV/AIDS (Walter and Gross, 1996). It is grounded in developmental theory and assumes that all children need some basic information about HIV/AIDS as well as some related information to provide a context that facilitates comprehension. It also allows for special situations, such as a child's personal association with HIV/AIDS or risk factors such as substance abuse or early sexual behavior. Finally, it posits a community-based approach to providing information for children who are 9 and older.

I started this book with a similar approach in mind, applying the concept of children's information needs to the subject domains of war and alternatives to war. I still believe that it is a useful heuristic way to think about what children need to know. However, as I have probed more deeply into the linkages between children and war, I have come to think in terms of children's information rights as much as children's information needs. For children to obtain the information they need about politically charged, emotional issues such as war and peace, we need to move from a concept of information needs to one of information rights. Children have the right to acquire the information they need in order to be competent citizens in a violent world that adults have created.

The whole tone of the discourse changes in both content and tone when we make the shift from children's information needs to information rights. The role of the child shifts from passive recipient of information to active agent with entitlements. The role of the adult shifts from agent of socialization to that of advocate, enabler, or facilitator.

Of course, children under the age of 18 are legally in the custody of their parents and have few rights of liberty at home (Houlgate, 1980, pp. 22 ff). Parents may legally determine where their children live, what they eat, how they will dress, and even what they may read. They are also legally responsible for the consequences of their children's behavior, whether that means replacing a neighbor's window shattered by an errant baseball or paying the fines on overdue library books. Children are dependent on their parents by law and also in practice. Many children depend on their parents to sign them up for soccer or to take them to the library. Even the American Library Association, whose Library Bill of Rights asserts that "a person's right to use a library should not be denied or abridged because of origin, age, background, or views," affirms the right and responsibility of parents to guide their own children's use of the library and its resources and services (American Library Association, 2006).

In this environment, what justification is there for advocating children's rights to information? Barbara Bennett Woodhouse (2004) proposes that we recognize two new categories of rights especially for children—needs-based rights and dignity-based rights. Needs-based rights would include positive rights to nurture, education, medical care, and other goods that children need to develop into productive adults. Dignity-based rights acknowledge that children are fully human from the time of birth. Woodhouse recognizes that law based on these dignity-based rights must reflect the inherent dependence and fragility of children but also their developing capacity for participation in decisions that affect their lives. She writes, "Thinking realistically about children's rights involves integrating children's needs with their capacities and acknowledging that dependence and autonomy are two sides of the same coin" (2004, p. 234). She goes on to identify five principles of human rights that should be applied to children (2004, pp. 235–239):

- The equality principle: the right to equal opportunity.
- The individualism principle: the right to be treated as a person, not an object.
- The empowerment principle: the right to a voice and, sometimes, a choice.
- The protection principle: the right of the weak to be protected from the strong.
- The privacy principle: the right to protection of intimate relationships.

Woodhouse has presented a framework that resolves much of the tension that has plagued the issue of children's rights. It acknowledges the child's right to protection as well as the child's right to autonomy. What librarians and teachers can contribute to this framework is the information that children need in order to exercise their rights.

We can make these information needs and rights concrete by looking at specific domains of knowledge. I will close this chapter with a sample presentation of information rights concerning the September 11, 2001, attack on New York and Washington, D.C., for 9- to 11-year-olds. We can construct models for other age groups and other topics based on this framework.

Basic information
What happened. Why we think it happened. Immediate responses: the rescue effort, the war in Afghanistan. Continuing issues: security, conflict between Islamists and the U.S., war in Iraq.

Basic related information
Islam. Tolerance. War (and peace). Democracy. Dissent. Patriotism. Military service. Foreign policy. Global perspectives.

Special situations
Children who lost a parent or relative in the attacks. Children with a parent or close relative serving in the Middle East. Muslim children.

Information providers
Community-based approach involving parents, teachers, child care providers, librarians, clergy, etc. *Children should be involved as active participants in the transfer of information.*

SHARING BOOKS
WITH CHILDREN

FEW CHILDREN WILL REFER TO THIS BOOK. However, they are the intended end users of the resources cataloged here. I assume that adults—librarians, teachers, parents—will consult this volume for books and other informational media about war and peace to share with children in a variety of ways. Librarians will refer to this book for guidance with reference and readers' advisory queries and as a source for their own programming. Teachers will find this a useful tool for curriculum and lesson planning. Parents will look here for assistance in navigating what might appear to be the broad, uncharted waters of children's book publishing and new media. Here are some things to think about before plunging in.

READING LEVELS

Curriculum specialists assume that by grade 4 children will be able to read well enough to handle the content in textbooks. While learning to read critically and with comprehension is a task that continues through one's formal education, 4th graders should no longer need formal instruction in the basics of reading. Unfortunately, reading scores in the United States indicate that this assumption may not be valid. There are too many students who are not reading at grade level in the upper elementary and middle school grades. These children have the same information needs and rights as their peers who have managed to break the reading code. For this reason, I have included some titles with a reading level that is lower than grade 4. DVDs may also be helpful for children who are having difficulty with print materials.

Most libraries shelve fiction picture books together. At one time, one could assume that picture books were intended for young children, either as read-aloud material for preschoolers or as independent reading for 6-, 7-, and 8-year-olds. Format is no longer a good predictor of the intended audience for a book. One can now find many picture books that are more appropriate for upper elementary and even middle school students than for their younger brothers and sisters. Some examples from the resource lists in this volume include:

- *Patrol* by Walter Dean Myers
- *A Boy Called Slow* by Joseph Bruchac
- *Rose Blanche* by Roberto Innocenti
- *The Harmonica* by Tony Johnson
- *Walt Whitman* by Barbara Kerley
- *Hiroshima No Pika* by Toshi Maruki
- *Pink and Say* by Patricia Polacco
- *Faithful Elephants* by Yukio Tsuchiya

CURRICULUM CONNECTIONS

Given their significance in history, it is not surprising that wars figure prominently in the social studies curriculum. American schoolchildren are certain to encounter the Revolutionary War and the Civil War before they enter high school. World War II may also be taught in middle school. However, teachers who have the flexibility to develop thematic units linking literature and history will also find that war and alternatives to war are topics that lend themselves to developing individual and group projects, fostering critical thinking skills, and promoting information literacy. These teachers do not limit themselves to the rigid demands of a prescribed curriculum. Phyllis K. Kennemer (1993) points out that war is a subject that engages students because of its drama and its impact on nations and individuals. She has compiled a useful guide for teachers in grades 6 through 8, in which she pulls together print sources about six wars that have influenced American history—from the Revolutionary War to the first Gulf War.

Like Kennemer, I have found that pairing nonfiction and fiction titles on a similar topic is a good way to help children see the relationship between books. The informational book often provides the facts that lay the groundwork for understanding a subject, while a good novel or picture book fills in the gaps and helps the child see the human dimensions. Some good complementary pairings from the resource lists in this book include:

Hiroshima
Clive Lawton. *Hiroshima*
Laurence Yep. *Hiroshima*
Adolf Hitler
Jackie French. *Hitler's Daughter*
James Giblin. *The Life and Death of Adolf Hitler*
Holocaust
Eleanor Ayer. *Parallel Journeys*
David Chotjewitz. *Daniel Half Human and the Good Nazi*
Japanese Internment Camps
Michael O. Tunnell and George W. Chilcoat. *The Children of Topaz*
Yoshiko Uchida. *The Bracelet*
World War II – American home front
Kathleen Krull. *V Is for Victory*
Milly Lee. *Nim and the War Effort*

Books about war and peace also have value to the social studies curriculum beyond their obvious subject content. All ten of the Curriculum Standards for Social Studies developed by the National Council for the Social Studies (*Expectations of Excellence*, 1994) are represented by the titles in this book. The appendix at the back of the book will lead you to titles for any of these thematic strands: culture; time, continuity, and change; people, places, and environments; individual development and identity; individuals, groups, and institutions; power, authority, and governance; production, distribution, and consumption; science, technology, and society; global connections; and civic ideals and practices.

Finally, it may be obvious that many of the books included here have literary merit that is independent of their content. Many of the best writers for young people have been moved to write about the timeless themes of war and peace: Katherine Paterson, Gary Paulsen, Kevin Crossley-Holland, Paul Fleischman, Susan Cooper, Robert Cormier, Karen Hesse, Lois Lowry, Linda Sue Park, Uri Orlev, Cynthia Rylant, Rosemary Sutcliff, and Gloria Whelan, just to name a few. There are Newbery and Caldecott medal winners among the titles included here. These books will find their place in any English and literature curriculum.

DEVELOPMENTAL ISSUES

This book compiles books and new media resources for children in grades 4 through 8, or ages 9 to 14. That represents a broad developmental range; 14-year-olds have very different cognitive, emotional, and social capabilities than their younger brothers and sisters. They have also had more years to acquire knowledge and experiences that enrich their frames of reference.

These developmental differences are partially addressed by the suggested grades provided for each resource listed here. However, a general discussion of the developmental issues relevant to sharing books and information about war and peace with children may be helpful here.

Childhood is a moving target. As children progress through physical, emotional, and cognitive developmental stages, their interests and capabilities change. The Swiss psychologist Jean Piaget (1969) is generally credited with identifying the most commonly used framework for understanding cognitive development in childhood. The children we are concerned with here are no longer in the sensorimotor and preoperational periods of early childhood. From age 7 to 10, they are ordinarily assumed to be in the period of concrete operations. They are able to perform complex intellectual operations and can understand time and space. However, they may still have some difficulty distinguishing reality from representations of reality. From ages 11 to 15, the middle school years, children are in the formal operations period. By this time, their conceptual abilities are well-matured. They can handle symbolic, abstract thought. They are still acquiring the information and knowledge, however, that will enable them to construct appropriate frames of reference and to integrate new information with knowledge they have already acquired. Keep in mind, of course, that the Piagetian stages are guidelines only, not intended to put children in cast-iron categories.

It is important to also consider situational factors that impact on a child's development. Piaget has sometimes been criticized for being too deterministic. James Garbarino (1982, 1989, 1991), for example, writes about the contexts in a child's life that might affect his or her development by presenting either risks or opportunities. He is concerned about the interaction between the individual child and the environment in which a child is situated. As much as possible, we should be aware of factors that might affect a child's response to literature or information that we are sharing. Some special situations might be:

- A parent or other close relative serving on active duty in the military
- Experiences as a refugee from a war-torn country
- Relatives who experienced the Nazi concentration camps or Japanese internment camps

SENSITIVE TOPICS

War itself is often regarded as a sensitive topic. It can certainly stir up emotional political debate. Some adults may consider the whole topic of war inappropriate for children. Some parents may want to preserve their children's innocence at all cost, believing that the world is frightening enough without adding hypothetical dangers. Others may be wary of possible political controversies inherent in discussions of American wars. However, librarians learn to present information in ways that are value-neutral and to present all sides of a topic whenever possible and good educators teach the critical thinking skills that children must learn to bring to complex issues. If we approach issues relating to war and peace with our highest professional standards and ethics, we will serve the interests of children and the adults who care about them.

The Holocaust perpetrated by the Nazi regime against the European Jews and others they considered undesirable is a specific topic that requires delicate handling. The events of the Holocaust are unspeakable and unthinkable, and yet we must find the words to speak and think about them if children are to incorporate the lessons from this horrible event into their knowledge about the world. Elaine Stephens, Jean Brown, and Janet Rubin (1995, p. 2), authors of a guide to teaching the Holocaust to young people, point out that this darkest chapter in our history also contains some of the brightest pages, acts of courage and dignity in the face of the cruelest degradation human beings have visited on other people.

It is important that adults who are sharing books and information about the Holocaust with young people sort out their own feelings and opinions about this event. Then they need to be sure that the children are properly prepared to learn. The authors cited above suggest a series of questions that adults can pose to children before going deeper into the topic (Stephens, Brown, and Rubin, 1995, p. 13):

- What do you already know about the Holocaust? About Nazi Germany? Where did you get this information?
- What questions do you have about the Holocaust?
- The Holocaust happened before you were born. Why do you think you need to learn about it now?

The discussion emerging from these questions will help you and the children establish some common ground before adding new information to their store of knowledge.

Maeve Visser Knoth (2006) recently wrote an essay about bibliotherapy in which she criticized the quick and literal fix that many adults seem to be looking for when they ask for a book to help a child through a crisis. If a grandmother has Alzheimer's disease, they want a book that reflects her situation exactly. A book about an uncle with Alzheimer's disease won't do. She wonders if a book that perfectly mirrored the child's circumstances would even be useful. Might it not be better, she asks, to provide *advance* bibliotherapy? Might it not be more therapeutic to have read about the horrors of war or the death of a parent or the evils of the Holocaust before one faces such phenomena in real life? It is this kind of inoculation that the best books for children can provide.

GENERAL TIPS FOR SHARING BOOKS WITH CHILDREN

Most of the adults reading this book will already have developed strategies for sharing books effectively with children. I am sharing some general tips that have worked for me as a way to prime the pump, to help readers become more self-aware of the things they do to connect children and books.

- Read the book yourself before sharing it with children. Use the annotations in this bibliography or in other sources as guidelines for making your initial selection, but don't rely on them.
- You will be most effective connecting children with books that you care deeply about.
- Don't stop reading aloud to children just because they can read well on their own. Reading a picture book such as Walter

Dean Myers's *Patrol* to a middle school class is a wonderful way to ensure that everyone has had the same literary experience. Reading longer books aloud, chapter by chapter is another good way to create shared meaning and a sense of community in a classroom or after-school group.

- Remember that children from 10 to 12 are eager for information that will give them mastery over their world. They will respond to books that empower them.

- Young adolescents, 13- and 14-year-olds, are concerned with issues of identity. They are often idealistic and concerned with the moral and ethical issues of war and peace. They relate well to the many novels in which characters test themselves against difficult obstacles.

- Avoid being too literal in thinking about the subjects of war and peace. Most children's books about war are also implicitly books about peace. Children often need words of comfort and images of compassion before they can visualize peace or even security when the world seems filled with uncertainty and danger. At the time of the first Gulf War, Katherine Paterson wrote, "We are not wise enough, we adults, to know what book will be right for any child at any particular moment, but the richer the book, the more imaginative the language, the better the chance that it will minister to a child's deep, inarticulate fears" (Paterson, 1991, p. 34). Children are more likely to respond to genuine expressions of emotion than to overly didactic content.

References

American Library Association. (2006). "Free Access to Libraries for Minors: An Interpretation of the Library's Bill of Rights." Chicago, IL: American Library Association. www.ala.org/Template.cfm?Section= interpretations&Template=/ContentManagement/ContentDisplay.cfm& ContentID=103214.

Anderson, Fred, and Andrew Cayton. (2005). *The Dominion of War: Empire and Liberty in North America 1500–2000*. New York: Viking.

"Beslan School Siege." (2004). BBC News. http://news.bbc.co.uk/1/shared/spl/hi/world/04/russian_s/html/6.stm.

Chen, Ching-Chih, and Peter Hernon. (1982). *Information Seeking: Assessing and Anticipating User Needs*. New York: Neal-Schuman.

"Darfur's Smallest Witnesses." (2005). Washington, DC: PBS Online NewsHour. Sept. 27, 2005. www.pbs.org/newshour/bb/africa/july-dec05/darafur_9-27.html.

Dervin, Brenda. (1989). "Audience as Listener and Learner, Teacher and Confidante: The Sense-Making Approach." In *Public Communication Campaigns*, edited by R. E. Rice and C. Whitney. Newbury Park, CA: Sage, 1989.

Dervin, Brenda, and Michael Nilan. (1986). "Information Needs and Uses," *Annual Review of Information Science and Technology*, Vol. 21.

Expectations of Excellence: Curriculum Standards for Social Studies. (1994). Silver Spring, MD: National Council for the Social Studies.

Garbarino, James. (1982). *Children and Families in the Social Environment*. New York: Aldine.

Garbarino, James, et al. (1989). *What Children Can Tell Us: Eliciting, Interpreting, and Evaluating Information from Children.* San Francisco: Jossey Bass.

Garbarino, James, Kathleen Kostelny, and Nancy Dubrow. (1991). *No Place to Be a Child: Growing Up in a War Zone.* Lexington, MS: Lexington Books.

Green, Andrew. (1990). "What Do We Mean by User Needs?" *British Journal of Academic Librarianship.* Vol. 5, No. 2 (1990), pp. 65–78.

Gross, Melissa. (1995). "The Imposed Query." *RQ*, Vol. 35, No. 2, (Winter 1995), pp. 236–243.

———. (2006). *Studying Children's Questions: Imposed and Self-Generated Information Seeking at School.* Lanham, MD: Scarecrow Press.

Houlgate, Laurence D. (1980). *The Child and the State: A Normative Theory of Juvenile Rights.* Baltimore, MD: Johns Hopkins University Press.

"Iraq Body Count." (2006). www.iraqbodycount.net.

Kennemer, Phyllis K. (1993). *Using Literature to Teach Middle Grades About War.* Phoenix, AZ: Oryx Press.

Knoth, Maeve Visser. (2006). "What Ails Bibliotherapy?" *The Horn Book*, May/June 2006, pp. 273–276.

Levey, Noam N. (2005). "Psyches of Iraq's Children Caught in the Cross-Fire." *Los Angeles Times*, Oct. 24, 2005, pp. A1, A7.

Mydans, Seth. (2004). "At Grozny's School No. 7, Survival 101 Is a Requisite." *New York Times*, Oct. 3, 2004, p. A3.

National Military Family Association. (2006). www.nmfa.org.

Paterson, Katherine. (1991). "Living in a Peaceful World. *The Horn Book*, Jan./Feb. 1991, pp. 32–38.

Piaget, Jean. (1969). *The Child's Conception of the World.* Totowa, NJ: Littlefield, Adams.

Stephens, Elaine C., Jean E. Brown, and Janet E. Rubin. (1995). *Learning About the Holocaust: Literature and Other Resources for Young People.* North Haven, CT: Library Professional Publications.

Walter, Virginia A. (1994). "The Information Needs of Children." *Advances in Librarianship*, Vol. 18 (1994), pp. 112–115.

Walter, Virginia A., and Melissa Gross. (1996). *HIV/AIDS Information for Children: A Guide to Issues and Resources.* New York: H. W. Wilson.

"War's Trauma Wears on the Children Left Behind." (2005). *USA Today*, Dec. 13, 2005, p. 1A.

Woodhouse, Barbara Bennett. (2004). "Re-Visioning Rights for Children." In *Rethinking Childhood*, edited by Peter B. Pufall and Richard P. Unsworth. New Brunswick, NJ: Rutgers University Press, pp. 229–243.

PART II

RESOURCES FOR CHILDREN ABOUT WAR AND PEACE

OVERVIEW

THIS SECTION OF THE BOOK IS ITS HEART. Here you will find an extensive thematic resource list of books, web sites, and audiovisual materials intended to inform children in grades 4 through 8 about important issues relating to war and peace. Most of the items—nearly 300—are books. You will also find a sampling of useful Web sites and videos, and even a couple of CDs. I have read every book, examined every Web site, watched every video, and listened to both CDs. While not all of the books are still in print, all should be available through libraries.

Although the listing of books is extensive, it is not comprehensive. I did not search out the many series books about wars and battles that serve primarily as supplementary text materials. A few such books are included, however, because the subject matter was important and not covered elsewhere. I used basic bibliographic tools as sources for the titles to be included: *Children's Catalog, The Horn Book Guide,* and review media such as *School Library Journal*. I also used more serendipitous techniques such as browsing book stores and library shelves, and this turned up more titles than you might think.

Because I compiled an earlier bibliography on this subject (Walter, 1993), I focused here on books published from 1992 through 2004. There are a few exceptions: books that I missed the first time around and books that have won the Newbery Medal. The Newbery books are worth reconsidering because they are so ubiquitous in school and public libraries.

The resources are organized thematically. Some books would have fit in several thematic categories; others were nearly unclassifiable. However, I used my best judgment to place each book in the category that best reflected its content. The author, title, and subject indexes at the back of the book will help you find the particular books you are interested in. An introduction to each thematic section provides some background information about the theme itself and a discussion of the issues raised by the resources that follow.

The bibliographic entry for each book contains the following information: author, title, illustrator, publisher, date, and ISBN number. Each Web site includes its URL. Videos list running time and distributor. All entries indicate an optimum age range. These are approximations, of course. Children's reading levels and interests vary widely. Please use the age ranges as suggestions only.

Each entry also contains a recommendation as follows: "Highly Recommended"—HR, "Recommended"—R, or "Recommended with Reservations"—RWR. No resources are included that are not at least recommended with reservations. Resources that are "Highly Recommended" are distinguished by literary or cinematic quality, accuracy of the information presented, and exceptional presentation of material relating to the theme in question. "Recommended" resources are suitable for sharing with children; they may be slightly less distinguished in quality or slightly less relevant in theme and content than items that are "Highly Recommended." Resources that are "Recommended with Reservations" have flaws that adults must consider before sharing with children. I have tried to be specific about my reservations in the annotation.

Each entry is also linked to one of the ten thematic strands defined by the National Council for the Social Studies as found in their publication *Expectations of Excellence* (1994). This should be helpful for teachers and school librarians; it also provides further information about the potential use of the resource with children.

Finally, each resource is annotated. The annotation is both descriptive and evaluative. In some instances, it also indicates how a book or resource might be shared with children. The initials F and NF denote fiction and nonfiction.

WAR AS HISTORY

IT IS NOT SURPRISING THAT THE HISTORY of humankind sometimes reads like a military history. It is not just that war is the kind of complex, dramatic event that gives historians fodder for their research. War is also a recurring event, with major consequences for the nations and individuals involved.

You need look no further than the history of the United States. The French and Indian War left its scars even before the bloody Revolutionary War that established independence from Britain. The war with Mexico, from 1846 to 1848, was an offensive war fought under the banner of Manifest Destiny. The Civil War's significance in shaping regional difference, racial tensions, and political values cannot be over-estimated. The Indian wars continued until government troops had nearly eliminated the Indian nations that originally occupied the land. The Spanish-American War gave us yellow journalism, Teddy Roosevelt's Rough Riders, and the beginning of a long entanglement with the Philippines. World War I ended American isolationism and, ironically for the "war to end all wars," set the stage for World War II. The Cold War that followed World War II led to fears of a nuclear holocaust and the paranoia of the Cuban Missile Crisis. The Vietnam War divided the United States as no event had since the Civil War. The legacy lives on in embittered veterans, post-traumatic stress syndrome, and thousands of Vietnamese and other Southeast Asian refugees trying to make new lives in the West. More recently, American troops have been sent to Somalia and the Middle East. The current war in Iraq threatens to be as divisive as the war in Vietnam as the toll of dead American soldiers rises and the definition of victory becomes murkier. Historians Fred Anderson and Andrew Cayton (2005) point out that most

Americans believe they make the world a better, safer, freer place by winning the wars in which they engage. However, many American wars cannot be justified on that basis; rather, they were imperial wars, fought for power.

In an eloquent metaphor, Christian Appy (2004), a history professor who has written about the legacy of the Vietnam War, claims that memories of war can never be buried; only bodies can. For young Americans to understand and learn from their national history, then, they must know something about its wars. I would argue that they should also be aware of wars fought in faraway places that did not directly involve the United States. In many cases, those wars have so disrupted the civilian population that tremendous numbers of refugees have been forced to flee their homelands, often to the United States. It is also imperative, as I demonstrated in Part I, that young Americans acquire a global perspective and a sense of interdependence with the rest of the world. However, almost all of the resources in this section are historical accounts of American wars. Other categories will reflect a more international scope.

WAR AS HISTORY IN RESOURCES FOR CHILDREN

Among the 8,000 or so books published for children each year, many are what we librarians call supplementary curriculum materials. These are supplements to textbooks, designed to go into more detail on specific topics and/or to help students complete homework assignments. Many are published as series, with a standardized format. While useful in their limited scope, few of these titles are distinguished by quality of writing. Because they are intended to support curriculum demands, they also tend to fall into fairly prescribed topic areas. I have included only a sampling of these titles in the bibliography that follows.

In addition to a proliferation of supplemental texts in series, there are some other trends in juvenile nonfiction publishing worth mentioning here. One is the creation of informational titles with sound content for younger and younger ages. It is no longer difficult to find a good biography for a second-grader to read. While this book focuses on older students, beginning with fourth-graders, it is good to know that there are some easier to read informational titles available for children who are not reading at grade level.

A second significant trend is what some people are calling "literary nonfiction." These are informational books that tell a story, finding the narrative arc in historical or scientific subjects. These are books in which the words are as carefully chosen as the facts. It was partly in recognition of the distinguished nature of so many informational books published for children that the Association for Library Service to Children established the Robert F. Sibert Informational Book Medal. The terms of the award define informational books as "those written and illustrated to present, organize and interpret documentable factual material for children." Books receiving this award are judged to have made a "significant contribution" to children's literature, determined by how well the entire work elucidates, clarifies, and enlivens its subject. Accuracy, documentation, and organization are considered, as are illustrative material ("ALSC/Robert F. Sibert Informational Book Medal Terms and Criteria," 2006).

A third positive trend is the use of primary sources and other tools of good historiography in the presentation of information for children. It is rare to read a juvenile biography these days with imagined dialogue. If it cannot be documented that a historical figure said something, it won't be repeated in these books. Almost all of the historical books presented here are illustrated with contemporary photos and illustrations, maps, or other primary source documents. Young readers are not only given sound historical facts; they are also exposed to the tools of historical research.

Finally, the range of topics covered in informational books has increased enormously. There are few subjects that have *not* been covered effectively in books for children. While this will be more noticeable in the chapter dealing with the horrors and consequences of war, it is also apparent in the wide variety of historical events represented here. Here are just some of the perhaps unexpected topics covered in the following resource list:

+ The terracotta soldiers buried with the first Emperor of China more than two thousand years ago (*The Emperor's Silent Army* by Jane O'Connor)
+ Adolf Hitler (*The Life and Death of Adolf Hitler* by James Giblin)
+ The practice of "reenacting" long-ago battles (*Here and Then* by George Ella Lyon and *Red Legs* by Ted Lewin)

- ◆ The espionage techniques used by George Washington during the Revolutionary War (*George Washington, Spymaster* by Thomas B. Allen)
- ◆ The role of women war correspondents during World War II (*Where the Action Was* by Penny Colman)

There are also books about specific wars, important battles, and military leaders, of course. Not so well represented in this section are historical accounts of wars in other countries. This is remedied somewhat in other segments, particularly in the section on the consequences of war. Interestingly, global perspectives are more prevalent in fictional accounts of war.

The widespread availability of DVDs and access to Web sites extend considerably the informational resources available to children. Students should have good information literacy skills before being turned loose to find information on the Internet. Specifically, they should know how to evaluate the sources they find there and how to integrate the information with what they already know about the subject without plagiarizing. A few good Web sites are included in the resource list that follows as examples that adults can use to get children started.

CHILDREN READING ABOUT WAR AS HISTORY

I have learned to avoid making generalizations about children's reading interests. There are children who are Civil War buffs and experts on World War II airplanes. Some children have become interested in relatively recent wars through hearing grandparents talk about them. A few children are turned on by visits to historical sites or museums or by seeing a movie about a historical event. Others are fascinated by history in general or just like to read biographies. It is safe to say, however, that most children will come to history books through classroom experiences and homework assignments. My hope is that they will find books, Web sites, and videos that meet those instructional needs and inspire them to keep learning.

Bibliography

✄

BOOKS

1.   ADLER, DAVID A. *Heroes of the Revolution*. Illustrated by Donald
A. Smith. Holiday House, 2003. Cloth 0-8234-1471-X. Grades 3 to 5.

This collective biography focuses on a well-chosen number of individuals who could be considered heroes of the revolution. Some of these are
familiar names: Ethan Allen, Thomas Jefferson, Nathan Hale, John Paul
Jones, Thomas Paine, Paul Revere, and George Washington. Others are
less well-known: Lydia Darragh, Crispus Attucks, Mary "Molly Pitcher"
Hays, Haym Salomon, and Deborah Sampson. Each hero is given a
one-page profile and a vivid painting of an event in his or her life. The
Author's Notes at the back of the book add more interesting details. A
timeline, source notes, and a selected bibliography are also included.
NF • R

2.   ALLEN, THOMAS B. *George Washington, Spymaster: How the
Americans Outspied the British and Won the Revolutionary War*.
Illustrated by Cheryl Harness. National Geographic, 2004. Cloth 0-
7922-5126-1. Grades 6 to 8.

This is a fascinating account of the ways in which George Washington
used the techniques of espionage to win the Revolutionary War.
Nathan Hale, Benjamin Franklin, Sam Adams, and Paul Revere are just
some of the American heroes who served as spies; and of course,
Benedict Arnold spied for the British. We learn here about the various
codes and ciphers used to send secret messages. The book design is a
tour de force, using type faces and drawings from the late 18th century
as well as pen-and-ink sketches by illustrator Harness in the style of
that period. Cleverly integrated throughout the book are actual ciphers
for the reader to decode. At the back of the book are a map and timeline, a glossary of spy talk, notes, and suggestions for further reading.
NF • HR

3.   ALLEN, THOMAS B. *Remember Pearl Harbor: American and Japanese Survivors Tell Their Stories*. National Geographic, 2001. Cloth 0-7922-6690-0. Grades 5 to 8.

The story of the attack on Pearl Harbor has often been retold from the American perspective. This account also includes memoirs by Japanese aviators who participated in the bombing raid. There is also some discussion of the failure by American military intelligence to have anticipated the attack, foreshadowing in some ways the September 11, 2001, terrorist attacks on the World Trade Center and the Pentagon. Photos, maps, timelines, and resource lists add to the value of this handsomely produced book. NF • R

4.   AMBROSE, STEPHEN E. *The Good Fight: How World War II Was Won*. Atheneum/Byron Preiss Visual Publications, 2001. Cloth 0-689-84361-5. Grades 6 to 8.

As the title indicates and the author's introduction makes clear, this is a book about heroes, the fighting men—mainly American in this account—who fought the powers of darkness and won World War II. It is primarily a military history, well-written and handsomely presented with maps and many full-page contemporary, iconic photos. NF • R

5.   ASHABRENNER, BRENT. *Remembering Korea: The Korean War Veterans Memorial*. Illustrated by Jennifer Ashabrenner. Twenty-First Century Books/Millbrook, 2001. LB 0-7613-2156-X. Grades 5 to 8.

Memorials are a way to both honor and remember our history. War memorials have often generated controversy, and the Korean War Veterans Memorial on the National Mall in Washington, D.C., is no exception. It was dedicated in 1995, 40 years after the end of this unpopular war. Fought while the United States was still recovering from World War II as part of a United Nations action that many Americans felt was not relevant to our national interests, it took the lives of more than 35,000 American soldiers. Ashabrenner does a good job of presenting the differing perspectives on the design of the memorial as well as giving a straightforward account of the Korean War itself. Color photos of the memorial and historical photographs from the time of the war help to make this an accessible and illuminating informational book. NF • HR

6.   BELLER, SUSAN PROVOST. *Never Were Men So Brave: The Irish Brigade During the Civil War*. Atheneum/McElderry, 1998. Cloth 0-689-81406-2. Grades 5 to 8.

Beller traces the formation of the Irish Brigade, a unit of the Army of the Potomac known for its courage and ferocity in battle, to the great Irish potato famine of the 1840s. Thomas Francis Meagher was a leader of the Irish Rebellion of 1848, an unsuccessful effort to throw off the oppressive rule of the British that had become intolerable during the years of famine. Escaping from exile in Van Dieman's Land to America, he saw the political opportunities for the Irish in America if they fought on the side of the Union. He organized the Irish Brigade and became its first Brigadier General. This force of soldiers distinguished itself in many of the early battles of the Civil War, most notably at Antietam, where they led the advance on the Sunken Road, afterwards known as Blood Alley because of the many men who died there. Beller chronicles some of the men who distinguished themselves in battle, including Father Corby, their Catholic Chaplain. There are glimpses of ethnic pride—the green banners they carried into battle and the wartime celebrations of Saint Patrick's Day—in this military history and many reminders of the ties that bind American immigrants to their mother countries. **NF • R**

7.   BELLER, SUSAN PROVOST. *To Hold This Ground: A Desperate Battle at Gettysburg*. McElderry Books/Atheneum, 1995. Cloth 0-689-50621-X. Grades 5 to 8.

The Civil War battle of Gettysburg is known today primarily for the speech that Abraham Lincoln gave on the occasion of the dedication of a national cemetery there four months later. Beller tells a compelling story of military strategy, heroism, and leadership in this account of the three-day battle itself. We learn about the terrain, with its two hills and a plain in between, that determined much of the strategy. And we learn about the two men who led the troops on either side in the critical battle over one of those hills, Little Round Top. On the Union side was Colonel Joshua Lawrence Chamberlain from Maine, who led his men to charge the Confederates with bayonets when they ran out of ammunition for their rifles. He went on to become governor of Maine. On the Confederate side, Colonel William Calvin Oates led his men in that desperate attempt to wrest the hill from the Union soldiers. He went on to become the governor of Alabama. While this account focuses on the role played by two military leaders, it also chronicles the deeds and deaths of ordinary soldiers. Contemporary photos and maps, an index, and a bibliography of adult sources add to the value of this historical account. **NF • HR**

8. BESSON, JEAN-LOUIS. *October 45: Childhood Memories of the War*. Creative Editions/Harcourt Brace, 1995. Cloth 0-15-200955-8. Grades 4 to 6.

Similar in many ways to Michael Foreman's *War Boy*, this is Besson's illustrated memoir of his childhood in France during World War II. A major difference between these two accounts, of course, is that France was occupied by the Germans while England remained free. As a middle-class Catholic child, Besson did not endure the most terrible consequences of the occupation; nor did he have the opportunity to demonstrate unusual feats of heroism or patriotism. Besson's narrative appears to be unfiltered by his adult perceptions and knowledge. While this provides a genuine child's-eye view of occupied France, it may prove confusing or misleading to contemporary American children. For example, he repeats the anti-Semitic propaganda of the time without any qualifiers. Still, with some adult interpretation, this book could be a good entry point to thinking about children in countries directly touched by war. **NF • RWR**

9. BOBRICK, BENSON. *Fight for Freedom: The American Revolutionary War*. Atheneum/Byron Preiss Visual Publications, 2004. Cloth 0-689-86422-1. Grades 5 to 8.

This profusely illustrated history of the American Revolution by a respected historian gives the young reader a brief introduction to the causes of the war. The emphasis here is on the military aspects of the war itself, with attention given to each of the major battles. A sidebar of "quick facts" on each page of text highlights interesting details. The somewhat fragmented narrative may make it difficult for the reader to get a sense of the overall course of the war, but each individual topic is covered adequately. There is a glossary of political and military terms used in the text, a bibliography of adult titles, and a brief list of relevant Web sites. The end papers give a timeline. **NF • RWR**

10. BREWSTER, HUGH. *Anastasia's Album*. Hyperion, 1996. Cloth 0-7868-0292-8. Grades 4 to 6.

The State Archives in Moscow contain the family albums of the Romanovs, the last rulers of imperial Russia. Brewster has made extensive use of the photos, letters, and drawings of Tsar Nicholas II's daughter Anastasia to tell the story of her life. The Romanovs lived a life of ease and luxury and domestic charm, marred only by the hemophilia of the tsar's young son and heir and the machinations of the monk Rasputin. World War I caused some changes. Anastasia visited wounded soldiers, and the tsar left his family to take control of the army. Enormous numbers of Russian soldiers had died in the war, and the winds of revolution were sweeping the country. In 1917, the tsar gave up his throne and became a prisoner in his own palace. The family was moved to a house in Ekaterinburg where, on July 16, 1918, Bolshevik soldiers apparently shot all of the members of the family. However, because the bodies had been removed, a mystery remains about the ultimate fate of Anastasia. The author presents this fascinating story in child-appropriate language and compelling images. A glossary and list of primary sources consulted adds further value. **NF • HR**

11. BURCHARD, PETER. *Frederick Douglass: For the Great Family of Man*. Atheneum, 2003. Cloth 0-689-83240-0. Grades 5 to 8.

The great early black leader emerges in this objective, analytical biography as a complex man with tremendous gifts and some obvious weaknesses. Much of the book deals with his early life as a slave and his escape to the North where Douglass became involved with the Abolition movement. He worked tirelessly for the end of slavery in this country, looking for any strategy that would accomplish this aim. When he heard about the Confederate firing on Fort Sumter, the incident that started the Civil War, his comment was, "God be praised." Douglass was one of the people who tried from the beginning to convince Lincoln to emancipate the slaves, but it took more than a year for him to do so, thereby changing the North's purpose in fighting the war from saving the Union to freeing the slaves. The Emancipation Proclamation, when it came, included a provision that qualified blacks could now serve in the army; and Douglass worked tirelessly to recruit men to join the first black regiments. With the death of Lincoln and the onset of Reconstruction, Douglass saw many of his dreams fall short. He nevertheless ended his life as a respected statesman and a man of influence.

Burchard's biography is well-documented and written with an eye to the narrative potential of this man's extraordinary life. Documents, drawings, and photographs from the time add interest. A bibliographical essay, note on sources, bibliography, and index contribute to the usefulness of the book. **NF • R**

12.   CALIFF, DAVID J. *Marathon*. Chelsea House, 2002. Cloth 0-7910-6679-7. Grades 6 to 8.

The Greeks succeeded in defeating the invading Persian army of King Darius in the Battle of Marathon in 490 B.C. This book looks at the tactics and circumstances that led to that victory. It also explains the significance of the battle for the subsequent history of both Greece and Persia. Photographs, diagrams, maps, and chronologies enhance the text.

This is part of the series Battles That Changed the World. Other titles not covered in this bibliography include *First Battle of the Marne, Gettysburg, Hastings, Midway, Normandy, Saratoga, Tenochtitlan, Tet Offensive,* and *Waterloo.* **NF • R**

13.   CHENEY, LYNNE. *When Washington Crossed the Delaware: A Wintertime Story for Young Patriots*. Illustrated by Peter M. Fiore. Simon & Schuster, 2004. Cloth 0-689-87043-4. Grades 3 to 5.

Washington made his legendary crossing of the Delaware on Christmas Day, 1776, surprising the Hessian soldiers at Trenton (who were celebrating the holiday) and winning a decisive early battle in the Revolutionary War. The author turns this brilliant piece of military strategy into an object lesson for young Americans, aiming to inspire them with a sense of pride and patriotism. Dramatic paintings add to the tone of high seriousness. The book is more successful as a patriotic tract than as a historical account. **NF • RWR**

14.   COLLIER, JAMES LINCOLN. *The Clara Barton You Never Knew*. Illustrated by Greg Copeland. Children's Press, 2003. LB 0-516-24346-2; pap. 0-516-25838-9. Grades 4 to 6.

Collier presents Clara Barton as a complex woman who was shy but ambitious, direct and straightforward, but occasionally manipulative. Although she gained national prominence for her work as a nurse for the Union side during the Civil War, her most lasting contribution was the founding of the American National Red Cross. In fact, it is clear from this biography that her genius was for management and organization, not for nursing. Her story—and that of Florence Nightingale in England—also demonstrate the ways in which the unusual circumstances of wartime have opened up new opportunities for women. **NF • R**

15. **COLMAN, PENNY.** *Where the Action Was: Women War Correspondents in World War II*. Crown, 2002. Cloth 0-517-80075-6; LB 0-517-80076-4. Grades 6 to 8.

Young people who routinely see women reporting from Iraq and other war zones may be surprised to learn that as recently as World War II women had to fight huge bureaucratic obstacles to serve as war correspondents. Those who succeeded not only recorded history; they made it. Colman profiles many of the better-known journalists and photographers who helped to document that war: Martha Gellhorn, Margaret Bourke-White, Lee Miller, and others. The author makes the point that the women were as tough, aggressive, and determined as their male counterpoints. They also sometimes saw a human side of war that their brother correspondents missed. **NF • R**

16. **COOPER, MICHAEL L.** *Fighting for Honor: Japanese Americans and World War II*. Clarion, 2000. Cloth 0-395-91375-6. Grades 6 to 8.

After giving background information about Executive Order 9066 which forced the evacuation of more than 110,000 Japanese Americans from their homes on the West Coast to internment camps after the attack on Pearl Harbor, Cooper tells about the extraordinarily distinguished military service given by young men from these camps when they were finally allowed to enlist. Limited to service in Europe and serving in segregated units, they proved to be unusually courageous soldiers, receiving more decorations for valor than any other companies. The author also tells of the prejudice that awaited many of these veterans when they returned to their communities after the war. **NF • R**

17. **DAMON, DUANE.** *Growing Up in the Civil War: 1861–1865*. Lerner, 2003. LB 0-8225-0656-4. Grades 4 to 6.

The book opens with a "note to readers" explaining how historians do detective work using primary sources and how the author of this book did his research into the daily life of boys and girls during the American Civil War. Those primary resources are well-represented in colored illustrations, contemporary photographs, recipes, song lyrics, and quotes from children who kept diaries or wrote memoirs when they were adults. The result is a fascinating glimpse of life during that horrendous war for children, rich and poor, white and black, Northern and Southern. **NF • HR**

18.   DAMON, DUANE. *When This Cruel War Is Over: The Civil War Home Front*. Lerner, 1996. LB 0-8225-1731-0. Grades 4 to 6.

While this account of the Civil War includes background about its causes and major events, the focus here is on the experience of the non-combatants, primarily the women and children, who remained at home while the war was being fought. Admittedly, in many cases the war was fought in their own backyards. We learn how the women and children were forced to take on traditional roles and duties of the men who were away at war—running farms and working to support the war effort in myriad ways. Many contemporary photographs and illustrations contribute to the accessibility of this well-written, well-researched overview of the Civil War. **NF • R**

19.   DAVIS, LUCILE. *Florence Nightingale*. Bridgestone, 1999. Pap. 0-7368-0205-3. Grades 3 to 5.

Florence Nightingale is usually considered the founder of modern nursing as a profession. She acquired much of her experience as a battlefield nurse caring for British soldiers during the Crimean War, and continued to work for more-sanitary hospital conditions and as a teacher of other nurses. This brief book outlines her accomplishments in a simple text, maps, and contemporary illustrations. **NF • R**

20.   DENNY, NORMAN, AND JOSEPHINE FILMER-SANKEY. *The Bayeux Tapestry: The Story of the Norman Conquest*. Atheneum, 1966. o.p. Grades 5 to 8.

It is worth the effort to track down this now out-of-print book through your local library. Part art appreciation and part historical narrative, it tells the story of the Norman Conquest as portrayed in the marvelous embroidered Bayeux Tapestry. The tapestry, more than 200 feet long, tells the story of this historic event from the perspective of the victorious Normans and features a visual style similar to contemporary cartoon strips. The authors use a two-part approach to accompany selected sections of the tapestry. First, they explain the action depicted in the tapestry; then they comment on its significance. **NF • R**

21. **DOLAN, EDWARD F.** *America in the Korean War*. Millbrook, 1998. LB 0-7613-0361-8. Grades 6 to 8.

The American people and the American government were not expecting to be involved in a war in 1950, just five years after the end of World War II. However, when the North Koreans, with the support of Russia and Communist China, invaded South Korea, President Truman moved hastily. The Security Council of the United Nations condemned the invasion and demanded withdrawal, but only 15 nations joined the United States in fighting to enforce the resolution. With the United States troops under the leadership of General MacArthur, most people expected a quick military solution. The war dragged on, however, as Chinese forces entered on the side of the North Koreans. After more than two years of fighting, during which American support for the war eroded dramatically, a diplomatic compromise was reached. Neither side could claim victory, and to this day the border between North and South Korea is one of the most militarized in the world.

This is not an easy book to read, with its detailed descriptions of military operations. However, it is an important source for understanding the current situation, in which North Korea threatens nuclear warfare against its neighbor to the south. **NF • R**

22. **DOLAN, EDWARD F.** *The Spanish-American War*. Millbrook, 2001. LB 0-7613-1453-9. Grades 6 to 8.

When the battleship *Maine* was attacked and sunk in the harbor of Havana, Cuba, it provided the catalyst for war that special interests in the United States had been hoping for. The Hearst and Pulitzer newspaper chains had already been clamoring for war. Now war fever swept the country. Dolan chronicles those beginnings and the conduct of the war itself, beginning with the battle of Manila Bay and proceeding through the successful invasion of Cuba by troops that included Teddy Roosevelt's Rough Riders. He also gives some attention to the mixed legacy of the war: the acquisition of Guam and Puerto Rico as American possessions, continued entanglement with the Philippines, the conquest of Yellow Fever, and the engineering triumph of the Panama Canal. **NF • R**

23. FRADIN, DENNIS BRINDELL. *Samuel Adams: The Father of American Independence*. Clarion, 1998. Cloth 0-395-82510-5. Grades 6 to 8.

Fradin's account of Samuel Adams, told with vivid prose and historical accuracy, does much to establish this man as one of the most important figures in America's fight for independence from Great Britain. Alone among the Founding Fathers, Adams devoted himself full-time to creating support for independence, and he is generally considered the strategist behind such resistance activities as the Boston Tea Party. The English political leaders considered him "the most dangerous man in Massachusetts." The first battle of the Revolutionary War was actually instigated by a British attempt to capture and imprison Samuel Adams and his co-conspirator, John Hancock. **NF • R**

24. FRASER, MARY ANN. *Vicksburg: The Battle That Won the Civil War*. Holt, 1999. Cloth 0-8050-6106-1. Grades 5 to 8.

This is a well-documented account of the siege of Vicksburg. The author uses maps, contemporary drawings and photos, and primary source quotations to enrich her history of this military operation that was crucial in the Union's effort to get control of the Mississippi River and win the Civil War. **NF • R**

25. FREEDMAN, RUSSELL. *Give Me Liberty! The Story of the Declaration of Independence*. Holiday House, 2000. Cloth 0-8234-1448-5; pap. 0-8234-1753-0. Grades 5 to 8.

Lavishly illustrated with paintings and prints, this is a compelling narrative of the events leading up to the Declaration of Independence on July 4, 1776. It begins with the Boston Tea Party in 1773 and ends with a discussion of the lasting relevance of the rights guaranteed by that important document. In between, Freedman peoples the pages of history with ordinary men and women as well as those who took leadership roles. He explains the position of indentured servants and African American slaves. This is a masterful piece of historical writing. **NF • HR**

26. FREEDMAN, RUSSELL. *Lincoln: A Photobiography*. Clarion, 1987. Cloth 0-89919-380-3; pap. 0-395-51848-2. Grades 5 to 8.

This biography of Abraham Lincoln deals extensively with the important role he played in the conduct of the Civil War. Freedman explains how Lincoln moved from seeing the war as a fight to preserve the Union to a struggle to free the slaves. This is one of the few nonfiction titles to be awarded the Newbery Medal, and it is an exemplary informational book for young people. The contemporary photos and other illustrations are well-chosen, and the text is historiography at its best. **NF • HR**

27.   GARLAND, SHERRY. *Voices of the Alamo*. Illustrated by Ronald Himler. Pelican, 2004. Cloth 1-58980-222-5. Grades 3 to 5.

History comes alive as men and women tell their stories of the Alamo, in both the siege of 1836 and the events that led up to it. Some of these voices have been heard before—those of Davy Crockett, Antonio Lopez de Santa Anna, Susanna Dickinson, and Sam Houston. Others are new—a Payaya woman who lived on the land three centuries before the Mexican and Texan armies fought over it, the Spanish padres who built a mission there in 1745, a Tejano rancher and a Texian farmer, and soldiers who fought on both sides. Evocative paintings help to bring these diverse characters to life. A historical note at the back of the book ties all of the narratives together and provides a contextual framework. **NF • R**

28.   GIBLIN, JAMES CROSS. *The Life and Death of Adolf Hitler*. Clarion, 2002. Cloth 0-395-90371-8. Grades 7 up.

Giblin was awarded the Robert F. Sibert Medal for this clearly written account of the man whose actions and policies brought about World War II and the horrors of the Holocaust, in which 6 million Jews, Gypsies, and homosexuals were killed. In the first chapter, he lays out the questions he will explore. What sort of man could plan and carry out such horrendous schemes? How was he able to win support for his deadly ventures? And why did no one try to stop him until it was too late? Using extensive primary source and other scholarly material, he provides answers that thoughtful young readers will find provocative. A final chapter discusses the rise of neo-Nazi movements around the world, including the United States. Well-chosen photographs and documents, a glossary of German words and terms, and an extensive list of source notes and a bibliography add to the value of this exemplary informational book. **NF • HR**

29.   GRANFIELD, LINDA. *Where Poppies Grow: A World War I Companion*. Fitzhenry & Whiteside, 2002. Cloth 1-55005-146-6. Grades 4 to 6.

This book provides an interesting Canadian perspective on World War I. Using a kind of scrapbook approach with many primary source materials such as postcards and photos, the author provides useful background information on many of the topics that are covered in other fictional accounts of the war. Each double-page spread covers a different subject: the causes of the war, what it was like in the trenches, soldiers' daily routine, warfare on the seas and in the air, the role of female nurses, propaganda, the home front, spies, and the deadly impact of new technology on the conduct of war. **NF • R**

30. GREGORY, KRISTIANA. *The Winter of Red Snow: The Revolutionary War Diary of Abigail Jane Stewart*. Scholastic, 1996. Cloth 0-590-22653-3. Grades 4 to 6.

Eleven-year-old Abigail, the daughter of a shoemaker, keeps a diary from December 1777 to July 1778. General Washington and his Continental Army are camped near her home at Valley Forge, Pennsylvania; and she sees firsthand the harsh conditions under which the soldiers are living. The snow is red from the men's bleeding feet; many of them have no shoes. We see Martha and George Washington through the young girl's eyes, as she delivers laundry to Mrs. Washington, who has joined her husband for the winter. The Historical Note at the back of the book gives an overview of the causes of the Revolutionary War and its conduct up until the time depicted in the book. A few small drawings give a sense of clothing and life at the time, and maps help to contextualize the time and place. **F • R**

31. HASKINS, JIM. *Black, Blue and Gray: African Americans in the Civil War*. Simon & Schuster, 1998. Cloth 0-689-80655-8. Grades 5 to 8.

For white Americans in the North, the Civil War was about preserving the Union. For white Americans in the South, it was about preserving their independence. For black Americans on both sides, the Civil War was about slavery. It is no wonder that they took an intense interest in the course of the war and that many served in battle, against extraordinary odds. Haskins tells their story here. He writes about the slaves whose white masters brought them to the war to serve as personal servants or cooks. He writes about the efforts of Frederick Douglass to change the policy that kept blacks from serving in the Union Army until 1863. He writes about the unequal treatment and unequal pay given to black soldiers and about their courage in battle. Finally, and almost most poignantly, he writes about the ways in which history was rewritten so as to minimize the efforts that blacks made on their own behalf during the Civil War. **NF • HR**

32.   HERBERT, JANIS. *The American Revolution for Kids: A History with 21 Activities*. Chicago Review Press, 2002. Pap. 1-55652-456-0. Grades 4 to 8.

This well-written overview of the events of the American Revolution is enhanced by many illustrations drawn from primary sources. Back matter includes a glossary, short biographies, the text of the Declaration of Independence, a list of Web sites and Revolutionary War sites to visit, and a bibliography. The real strength of this book, however, lies in the well-designed activities that help bring history to life for contemporary children. These include learning to dance a minuet like George Washington, making paper cutouts like those in fashion in colonial homes, reenacting the Battle of Cowpens, and making a papier-mache powder horn. **NF • HR**

33.   KIMMEL, ERIC A. *Montezuma and the Fall of the Aztecs*. Illustrated by Daniel San Souci. Holiday House, 2000. Cloth 0-8234-1452-3. Grades 2 to 4.

The story of the conquest of the great Aztec nation by a small band of Spanish explorers under the leadership of Hernan Cortes is a dramatic one. Kimmel and San Souci make the most of the inherent excitement and tragedy of this event while also clarifying some aspects of it. We learn, for example, that Cortes was able to enlist the support of other neighboring peoples whose lands had been conquered by Montezuma. As the author points out in a note at the end of the book, Cortes did not really conquer the Aztecs. Instead, he started a revolution and then took advantage of it by declaring himself its leader. Kimmel is careful to tell both the Spanish and Aztec versions of the event and to give a place of honor to Cuahtemoc, the Aztec prince who continued to fight the Spanish after Montezuma's death. A glossary and a list of adult resources for further reading are included. **NF • R**

34.   KRULL, KATHLEEN. *V Is for Victory: America Remembers World War II*. Apple Soup/Knopf, 1995. Cloth 0-679-86198-X; LB 0-679-96198-4. Grades 5 to 8.

The cover proclaims this to be a book for families commemorating the 50th anniversary of the Allied victory. Lavishly illustrated with photos and documents from the war years and put together in a scrapbook format, it seems designed to stimulate the memories of people old enough to have lived through World War II and to stimulate the curiosity of young readers. The coverage is thorough, from the events leading up to the war to the bombing of Pearl Harbor to the war's end and some lasting consequences. There are chapters on the horrors of the Holocaust and the injustice of the Japanese American internment camps. A bibliography includes both adult and juvenile titles. **NF • HR**

35.   LEWIN, TED. *Red Legs: A Drummer Boy of the Civil War*.
Illustrated by the author. HarperCollins, 2001. Cloth 0-688-16024-7; LB 0-688-16025-5. Grades 2 to 4.

The book opens with Stephen, a young boy, sitting by a camp fire with other Union soldiers, thinking about the letter he would write to his mother. We see him line up for roll call and eat a breakfast of slab bacon and coffee. When the bugle blares, Stephen takes his drum and taps out the signal for the men to assemble. The Union soldiers march to battle while the Confederate army marches to meet them. The drummer boys are sent to the rear, but in the ensuing battle, Stephen is shot. Then a hand reaches down and helps him up. All of the fallen soldiers get up and shake hands with the enemy. The battle is over, and they can go home because this is a historical reenactment. An author's note explains what reenactors do and tells that the story is based on a real drummer boy from Brooklyn, New York. **F • R**

36.   LYON, GEORGE ELLA. *Here and Then*. Orchard, 1994. Cloth 0-531-06866-8. Grades 4 to 6.

History is a living phenomenon to Abby's parents who pursue their passion by reenacting Civil War battles. The summer before she starts seventh grade, Abby joins them and plays the part of Eliza Hoskins, a 40-year-old woman who nursed the sick and wounded on both sides of the war from her home in Kentucky. The story takes a supernatural turn when Eliza begins to write in Abby's diary and communicates the desperate need she has for medical supplies. Back home in the 20th century, Abby convinces her best friend to help her round up the necessary supplies and then makes the trip back to the reenactment site to deliver them. She encounters a wounded Civil War soldier there, another time-traveler like her. Later, she and her family find his grave and know from the date on the marker that he survived the Civil War, perhaps because of Abby's intervention. **F • R**

37.   McPHERSON, JAMES M. *Fields of Fury: The American Civil War*.
Atheneum/Byron Preiss Visual Publications, 2002. Cloth 0-689-84833-1.
Grades 5 to 8.

McPherson is a noted historian who has written many well-received
books about the Civil War for adults. He has used his expertise effectively in this account written for young readers. While it is primarily a
military history, the author also includes information about the causes
of the war, slavery, the effects on the southern and northern home
fronts, and Reconstruction. The format is attractive and readable; each
double-page spread features a full-page illustration on the right hand
side with a narrative text and sidebar of other interesting, relevant facts
on the left. Back matter includes a glossary, a bibliography of mostly
adult titles, and a list of Civil War sites on the Web. NF • R

38.   MARRIN, ALBERT. *Old Hickory: Andrew Jackson and the
American People*. Dutton, 2004. Cloth 0-525-47293-2. Grades 6 to 8.

The seventh president of the United States served as a soldier in the
Revolutionary War before he was 14 years old. He went on to fight
Indians and to become a general in the War of 1812, defeating the
British in the Battle of New Orleans. A wildly popular war hero, he
handily won the presidency in 1823. A bit of doggerel from the time
summed up the difference between the two candidates: "John Quincy
Adams who can write, Andrew Jackson who can fight" (p. 145). Marrin
does an admirable job of interpreting the life and political legacy of
Old Hickory, contextualizing his racism—manifested in his attitudes
toward African and Native Americans—within the general values of
the time. Jackson's championship of the rights of common people and
his efforts to preserve the Union during the years leading up to the
Civil War are acknowledged. His leading role in the horrific policies
that led to dispossessing Native Americans of their tribal lands and the
terrible Trail of Tears are is also described in detail. NF • R

39.   MARRIN, ALBERT. *Sitting Bull and His World*. Dutton, 2000. Cloth
0-525-45944-8. Grades 6 to 8.

Marrin acknowledges the difficulties a historian faces in trying to accu-
rately represent the lives of Native American people. He then tries to
overcome these difficulties in this panoramic depiction of the life and
times of the great leader Sitting Bull. There are many telling details
about what it was like to grow up as one of the Lakota people in the
years before the white people began to ravage the Great Plains and sys-

tematically eradicate the traditional culture of the Indians who lived there. He tells how the destruction of the great herds of buffalo eliminated the main source of food for the Plains Indians and forced them into lives of dependency on reservations. Marrin explains the role that Sitting Bull played in leading his people through these desperate times, ending with his death at the hands of Indian police, acting under the orders of government officials. It is a peculiarly American story, one that all American children should know. **NF • HR**

40.   MELTZER, MILTON. *The American Revolutionaries: A History in Their Own Words 1750–1800*. HarperCollins, 1987. Cloth 0-690-04641-3; HarperTrophy, 1993, pap. 0-06-446145-9. Grades 7 to 8.

Excerpts from primary source materials such as letters, diaries, pamphlets, books, and historical documents tell the story of the American Revolution from the point of view of men, women, and young people who were there. Meltzer's informative introduction to each piece provides the context. This is historiography at its best. **NF • HR**

41.   MELTZER, MILTON. *Weapons and Warfare: From the Stone Age to the Space Age*. Illustrated by Sergio Martinez. HarperCollins, 1996. Cloth 0-06-024875-0; LB 0-06-024876-9. Grades 5 to 8.

Brief chapters or sections trace the history of weapons and warfare from the use of the stone club in prehistoric times to the atomic and hydrogen bombs of the 20th century. Meltzer discusses the consequences of each technological advance in weapon-making for warfare itself and for the society in which the weapons were used. The conclusion of the book briefly touches on the economic aspects of arms supply and also explains the psychological cost of killing for soldiers who carry the weapons. **NF • R**

42.   MURPHY, JIM. *The Long Road to Gettysburg*. Clarion, 1992. Cloth 0-395-55965-0; pap. 0-618-05157-0. Grades 5 to 8.

Like Susan Beller in *To Hold This Ground*, Murphy uses the personal war journals of a Confederate and a Union soldier to humanize his story of this terrible battle that marked a turning point in the Civil War. We see the tedium and the horror of war from the perspectives of these two young men. Murphy also explains the larger military strategy involved in the battle of Gettysburg and the critical decisions made by

generals on either side. The many historical photos, maps, and drawings—at least one on each double-page spread—add visual appeal as
well as significant information. **NF • HR**

43.   MURPHY, JIM. *A Young Patriot: The American Revolution as
Experienced by One Boy*. Clarion, 1996. Cloth 0-395-60523-7; pap. 0-
395-90010-0. Grades 5 to 8.

This is one young soldier's perspective on the American Revolutionary
War, reconstructed from his own narrative and other primary sources.
Joseph Plumb Martin was only 15 when he joined a Connecticut troop
and left home to fight the British. Through his own words, we learn
about the severe conditions under which the Continental troops exist-
ed, without ample food, clothing, or ammunition and with such a lack
of sanitary housing that thousands died of sickness. The soldiers were
not even paid their wages because Congress could not afford them.
Outnumbered by the vastly better trained and equipped British army,
the American troops eventually won the war through the superb tactics
of General Washington and their own persistence. After the war, Martin
found his way to a farm in Maine, where he eked out a poor living
from the rocky soil and eventually wrote the account on which this
book is based. The author explains that Martin's self-published book,
little noticed at the time, is considered by historians today to be one of
the most important sources of information about the War for
Independence. A bibliography of adult titles and a chronology are
included. **NF • HR**

44.   NELSON, PETE. *Left for Dead: A Young Man's Search for Justice
for the USS Indianapolis*. Delacorte, 2002. Cloth 0-385-72959-6; 2003,
pap. 0-385-73091-8. Grades 6 to 8.

In 1996, an 11-year-old boy, Hunter Scott, became intrigued with the
story told by survivors of the *USS Indianapolis*, sunk by a Japanese sub-
marine at the end of World War II. His research on the incident for a
school history fair led him to believe that the captain had been wrong-
fully court-martialed by the Navy for putting his ship at hazard. He
was ultimately able to persuade Congress to clear the captain's good
name. This is that boy's story and also the story of the men of the
Indianapolis, both the many who died in the attack and the few who
survived for five days in shark-infested waters before they were rescued. **NF • R**

45. O'BRIEN, PATRICK. *Duel of the Ironclads: The Monitor vs. The Virginia*. Walker, 2003. Cloth 0-8027-8842-4; LB 0-8027-8843-2. Grades 4 to 6.

This nonfiction picture book chronicles an unusual arms race between the North and the South during the Civil War. Each side was rushing to build an armored, iron-clad warship, and each side succeeded. These strange-looking ships—the *Monitor* and the *Virginia* (or the *Merrimack*, as she was known in the North)—fought each other in an indecisive battle in 1862 while thousands of civilians watched from the shore. The Confederate army destroyed the *Virginia* shortly after the battle to avoid having her fall into Union hands, and the *Monitor* sank in a violent storm before the end of 1862. Still, these two ships are memorable for having been the first two armored ships to engage in battle, ending the era of wooden warships forever. **NF • R**

46. O'CONNOR, JANE. *The Emperor's Silent Army: Terracotta Warriors of Ancient China*. Viking, 2002. Cloth 0-670-03512-2. Grades 4 to 6.

Clear, expository prose and striking illustrations tell the story of the discovery of the 7,500 stunningly realistic terracotta soldiers and horses, buried underground in China for more than 2,000 years. The reader learns that these remarkable figures, now considered one of the true wonders of the ancient world, were created and installed to protect Qin Shihuang, the ruthless first Emperor of China, after death. This remarkable ruler used his military force to unite warring kingdoms into one empire. He built the first Great Wall of China to protect the borders of his country. He also burned books and buried alive more than 400 scholars who were critical of him. The terracotta warriors remain today as a legacy of an ancient military dictatorship. **NF • R**

47. PANCHYK, RICHARD. *World War II for Kids: A History with 21 Activities*. Chicago Review Press, 2002. Pap. 1-55652-455-2. Grades 5 to 8.

This is an exceptionally comprehensive and child-friendly overview of the causes, events, and consequences of World War II. The author ties together primary source materials with a coherent narrative and provides relevant, interesting activities that help bring history alive. Among the suggested activities: code breaking, bandage making, living out of a ration kit, identifying military ranks, and learning military lingo. Classroom teachers would be well-advised to start here if they are planning units about World War II. **NF • HR**

48. RANSOM, CANDICE F. *Children of the Civil War*. Carolrhoda, 1998. LB 1-57505-241-5. Grades 3 to 5.

This volume in the Picture the American Past series uses historical photos and a simple text to introduce younger readers to the Civil War. The focus is on the experiences of children in the North and South, including slaves and the boys who joined the troops as buglers and drummer boys. This is one of the few books that addresses the issue of children who were orphaned because of the war. Back matter includes directions for making a wheel code, suggestions for follow-up activities, a resource list, and a timeline. **NF • R**

49. SANDLER, MARTIN W. *Civil War*. HarperCollins, 1996. Cloth 0-06-026024-6; LB 0-06-026027-0. Grades 3 to 6.

Sandler draws on the rich visual resources of the Library of Congress to create a highly pictorial overview of the American Civil War. The text explains the illustrations and provides a coherent account of the causes, events, important individuals, and consequences of the war. **NF • R**

50. SCHANZER, ROSALYN. *George vs. George: The American Revolution as Seen from Both Sides*. National Geographic, 2004. Cloth 0-7922-7349-4. Grades 3 to 5.

The author/illustrator tells the story of the American Revolution by focusing on two of its most iconic characters: George Washington and King George III. In clear, easy-to-understand prose and humorous illustrations, she compares and contrasts these two leaders who found themselves on opposite sides of the War for Independence. We see the events leading up to the Revolution and the conduct of the war from the point of view of each side. There is a bibliography containing books written for both children and adults, a list of sources for the quotes given in balloons throughout the text, and an index. This is a very painless way to learn American history! **NF • HR**

51. TANAKA, SHELLEY. *D-Day: They Fought to Free Europe from Hitler's Tyranny*. Illustrated by David Craig. Hyperion/Madison Press, 2003. Cloth 0-7868-1881-6. Grades 5 to 8.

The story of the invasion of Normandy by American and other Allied troops on June 6, 1944, is told in first-hand narratives, historical sidebars, photos, and vivid paintings. The book is more successful in presenting a wealth of small details—the "crickets" used by paratroopers to signal each other in the dark, the meaning of "D" in D-Day, the contents of a portable surgical kit, and the inflatable life belt that was washed ashore decades after the invasion—than it is at communicating the significance of the event. **NF • RWR**

52. VAN STEENWYK, ELIZABETH. *Mathew Brady: Civil War Photographer*. Franklin Watts, 1997. LB 0-531-20264-X; pap. 0-531-1585-9. Grades 3 to 5.

This biography begins with the day on which Brady took a photograph of President James K. Polk, the first photograph ever to be taken of a sitting United States president. Photography was in its infancy, and Brady was one of its pioneers. When the Civil War began, Brady was busy taking pictures of the soldiers gathering in Washington, D.C. He went on, of course, to photograph the battlefields of the Civil War, following the Union army. Many of these iconic images are reproduced in this slim volume. **NF • R**

53. WALDMAN, NEIL. *Wounded Knee*. Atheneum, 2001. Cloth 0-689-82559-5. Grades 6 to 8.

Waldman traces the origin of the events that would lead to the massacre of innocent women and children of the Lakota people in 1890 to the first contacts between Christopher Columbus and the native people that he encountered on the island of San Salvador. Conflict between the dominant white people and the native people of America resulted in misunderstandings, broken promises, escalating hostilities, and finally open warfare. Unfortunately, the massacre at Wounded Knee was just one of many such incidents. Waldman dramatizes the tragedy with his own acrylic paintings. **NF • R**

WEB SITES

54. *The Alamo*.
http://www.thealamo.org
Grades 4 to 8.

This useful Web site provides visitor information and a good account of the famous battle that occurred here in 1836. The Educational Resources section includes lesson plans and links to other related sites. The page "just for kids" includes coloring sheets, word finders, and a very appealing "Flat Stanley Gallery" with photos of the book character visiting the Alamo. **NF • R**

55. American Visionaries: Frederick Douglass.
http://www.cr.nps.gov/museum/exhibits/douglass/
National Park Service, n.d. Grades 4 to 8.

This Web site shows the contributions of Frederick Douglass to the early women's rights movement as well as to the anti-slavery movement. Brief, factual texts, images, and lesson plans are included. NF • R

56. The Anne Frank Guide.
http://www.annefrankguide.net
Grades 5 to 8.

This useful Web site is a product of the Anne Frank House in Amsterdam and its international affiliates. It is available in several major European languages; the English edition is created and maintained by educators in the U.K. It is divided into three major segments: data, a timeline, and tips for students who are putting together a project or talk based on the life of Anne Frank. The data section is rich in background information and pictures, as well as film and sound clips. NF • R

57. Fort Davis National Historic Site.
http://www.nps.gov/foda/
National Park Service, 2006. Grades 5 to 8.

Fort Davis, in the mountains of West Texas, is a surviving example of a frontier military post that was a significant location during the Indian Wars. It is also historically significant because several all-black U.S. Cavalry regiments, established after the Civil War, were stationed there. The link to "history & culture" leads to photos and text about many relevant topics, including several about the Buffalo Soldiers and less-well-known aspects of the Indian Wars in the West. NF • R

58. Frederick Douglass.
http://www.pbs.org/wgbh/aia/part4/4p1539.html
Public Broadcasting System, n.d. Grades 4 to 8.

A brief biographical profile gives the highlights of Douglass's life and contributions. Useful links include the text of his famous speech, "The Meaning of July Fourth for the Negro," and a letter to William Lloyd Garrison from Harriet Beecher Stowe. NF • R

59. *Gettysburg National Military Park*.
http://www.nps.gov/gett/
National Park Service, n.d. Grades 4 to 8.

This well-designed and informative Web site features a virtual tour of the Gettysburg National Military Park in Pennsylvania. Maps, photos, and text give a good overview of the Battle at Gettysburg and its significance within the context of the Civil War. There is a fascinating section on the Great Reunion of 1913 at the battlefield, in which Union and Confederate soldiers met together and apparently put the enmity of the war behind them. **NF • R**

60. *Lakota Accounts of the Massacre at Wounded Knee*.
http://www.pbs.org/weta/thewest/resources/archives/eight/wklakota.htm
PBS, 2001. Grades 6 to 8.

Excerpts from the Report of the Commissioner of Indian Affairs for 1891 provide moving primary source documentation of the Lakota perspective on the massacre at Wounded Knee. **NF • R**

61. *National Park Service Revolutionary War Site*.
http://www.nps.gov/revwar
National Park Service, n.d. Grades 4 up.

This is a well-organized site linking students, teachers, and researchers to many useful sources of information about the Revolutionary War. It includes timelines, summaries of events, and links to thought-provoking issues relating to the "unfinished revolution," showing the relevance of events that took place more than 200 years ago to the United States' current situation. **NF • HR**

62. *Navajo Code Talkers' Dictionary*.
http://www.history.navy.mil/faqs/faq61-4.htm
Department of the Navy—Navy Historical Center, 1999. Grades 4 to 8.

In *Navajo Code Talkers,* Nathan Aaseng describes how the Navajo marines devised an indecipherable code based on their native language. The military vocabulary needed for their battlefield communications often had no direct correlation in Navajo so these cryptographers needed to be inventive, devising words that would defy detection but also be easy to remember. This Web site from the Naval Historical Center contains their dictionary. The literal translations are a fascinating look into the connections made between the world of modern warfare and the Navajos' own culture. They used their Navajo word for clan, *din-neh-ih*, to stand for corps. *Gini*, or chicken hawk, stood for dive bomber. Tank destroyers became *chay-da-gahi-nail-tsaidi*, tortoise killers. NF • R

63.   *Vietnam Online.*

http://www.pbs.org/wgbh/amex/vietnam
WGBH, 1997–2005. Grades 5 to 8.

This Web site is intended as a companion resource to the American Experience documentary "Vietnam: A Television History." However, it can be used independently by teachers and students with an interest in the Vietnam War. There are many useful links: a timeline, a detailed "who's who" of the people involved, and maps. One link leads to primary sources such as the Tonkin Gulf Resolution, letters from President Eisenhower and President Kennedy to the South Vietnamese Premier Ngo Dinh Diem, and the statement of the Vietnam Veterans Against the War. The section titled "In the Trenches" has a useful segment on the My Lai Massacre as well as a discussion of the MIA issue and a glossary of the unique language of the war. A Teacher's Guide has hints for activities related to civics, geography, and culture. NF • HR

64.   *War, Military.*

http://memory.loc.gov/ammem/browse/ListSome.php?category=War,+
Military
Library of Congress, n.d. Grades 5 to 8.

This "War, military" subject heading from the American Memory site of the Library of Congress leads the browser to relevant links within the online collection. There are many primary source documents from the Civil War, in particular: maps, photographs, selections from diaries and other papers, even selections of band music. Other treasures include Ansel Adams's photographs of Japanese American internment at Manzanar and issues of "Stars and Stripes" that were published during World War I. NF • HR

DVDs

65. *The Civil War: A Film by Ken Burns.* Florentine Films and WETA. 1990. Approximately 11 hours. Grades 5 to 8.

The sweep of events covered in the nine episodes of this epic documentary is enormous. The production captures more than the events of the Civil War, however. Because black-and-white photography had come into use at the time, we see the faces of the ordinary soldiers as well as the military and political leaders, many sporting astonishing displays of facial hair. There are haunting photos of the battlefields strewn with the dead. Gifted actors read the words of men and women who wrote letters and kept diaries that have survived to this day. The scholarly commentators provide insightful perspectives, and the narration of David McCullough pulls it all together. The use of evocative period music may be the most memorable aspect of the production; it enhances the emotional impact of the visual images and spoken words. NF • HR

66. *Liberty! The American Revolution.* Twin Cities Public Television. 1997. Approximately 6 hours. Grades 5 to 8.

Anyone wishing to get a good overview of the events leading up to the American Revolution, the course of the war, and its consequences for the nation would be well-advised to spend the time with these three discs, each containing two one-hour episodes. Actors speak words taken directly from contemporary diaries, documents, and letters; among them the diary of Robert Plumb Martin, whose account also forms the basis of Jim Murphy's *A Young Patriot.* The visuals re-create the look of the land more than 200 years ago. Historians interpret events intelligently.

The first episode, "The Reluctant Revolutionaries," opens with Benjamin Rush visiting King George in his throne room in the 1760s. We learn that the American colonists at that time were proud to be part of the powerful British Empire. That relationship begins to sour, however, with the passage of the Stamp Act in 1766. By 1773, American colonists have resisted what they see as harsh taxation with actions such as the Boston Tea Party, and the British have retaliated by sending gunboats to Massachusetts. "Blows Must Decide," episode two, shows the events leading up to the Declaration of Independence, on July 4, 1776, including the famous ride of Paul Revere, and the publication of *Common Sense* by Thomas Paine.

Episode three, "The Times That Try Men's Souls," focuses on the efforts of the early American leaders to communicate an abstract concept of liberty that will galvanize people to their cause and on George Washington's task of forging a national army out of 13 separate militias. "Oh, Fatal Ambition," episode four, profiles the British General Burgoyne, whose campaign in New York ultimately fails and gives Benjamin Franklin the ammunition he needs to negotiate a treaty with France.

"The World Turned Upside Down" is the fifth episode. It explores the course of the war in the southern states where slavery and a gaping chasm between the wealthy plantation owners and poor whites complicate the political agenda. Things look so bad for the Patriots that General Benedict Arnold, a Colonial military hero, defects to the British in a major act of treason. Ultimately, however, with the help of European allies and the brilliant military strategy of General Nathaniel Green, the Patriots win the war.

The final episode—"Are We to Be a Nation?"—chronicles the work of the Founding Fathers who create the structure of a new government by crafting the Constitution, a major document of political philosophy. NF • HR

67. *Rebels and Redcoats: How Britain Lost America*. WGBH Educational Foundation and BBC. 2003. 200 minutes. Grades 6 to 8.

Four 50-minute episodes tell the story of the American Revolution from the British perspective. This is primarily a military history, presenting the conflict as a civil war between divided British factions. The narrator, who gives his commentary while driving, walking, and, in one case, riding a horse through the contemporary sites of the historic events that he is recounting, draws some compelling parallels between Britain's position during the Revolution and the United States position much later during the Vietnam War. The DVD would probably be most interesting to those rare young people who are avid Revolutionary War buffs; but teachers could also use this DVD to encourage critical thinking about some of the legendary heroes and events of American history. NF • R

68. *Vietnam: A Television History*. WGBH. 1983, 1996, 2004. Approximately 11 hours. Grades 7 up.

This comprehensive video documentary on four discs is structured in 11 separate one-hour episodes. The content is well-researched and well-balanced and includes multiple perspectives on the Vietnam War. Most episodes explore a specific time period, from the roots of the war in 1945 to 1953 to its ending and immediate aftermath from 1973 to 1975. Other episodes explore specific themes such as the covert wars in Cambodia and Laos and the United States home front. Because this was the first televised war and because those reports were uncensored, many of the images are vivid, violent, and graphic. There are interviews with the policymakers and advisers who were involved in the decisions that led to increased American involvement in Southeast Asia, with soldiers who fought on the ground, with anti-war protesters, and with Vietnamese people whose sympathies represent a wide spectrum of values. Young people who have the opportunity to view the entire documentary will gain insights into a historical event that had a profound effect on their grandparents' generation and that echoes today in our thinking about American interests overseas and our willingness or reluctance to send American soldiers to war. **NF • HR**

CDs

69. *The Civil War: Traditional American Songs and Instrumental Music Featured in the Film by Ken Burns*. Elektra Nonesuch, 1990. Grades 4 to 8.

Twenty-eight tracks give the listener a feeling for the Ken Burns documentary on the Civil War. The haunting theme song, "Ashokan Farewell" is here, as well as Civil War classics such as "When Johnny Comes Marching Home," "Dixie," and "Yankee Doodle." In addition to songs and instrumental music, the last track features a reading of the poignant letter that Sullivan Ballou wrote to his wife before the Battle of Bull Run. **NF • HR**

HOPE AND GLORY

O F COURSE, WAR IS NOT JUST A HISTORICAL EVENT. It is also an idea and an ideal. Throughout history, men—more so than women—have found war to be the crucible for demonstrating their honor and courage, for seeking fame, and for being heroes. At least initially, most men march off to war in quest of hope and glory.

Leo Braudy (2003) writes that war, and especially the *idea* of war, determines how "real" men should live and be. This was true for the Greeks and it is true today, although the evolution of high-technology weapons since World War I has changed this somewhat. Acts of individual heroism seem to matter less when generals direct battles from far behind the lines and soldiers view their targets through distant computerized scopes (p. 495). In more traditional warfare, men displayed individual honor in the presence of others, thereby turning that honor into a social fact. The honor code underlying warfare shaped male physical violence into socially acceptable forms (pp. 50ff.).

As boys enter adolescence, issues of male identity become particularly salient, and many teenagers yearn for opportunities to test their own capacity for heroism. It is not surprising that many of the books in this section depict young male protagonists seeking hope and glory on the battlefield. Throughout history, there have been institutions that have been designed to fulfill those dreams. Knighthood is an interesting historical example, with its code of chivalry intended to temper the demands for deeds of physical violence with honor and romanticized protection of women.

Some Native American tribes also developed a warrior culture that allowed or encouraged young men to demonstrate their bravery and prowess in the martial arts. The Web site of the U.S. Naval

Historical Center states that at the end of the 20th century, there were more than 190,000 Native American military veterans, giving them the highest record of service per capita compared with other ethnic groups. The author of this Web site attributes this disproportionately high participation in military service to the Native American warrior tradition ("Twentieth Century Warriors," 1997). While this may be an oversimplification or even an ethnic stereotype, there is anthropological and sociological evidence of a continuing warrior tradition that is stronger in some tribes than others. Tom Holm (1996) looked into the contemporary manifestations of the warrior tradition in his study of Native American veterans of the Vietnam War. He found that in the tribes of the Great Plains, prairies, and Northeast, a form of ritualized warfare had played an important role in maintaining tribal stability in the years before tribes were decimated by American armies and disease. A continuing legacy from that history is the place of honor accorded to a warrior. Even the mothers of warriors are given a place of honor in pow wows and other ceremonial gatherings.

War has often been an arena in which groups facing discrimination sought to demonstrate their capacity for courage. Often their hope was not for glory but for justice. As long ago as the Revolutionary War, African Americans have struggled to be allowed to fight in their country's wars. It will be surprising to many young people to learn that as recently as World War II they fought in segregated units. Japanese Americans eventually won the right to fight in World War II, although not in the Pacific theater. Their battalions showed remarkable heroism and took unusually high casualties, earning respect for their courage and patriotism.

Women, too, have sought the opportunity to serve in wartime. They disguised themselves as men in order to serve in the Revolutionary and Civil Wars. They nursed the sick and wounded. They have served unofficially, as spies and support personnel. And today, they wear the uniforms of regular military personnel. There are currently more than 350,000 women serving in the United States military, 15 percent of them as active duty personnel ("Wounded in War," 2005). Although officially the Defense Department exempts women from jobs whose primary mission is combat, female soldiers in Iraq are being killed alongside their male counterparts. Forty-one American female soldiers had died by the time a PBS "News Hour" was aired in August 2005. Many were killed by suicide bombers or by improvised explosive devices (IEDs) as they moved in convoys along highways and city streets ("Women in Combat," 2005).

War tends to stimulate thoughts of hope and glory for civilians as well as for those who actually do the fighting. Chris Hedges (2002), an award-winning war correspondent, writes about the exalted sense of nationalism or patriotism that war generates within a society. The world seems to be filled with high drama, however romanticized, and "a moral purpose is infused into the trivial and the commonplace" (p. 54). Think how Americans came together in a kind of ecstasy of patriotism after the attacks on the World Trade Center in 2001. United for the moment in suffering, many were already anticipating the inevitable retaliation. Think of the symbols of the Persian Gulf and Iraq wars: yellow ribbons tied to trees and attached magnetically to cars and SUVs, all reminding us to support our troops. There is obviously a strong link between support for war and the ideals of nationalism or patriotism. The link can be authentic and genuine or manipulated by propaganda.

CHILDREN'S LITERATURE WITH THEMES OF HOPE AND GLORY

It is not surprising that many novels set in times of war revolve around issues of heroism. In young adult novels, in particular, wartime settings lend themselves to situations that make compelling coming-of-age stories. The heightened reality of war makes a young protagonist's search for identity and meaning particularly dramatic. There are many good examples in this section, representing a wide range of genres, from fantasy to historical fiction to contemporary realistic novels. Look particularly at:

- The Protector of the Small and Song of the Lioness series by Tamora Pierce for books in which female protagonists struggle to find a place in a male world
- The Arthur trilogy by Kevin Crossley-Holland in which a boy living in medieval England finds his life is magically mirroring that of the legendary King Arthur
- The Sea of Trolls by Nancy Farmer, set in the year 793 A.D. at the time of the Viking raids on Saxon England
- Soldier's Heart by Gary Paulsen, a moving novella about the disillusionment experienced by a 15-year-old boy who had hoped to find excitement in a real "fighting war" but ends up physically and emotionally damaged
- Romare Bearden's Li'l Dan, the Drummer Boy, about a slave who takes the Union soldiers at their word when they tell him he is free, taking his drum and following them into battle

- *B Is for Buster* by Iain Lawrence, in which a Canadian boy tries to exchange his abusive parents for brave comrades in arms fighting in World War II
- *After the War* by Carole Matas, a novel about a survivor of Buchenwald concentration camp, who fights depression by fighting to establish the Jewish state of Israel

Nonfiction books in this chapter also cover a wide range of subjects; some of the most interesting and distinguished deal with the quest by non-white American males and by American women for opportunities to demonstrate heroism in wartime. Some good examples include:

- *Navajo Code Talkers* by Nathan Aaseng
- *Come All You Brave Soldiers: Blacks in the Revolutionary War* by Clinton Cox
- *Red-Tail Angels: The Story of the Tuskegee Airmen of World War II* by Patricia and Fredrick McKissack
- *Angels of Mercy: The Army Nurses of World War II* by Betsy Kuhn

MULTIMEDIA RESOURCES

There are many good, authoritative Web sites with biographical information about real-life heroes that children may be interested in. Even the legendary King Arthur can be found on the World Wide Web and in documentary videos. The Web site for the Congressional Medal of Honor is another good source of information about American soldiers who have been recognized for their heroism in battle.

CHILDREN'S READING INTERESTS AND INFORMATION NEEDS

All children need heroes. They needn't be real; fictional heroes are sometimes even more satisfying. Children need to contemplate the possibilities of heroism. Will they be brave enough, strong enough, wise enough to handle the difficulties that their lives will present to them? All of us who care about children hope that these will be hypothetical questions that can be satisfied by reading. Books can be a

wonderful testing ground, and many children who read are instinctive-
ly drawn to books with heroes that are larger than life or reassuringly
child-sized. We know that some children will be faced with real-life
situations in which courage, strong character, and quick thinking may
be required. We can only hope that they will remember Alanna, the
girl who became a knight in the imaginary kingdom of Tortall, or
Sitting Bull, who was called Slow as a boy but went on to become one
of the most remarkable warrior chiefs. We hope young readers will
remember and be inspired.

Bibliography

✄

BOOKS

---

70.   AASENG, NATHAN. *Navajo Code Talkers: America's Secret
Weapon in World War II.* Walker, 1992. Trade 0-8027-8182-9; 2002, pap.
0-8027-8183-7. Grades 5 to 8.

Aaseng makes certain that readers understand the irony inherent in the
story of the Navajo code talkers. These Native Americans had been forbidden to speak their language in the government schools they attend-
ed as children. That they nevertheless retained their mother tongue is
due in part to their geographic isolation and in part to their strong culture. That they came forward to serve in World War II, using their
unique language to communicate in code that proved to be unbreak-
able, is a tribute to their loyalty to a country that had not treated them
well. Here is the story of the contributions made by Navajo Marines
during the difficult campaigns to take the Japanese island strongholds
such as Iwo Jima and Okinawa. **NF • R**

71.   ALDER, ELIZABETH. *Crossing the Panther's Path.* Farrar Straus
Giroux, 2002. Cloth 0-374-31662-7. Grades 6 to 8.

Billy Caldwell, the 16-year-old son of a British soldier and a Mohawk
mother, is inspired by the Shawnee chief, Tecumseh, to join him in his
efforts to repel the Americans from the Northwest Territory. At first
Tecumseh is successful as he unites Indians from several tribes and
secures the assistance of the British army. Caldwell becomes a trusted
interpreter for Tecumseh and a seasoned warrior. Billy is appalled, however, by the brutality shown by both sides toward innocent women and

children. The fighting depicted here between the British and Indians on one side and the Americans on the other led to the War of 1812, which further diminished Indian lands in North America. **F • R**

72.   BANKS, SARA HARRELL. *Abraham's Battle: A Novel of Gettysburg*. Atheneum, 1999. Cloth 0-689-81779-7. Grades 4 to 6.

An ex-slave named Abraham Small and a young Confederate soldier named Lamar Cooper have a chance encounter on the farm near Gettysburg where Abraham works. Their conversation convinces Abraham that he needs to do his part for the Union cause. He takes his mule and volunteers as an ambulance driver, helping to retrieve the wounded soldiers from the Gettysburg battlefield. There he sees Lamar and takes him back to the Union field hospital to be treated. The boy does not survive his wounds, but he is able to write to his sister and ask her to send Abraham some okra seeds, a southern vegetable that the old man has been missing. When he gets word that President Abraham Lincoln will be coming to dedicate the cemetery at Gettysburg, Abraham Small knows that he must be there. After his speech, the president approaches Abraham and asks him to drive him to the battleground where he can pay his respects to the men who died there. As they return to the entrance of the cemetery, Lincoln gives Abraham Small his hat.

The plot in this short novel is slender and nearly collapses under the weight of didactic content about the Civil War. Some young readers, however, may find this an accessible introduction to some important historical issues. **F • RWR**

73.   BEARDEN, ROMARE. *Li'l Dan, the Drummer Boy: A Civil War Story*. Illustrated by the author. Simon & Schuster, 2003. Cloth 0-689-86237-7. Grades 3 to 5.

Li'l Dan, a slave on a cotton plantation, learns to play the drum from an older man whose instrument had come from Africa. He makes his own drum from a hollow log and a pig hide pulled taut over the top. When a troop of black Union soldiers arrive at the plantation and tell him that he is free, he takes his drum and follows them. The war isn't over, and the soldiers still have battles to fight. Li'l Dan proves that he is more than a mascot when he uses his drum to mimic the sound of a "five pounder" cannon, fooling the Confederate cavalry into thinking that the Union troop is better armed than they really are. General Sherman himself thanks Li'l Dan for his service and heroism and invites him to join the Army's Drum Corps.

The recent discovery of this manuscript gives young readers an opportunity to experience the artwork of Romare Bearden, one of America's greatest artists. The story itself is charming and comes to life as a read-aloud by Maya Angelou in the CD that is bound into the back cover. **F • R**

74.   BORDEN, LOUISE. *The Greatest Skating Race*. Illustrated by Niki Daly. Atheneum/Margaret K. McElderry, 2004. Cloth 0-689-84502-2. Grades 3 to 5.

In 1941, the Germans have occupied Holland. When a local man is arrested, his children are also thought to be in danger. Ten-year-old Piet, the son of a skate maker, is drafted to lead the two children to safety in Belgium by way of the frozen canals and waterways between their small town and Brugge, 16 kilometers away. Quick thinking and endurance enable the children to act the part of school children on an innocent outing, crossing the border into Belgium and finding the aunt who will shelter the endangered children for the rest of the war. Author's notes at the end of the story explain the *Elfstedentocht*, the 200-kilometer skating race that is a beloved tradition in Holland and that served as Piet's inspiration on his own marathon, and also give a brief history of skating. **F • R**

75.   BORDEN, LOUISE. *The Little Ships: The Heroic Rescue at Dunkirk in World War II*. Illustrated by Michael Foreman. McElderry/Simon & Schuster, 1997. Cloth 0-689-80827-5. Grades 3 to 5.

In May of 1940, half a million British and French troops were trapped in northern France with no escape except by sea. More than 800 ships—from great battleships to small private boats—assembled on the southeastern coasts of England and sailed across the English Channel to bring the boys home. This picture book tells the story from the point of view of a young girl who helps her father sail their fishing boat on that eventful day. The book concludes with an author's note that puts the story in its historic context and with an excerpt from Winston Churchill's eloquent speech to Parliament after the evacuation. **F • R**

76. BRADLEY, JAMES, AND RON POWERS. *Flags of Our Fathers: Heroes of Iwo Jima*. Delacorte, 2001. Cloth 0-385-72932-4; LB 0-385-90009-0. Grades 6 to 8.

James Bradley's father was one of the six men raising the United States flag in the iconic photo taken on the island of Iwo Jima during one of the most costly battles of World War II. After his father's death, Bradley set out to learn the stories of the other five men. These young Marines came from diverse backgrounds. They included a mill worker from New England, a Kentucky tobacco farmer, a Pennsylvania coal miner's son, a Texan from the oil fields, a boy from the dairy farms of Wisconsin, and a Pima Indian living on an Arizona reservation. Only three of them survived Iwo Jima.

Bradley also learned that while the photo was not staged, as some had contended, it did not depict the raising of the first American flag on Iwo Jima. That flag was lowered and presented to the naval commander for safekeeping. The image of this second flag raising was so striking, however, that it was used as the basis for a last-ditch effort by the U.S. government to raise money through the sale of war bonds. The three surviving Marines were reluctant spokesmen for this campaign. Bradley's reticent, modest father told him that the real heroes of Iwo Jima were the ones who did not return. **NF • R**

77. BRADLEY, KIMBERLY BRUBAKER. *For Freedom: The Story of a French Spy*. Delacorte, 2003. Cloth 0-385-72961-8. Grades 6 to 8.

Suzanne, a teenage girl in Cherbourg, France, continues to train as an opera singer while the events of World War II change almost everything else about her daily life. Her family doctor recruits her to be a spy for the French Resistance, delivering coded messages to other members of the secret network. In the very last days of the war, the network is betrayed. Suzanne is arrested by the Nazis who occupy her town, but she is saved by the timely Allied invasion of Normandy on D-Day. This first-person narrative is a fictionalized account of a real person. It demonstrates the opportunities for heroism that arise during times of emergency. **F • R**

78. BRESLIN, THERESA. *Remembrance*. Delacorte, 2002. Cloth 0-385-73015-2; LB 0-385-90067-8. Grades 7 to 8.

Five young people from a small town in Scotland experience World War I in very different ways. Charlotte, a 15-year-old from a privileged family, shocks her mother with her determination to help the war effort by training to be a nurse. Her older brother Francis is tormented by what he sees as the waste of lives for a pointless cause. John Malcolm, the son of a shopkeeper (and Charlotte's sweetheart), enlists at the earliest opportunity, eager to fight for England. When he dies early in the war, all of the characters are affected. His twin sister Maggie sees opportunities to escape her small-town life as the war stimulates profound social changes. Their little brother Alex, too young to enlist, schemes to find a way to be a soldier and avenge his brother before the war is over. The author, a Carnegie Medal winner, creates memorable characters and indelible images of the horrors of war and its consequences for everybody involved. **F • HR**

79. BRUCHAC, JOSEPH. *A Boy Called Slow*. Illustrated by Rocco Baviera. Philomel, 1994. Cloth 0-399-22692-3. Grades 3 to 5.

In this visually beautiful picture-book biography, Bruchac tells how the young Indian boy called Slow as a baby acquired the name of Sitting Bull. It happened when he was 14 years old and joined his father and men of the tribe to fight a band of Crow, the traditional enemies of the Hunkpapa people. In that battle, Slow was the first to attack, and the raid was a great success. In recognition of his son's prowess, his father gave him one of his own names, a name of great power: Tatan'ka Iyota'ke, or Sitting Bull. **NF • R**

80. BRUCHAC, JOSEPH. *Crazy Horse's Vision*. Illustrated by S. D. Nelson. Lee and Low, 2000. Cloth 1-880000-94-6. Grades 3 to 5.

The focus of this fictionalized picture-book biography is on the personal development of the great Indian Chief Crazy Horse from a dreamy, quiet child to a military genius and wise leader of his people. Along with Chief Sitting Bull, Crazy Horse was one of the heroes of the Battle of Little Big Horn, in which General Custer was defeated. The end papers of the book are illustrated in the traditional ledger book style while the illustrations themselves are more impressionistic, incorporating symbols and colors with special meaning to the Lakota people. Endnotes by both the author and illustrator add to the explanatory content of the text and illustrations. **F • R**

81. COOPER, MICHAEL L. *Hell Fighters: African American Soldiers in World War II*. Lodestar/Dutton, 1997. Cloth 0-525-67534-5. Grades 6 to 8.

The 369th Regiment started as a National Guard unit based in Harlem. When the United States entered World War I, the unit became one of the few segregated black regiments to see combat action. Four hundred thousand African American soldiers served in World War I, but most were assigned non-combat duties as stevedores and laborers. Even the regiment profiled here was subjected to racism. One white officer even distributed a letter to the mayors of French towns explaining that in the United States white people, especially women, did not socialize with blacks and asking them to honor this tradition. The 369th Regiment distinguished themselves in battle and returned home to a proud welcome from the people of New York as they marched from Manhattan to Harlem. NF • R

82.   COOPER, SUSAN. *Dawn of Fear*. Harcourt Brace Jovanovich, 1970. Cloth 0-15-226201-4. Grades 4 to 6.

Three English boys are fascinated by the air raids that threaten their small town outside London. The damage hasn't been severe yet, and the raids seem exciting. They look for shrapnel and build a camp in the field behind their homes. Their games turn more serious, however, when another gang of boys wrecks their camp and an older boy urges them to take revenge. Their war game escalates from a mudball fight to a fist fight between two of the boys who are nearly adults. It makes the younger boys uncomfortable and that night Derek, the protagonist of the novel, feels afraid for the first time when the bombing raids send his family to their backyard shelter. The next day he learns that a bomb made a direct hit on the home of Peter, one of the boys in his gang. As the story ends, Derek is sitting in the ruins of the boys' camp, crying.

The parallel between the boys' fight and the war between Germany and Britain is made obvious in a number of ways. Boys, in particular, will find much to think about. F • R

83.   COX, CLINTON. *Come All You Brave Soldiers: Blacks in the Revolutionary War*. Scholastic, 1999. Cloth 0-590-47576-2. Grades 6 to 8.

Many of us know that the first man to fall in the Boston Massacre is said to be Crispus Attucks, a fugitive slave. He was not the only black man to respond to the call to fight on the colonial side in the Revolutionary War. It is estimated that more than 5,000 soldiers of color participated in the war. Cox tells the stories of many of these men, who were motivated by patriotism and by the hope that their status in the new nation would be improved. Their hopes were dashed, of course, by the framers of the American constitution who refused to outlaw the institution of slavery. **NF • R**

84. CROSSLEY-HOLLAND, KEVIN. *At the Crossing Places*. Scholastic, 2002. Cloth 0-439-26599-1. Grades 6 to 8.

In Book Two of the Arthur Trilogy, young Arthur finds himself at a crossing place—between his boyhood and manhood, between the home where he was raised and the home where he is now living as squire to Lord Stephen, and between a peaceful existence and the battles that will come when he joins the Crusade to free Jerusalem from the Saracens. He continues to find parallels between his life and that of the legendary King Arthur that is revealed to him in the magical and mysterious Seeing Stone that Merlin has given to him. At the book's close, he and Lord Stephen are rallied for the Crusade on which they will soon embark. Arthur looks forward to the action but finds himself thinking about the good Saracens he has encountered in the Middle March where he lives. The French Count who is leading their Crusade counters with the argument of Saint Augustine that sometimes it is wrong to keep the peace, that God has commanded Christians to liberate Jerusalem from the pagans. It is a classic call to arms, and Arthur responds to it with the eagerness of youth. **F • HR**

85. CROSSLEY-HOLLAND, KEVIN. *King of the Middle March*. Scholastic, 2004. Cloth 0-439-26600-9. Grades 7 up.

In this last volume of the Arthur Trilogy, Arthur is 16 years old and finally embarked on a Crusade as the squire to Sir Stephen. He continues to use the Seeing Stone given to him by Merlin for its visions of the legendary King Arthur, whose life and times seem to parallel his own. He is knighted and ponders the responsibilities that come with that honor. The small band of English Crusaders becomes embroiled in the power plays of the Venetian doge and ends up fighting his Christian enemies rather than the Saracens. Sir Stephen is grievously wounded, and Arthur is ordered to take him back to England without either of them entering the holy city of Jerusalem.

During the fighting in Italy, Arthur sees much that robs him of his innocence and makes him question the glory of war and the righteousness of the Crusaders' cause. He also comes to understand his own potential for leadership; as Merlin says at the book's close, he finds the King within him. **F • HR**

86.   CROSSLEY-HOLLAND, KEVIN. *The Seeing Stone*. Scholastic, 2001.
Cloth 0-439-26326-3; 2002, pap. 0-439-43524-2. Grades 7 up.

Book One of the Arthur series blends a historical novel set in medieval
England with Arthurian legends. Arthur, the 13-year-old protagonist,
longs to begin his training for the knighthood by being named a squire,
and he worries that his father may want him to train for the priest-
hood instead. When Merlin, his father's mysterious friend and adviser,
gives the boy a magical black stone, he begins to have visions of another time and place that seem to parallel his own situation. He sees in
the stone scenes from the life of the mythical King Arthur, his name-
sake, that anticipate events in his own life. The novel ends with the rev-
elation that Arthur is the foster son of the man and woman he had
always thought to be his birth parents and with the prospect of his
going on a Crusade as the squire to a local knight. At the same time,
the seeing stone reveals the true parentage of the legendary Arthur as
he pulls the sword from the stone and is named King of Britain.

   This beautifully written novel brings the medieval world vividly to
life. It is an excellent introduction to the religious teachings and social
conditions in which the particular institutions of knighthood and fief-
doms flourished. Arthur is a complex hero, coping with the onset of
adolescence as well as the discovery of his true origins and questioning
some of the basic values and civic norms of his society. **F • HR**

87.   CROSSLEY-HOLLAND, KEVIN. *The World of King Arthur and His
Court: People, Places, Legend, and Lore*. Illustrated by Peter Malone.
Dutton, 1998. Cloth 0-525-46167-1; pap. 0-515-47321-1. Grades 5 to 8.

The subtitle says it all. This is a miscellaneous collection of facts and
lore about the legendary King Arthur. The curious reader can find
information here about the food and drink that Arthur might have
consumed, the tournaments in which knights tested their military
skills, heraldry, the historical origins of the Arthurian legends, and
much more. Many color illustrations add to the appeal of this handsome book. **NF • R**

88.   DAVIS, KENNETH C. *Don't Know Much About Sitting Bull*.
Illustrated by Sergio Martinez. HarperCollins, 2003. LB 0-06-028818-3;
pap. 0-06-442125-2. Grades 5 to 8.

Davis uses the question-and-answer format of the "don't know much
about" books to communicate a broad range of facts about the life and

accomplishments of the great Lakota chief who led his Indian nation in many battles against the United States Army, including the defeat of General Custer in the Battle of Little Big Horn. In addition, he offers a great deal of objective information about the warrior culture of the Great Plains Indians, about the harmful consequences of the U.S. policies that devastated their way of life, and about the daily life of the Lakota people, at war and in times of peace. NF • R

89. DENSLOW, SHARON PHILLIPS. *All Their Names Were Courage: A Novel of the Civil War*. HarperCollins/Greenwillow, 2003. Cloth 0-06-623810-2; LB 0-06-623809-9. Grades 4 to 6.

Eleven-year-old Sallie loves horses. She and her friend Isaac, a gifted artist, decide to write to Civil War generals, asking them to send descriptions and anecdotes about their war horses. The two children then compile a scrapbook with drawings of the horses and the accompanying letters from the soldiers. We learn all of this through letters that Sallie writes to her brother, who is serving with the Union army, through the letters that her brother sends back to her, and through the letters from the Generals about their horses. The author weaves in interesting and telling details about everyday life on a Kentucky farm and in the Union Army, as well as the role that horses played during the Civil War. F • R

90. DHAN GOPAL, MUKERJI. *Gay-Neck: The Story of a Pigeon*. Illustrated by Boris Artzybasheff. Dutton, 1927. Cloth 0-525-30400-2. Grades 6 to 8.

Very few contemporary children read this early Newbery Medal winner. Its flowery language and long, descriptive passages present nearly insurmountable barriers to today's readers. However, for those who persist, there are some remarkable glimpses into the dramatic landscape of the Himalayas, written at a time when Everest had not yet been climbed. There are also some vivid descriptions of the air battles of World War I from the perspective of Gay-Neck, a pigeon who has been trained in India and sent to serve alongside the Indian troops in Europe. Clearly, Gay-Neck's young Indian owner and trainer originally had dreams of hope and glory, but the ultimate message is profoundly anti-war. F • RWR

91. EDMONDS, WALTER D. *The Matchlock Gun*. Illustrated by Paul Lantz. Putnam, 1989 (new edition). Cloth 0-399-21911-0; pap. 0-698-11680-1. Grades 4 to 6.

Based on a true incident, this is a novella about a Dutch family living in the Hudson River Valley in 1756, during the French and Indian War. While the father is away with the militia, a band of Indians attacks the family's remote home. The mother is seriously wounded, but 10-year-old Edward succeeds in firing the old Spanish matchlock gun, killing three Indians and scaring off the rest. The book is marred by its stereotyped portrayal of Indians as inhuman savages. This is the description of the Indians as they approach the house: "They hardly looked like men, the way they moved. They were trotting, stooped over, first one and then another coming up, like dogs sifting up to the scent of food" (p. 39). This book was awarded the Newbery Medal in 1941, a year in which it must have seemed appropriate to honor a portrayal of heroic behavior by a white child facing nonwhite savages. **F • RWR**

92. FARMER, NANCY. *The Sea of Trolls*. Richard Jackson Books/Atheneum, 2004. Cloth 0-689-86744-1. Grades 5 to 8.

Eleven-year-old Jack is a Saxon boy living in the year 793 A.D. when the Vikings attack his land, capturing him and his little sister Lucy. What follows is high adventure, filled with action and a little magic. By the time the plot has reached its satisfying ending, Jack has come to understand and even like some of the Viking Berserkers, enemies who drug themselves into a murderous frenzy before they go into battle. He outwits a dragon, a giant spider, and a troll-boar and encounters descendents of the monster Grendel.

    Farmer has successfully woven together elements of Norse mythology, bits of history, folk motifs, and the epic "Beowulf." This is also a novel of ideas, with its framing device of the clash between the warlike seagoing Norsemen and the agrarian Saxon peasants, with their Druid religion. Thoughtful young readers will find much here to ponder. **F • HR**

93. FLEISCHMAN, PAUL. *Bull Run*. Illustrated by David Frampton. Laura Geringer/HarperCollins, 1993. Cloth 0-06-021446-5. Grades 6 to 8.

The cacophony and confusion of war are captured in the multiple voices that relate their various connections with Bull Run, the first battle in the Civil War. A sister left behind in Minnesota and a southern woman who worries about her daughters' husbands as they go to lick the

Yankees, a general who knows too well the horrors of war, a man who is devoted to the war horses, a photographer and a sketch artist, a black man who is determined to fight for his freedom, soldiers fighting on both sides—all contribute their stories. It is impossible to read this book and avoid seeing the human face of war. **F • HR**

94. FORBES, ESTHER. *Johnny Tremain*. Houghton Mifflin, 1943. Cloth 0-395-06766-9; Yearling, 1987, pap. 0-440-44250-8. Grades 6 to 8.

We see Revolutionary Boston through the eyes of young Johnny Tremain. When a bad burn cripples his hand, he must abandon a promising career as a silversmith. Instead, he becomes a courier for a printer and is swept up in the ideas and adventure of the Whig resistance to the British. This rich historical novel makes the events of the Boston Tea Party, the Battle of Lexington, and Paul Revere's ride come alive as the exciting backdrop of one young man's life. **F • R**

95. FOREMAN, MICHAEL. *War Boy: A Country Childhood*. Arcade/Little, Brown, 1989. Cloth 1-55970-049-1. Grades 4 to 6.

Foreman uses both text and evocative illustrations to evoke his boyhood during World War II in the heavily bombed Suffolk countryside. Children will appreciate the everyday details that bring that faraway time and place to life. The author/illustrator, for example, draws the exact trajectory of the incendiary bomb that came through the roof over his bed and bounced over his mother's bed, hitting a mirror, before exploding up the chimney. He includes drawings of the cigarette cards that taught people what to do in those emergencies and how to adjust a gas mask. Even during wartime, Foreman and his friends saved their pennies for candy at the local store, played Cowboys and Indians, and went to the movies. The tone of this memoir is genuinely nostalgic, recalling a time when, in spite of the hardships and very real dangers, he was happy. **NF • HR**

96. FOREMAN, MICHAEL. *War Game*. Arcade/Little, Brown, 1993. Cloth 1-55970-242-7. Grades 6 to 8.

Foreman takes the young reader back to the trenches of World War I, where four young British boys are fighting for their country instead of playing on the national soccer team as they had once dreamed. Their cold and discomfort, fear and courage, as well as the surreal environment of trench warfare, are vividly presented in words and pictures.

When Christmas comes, they long for home. What happens, in an incident based on historical fact, is that the young men on both sides of the war leave their trenches and shake hands. They exchange Christmas songs and Christmas gifts and play an exuberant game of soccer. The officers disapprove of this breakdown in military discipline, and soon the British and German soldiers who had shared one day of peace and friendly competition have returned to killing each other across no-man's land. **F • HR**

97.   GARLAND, SHERRY. *A Line in the Sand: The Alamo Diary of Lucinda Lawrence*. Scholastic, 1998. Cloth 0-590-39466-5. Grades 4 to 6.

The diarist in this entry in the Dear America series is 13-year-old Lucinda Lawrence, the daughter of one of the Americans who has settled near the town of Gonzales in Texas. The settlers are there legally, under arrangement with the new Republic of Mexico. General Santa Anna has been elected president of Mexico and has begun a more dictatorial form of government, taking away the autonomy of states like Texas. It is now 1835, and the American colonists are beginning to talk about the need to fight for independence from Mexico. Lucinda hears the adult men in town arguing politics and preparing for war. Her own brother goes to San Antonio to help fortify and defend the Alamo, a former mission now being used as a garrison. She meets Davy Crockett, who has the same mission as her brother, and she sees the unexpected arrival of Santa Anna with an army of 4,000 Mexican soldiers. Susanna Dickinson, one of a handful of survivors of the subsequent siege of the Alamo returns to Gonzales with the news, and Lucinda and her family must now flee the Mexican army that is killing all remaining Americans, or Texians, as they called themselves. The fictionalized diary reveals the everyday life of a hard-working frontier girl as well as the terrible consequences of war for civilians as well as combatants. **F • R**

98.   GRAVETT, CHRISTOPHER. *Knight*. Illustrated by Goeff Dann. DK, 2004. Cloth 0-7566-0696-9; LB 0-7566-0695-0. Grades 4 to 6.

This Eyewitness book presents a lot of miscellaneous information about European knights and a little coverage of the Japanese Samurai knights as well. There is an emphasis on weaponry and armor that will delight many boys in particular. A timeline and glossary add value, as does a section titled "Find out more" that includes suggestions for designing a coat-of-arms, lists of useful Web sites, and places to visit. **NF • R**

99. HAVILL, JUANITA. *Eyes Like Willy's*. Illustrated by David Johnson. HarperCollins, 2004. Cloth 0-688-13672-9; LB 0-688-13673-7. Grades 4 to 6.

In 1906, 10-year-old Guy and his younger sister Sarah spend their summer vacation with their parents on Lake Constance in Austria. Their friendship with an Austrian boy named Willy grows over the years as the families return to the lake each summer. Guy develops his artistic talent, and Willy becomes a talented musician. And still they are the best of friends. In 1914, however, Austria and France are at war; and in 1915, both Guy and Willy must become soldiers, fighting on opposite sides. Guy is seriously wounded saving a German soldier who has eyes like Willy's. After a difficult convalescence, he recovers; and then the war is over at last. Guy goes to Normandy to repair an old family house. One afternoon, Sarah arrives there with a man whose right sleeve is pinned to his coat in the manner of those who have lost an arm. It is Willy, who has found his childhood friends. He tells Guy that he has asked Sarah to marry him. Guy is at first speechless with joy, and then he says, "Now we will be brothers."

The young men's willingness to serve their countries while knowing that the enemy they shoot might be a dear friend is poignant. Simple line drawings, rare in children's novels these days, add to the sense of time and place. **F • R**

100. HODGES, MARGARET. *Merlin and the Making of the King*. Illustrated by Trina Schart Hyman. Holiday House, 2004. Cloth 0-8234-1647-X. Grades 4 to 8.

Hodges bases her retelling of three well-known Arthurian legends—those dealing with the sword in the stone, the sword Excalibur, and the death of Arthur—on Sir Thomas Malory's *Morte d'Arthur*. The retellings are elegant, and Hyman's color decorations on every page re-create the look of an illuminated manuscript. This is a splendid introduction to the stories of this fabled warrior king. **NF • R**

101. HUNTER, MOLLIE. *The King's Swift Rider: A Novel on Robert the Bruce*. HarperCollins, 1998. Cloth 0-06-027186-8. Grades 7 to 8.

Told from the point of view of a young boy who accompanies the 14th-century hero Robert the Bruce on his campaign to free Scotland from British rule, this is primarily a story of military tactics and leadership. We learn little about the narrator, young Martin Crawford, who serves at first as a page and then as a courier and spy for the Bruce, and a great deal about the battle for hearts and minds as well as critical terrain. **F • RWR**

102. KELLY, ERIC P. *The Trumpeter of Krakow*. Illustrated by Janina Domanska. Macmillan, 1966. Cloth 0-02-750140-X. Grades 6 to 8.

This handsome edition is a reissue of the Newbery Medal winner originally published in 1928. The opening chapter retells the legend of "the broken note," based on a historical event that took place in 1241 when the Tartars invaded Poland and attacked the city of Krakow. The young trumpeter whose job it was to sound the Heynal, a hymn, each hour on the hour in the tower of the Church of Our Lady Mary, was determined to perform even in the face of the enemy. A Tartar shot him while he was sounding his trumpet, and the song ended on a broken note. Since that time trumpeters continue to play the Heynal on the hour, ending it on the same broken note in remembrance of that young trumpeter's bravery and sacrifice.

The story then shifts forward two centuries to the year 1461 to tell the story of another young man. His family has fled their home in the Ukraine with a treasure that the family has guarded for generations. The father intends to place it in the hands of the ruler of Poland. In the meantime, he takes the position as trumpeter in the tower and teaches the Heynal to his son, who is inspired by the patriotic legend surrounding it. A ruthless mercenary has pursued the family to Krakow with the intent of stealing the treasure, a crystal of great power and beauty. The plot that unfolds is full of mystery and intrigue, and the setting of a medieval European city at the dawn of the Renaissance is fascinating. **F • R**

103. KERVEN, ROSALIND. *King Arthur*. Illustrated by Tudor Humphries. DK Publishing, 1998. Cloth 0-7894-2887-3. Grades 4 to 8.

Kerven bases her retelling of the Arthurian legends on many traditional sources. This Eyewitness Classic features the usual sidebars and illustrations that amplify the text with relevant bits of information and interesting trivia. There are also sections on the archaeological and historical evidence about Arthur and the many retellings of the legends, including those on stage and screen. **NF • R**

104. KUHN, BETSY. *Angels of Mercy: The Army Nurses of World War II*. Atheneum, 1999. Cloth 0-689-82044-5. Grades 4 to 8.

More than 59,000 women served as Army nurses during World War II. This book tells the story of their experiences, beginning with the Japanese attack on Pearl Harbor on December 7, 1941. These women worked in field and evacuation hospitals in combat areas as well as in rehabilitation centers in the United States. They were taken prisoner in the Philippines, waded ashore at Omaha Beach shortly after D-Day, and worked around the clock to treat seriously wounded soldiers in combat zones throughout the Pacific and European theaters of war. They received less pay and privileges than the men they served with, and they suffered racial discrimination as well. African American women were not allowed to join the Army Nurse Corps until nearly the end of the war, and then were subjected to a quota system. Men were not allowed to serve as nurses at all. First-hand accounts by the nurses and contemporary photos add immediacy to this well-documented chapter of feminist and military history. **NF • R**

105. LAWRENCE, IAIN. *B Is for Buster*. Delacorte, 2004. Cloth 0-385-90108-9. Grades 6 to 8.

It is the start of World War II. Sixteen-year-old Kak, nicknamed for his hometown of Kakabeka, Canada, lies about his age and enlists in the Canadian Air Force, eager to exchange his abusive parents for brave comrades in arms. Trained as a wireless operator, he is thrilled when he is sent to a squadron in England, where he looks forward to heroic deeds flying bombing raids in Germany. On his first night op, in the old Halifax bomber named "B for Buster," he learns that heroism isn't all he expected it to be; he is terrified. Slowly, under the tutelage of Bert, the caretaker of the homing pigeons who fly with the crews, he learns that true courage means going on when he is paralyzed with fear. While this is primarily Kak's story, a pigeon named Sergeant Percy plays a stunning cameo role. **F • HR**

106. LAWRENCE, IAIN. *Lord of the Nutcracker Men*. Delacorte, 2001. Cloth 0-385-72924-3; LB 0-385-90024-4. Grades 5 to 8.

This novel captures the profound sense of sadness and waste that seems to be the legacy of World War I, especially in England, where the consequences were so grave. Johnny's father is a toymaker who has given him an army of nutcracker soldiers that he whittled himself. Johnny is sent to live with his aunt when his father goes to fight and his mother goes to work in a munitions factory. He pretends his nutcracker men are German soldiers and develops an elaborate game of warfare in the backyard, complete with trenches and barbed wire. His father makes more wooden soldiers and sends them to Johnny, along with letters that describe his experiences on the front. Johnny enacts battles in the backyard that seem to foretell the real battles in which his father fights. There are graphic descriptions of trench warfare that may be as difficult for some young readers to handle as they are for Johnny to accept. The novel acknowledges the dreams of hope and glory that motivate men to fight; it is also unflinching in its portrayal of the costs of achieving those dreams. **F • HR**

107. LEE, JEANNE M. *The Song of Mu Lan*. Front Street, 1995. Cloth 1-886910-00-6. Grades 2 to 4.

Many children know Mulan only as a character in a Disney animated film. A note at the back of this picture book tells them that she first appeared in a Chinese folk poem sometime between 420 and 589 A.D. Children in China still learn the poem today. This beautifully illustrated book is a faithful translation of that poem, which is also rendered in Chinese calligraphy. It is a story of a daughter's sense of duty and love for an aging father as well as a story of heroism in war. **F • HR**

108. LONGFELLOW, HENRY WADSWORTH. *The Midnight Ride of Paul Revere*. Illustrated by Christopher Bing. Handspring Books, 2001. Cloth 1-929766-13-0. Grades 4 up.

Longfellow's poem has made Paul Revere the best-known hero and patriot of the American Revolutionary War. In this handsome book, Christopher Bing has woven together evocative illustrations and historical fact that both interpret the poem and add to a young reader's understanding of the event. **F • HR**

109. McKISSACK, PATRICIA, AND FREDRICK McKISSACK. *Red-Tail Angels: The Story of the Tuskegee Airmen of World War II*. Walker, 1995. Cloth 0-8027-8292-2; LB 0-8027-8293-0. Grades 6 to 8.

It will be a shock to many young readers to discover that the armed forces were segregated during all of World War II; Harry Truman didn't order the integration of the American military until 1948. In 1942, the special 99th Fighter Squadron was established in Tuskegee, Alabama, as an experiment to train black pilots. These airmen eventually flew hundreds of successful missions in Europe and North Africa. They were awarded 150 Distinguished Flying Crosses and Legions of Merit, and several went on to become generals. The McKissacks tell their stories through first-hand accounts, interviews, photos, and other primary source documents. **NF • R**

110. MATAS, CAROL. *The Garden*. Simon & Schuster, 1997. Cloth 0-689-80349-4. Grades 7 to 8.

In this sequel to *After the War* (see next chapter), Ruth is working on a kibbutz, happiest when tending her rose garden. She has joined the Haganah, however, a Jewish army committed to defending the Jewish settlers from attack by Arabs or the British, who still control Palestine. In 1947, the United Nations voted to partition Palestine into a Jewish state and an Arab State. The jubilation felt by Ruth and the other Jews in Palestine is short-lived, however, as the Arabs begin a war to drive them out of the country. Ruth is forced to face her hesitation about armed conflict and ultimately chooses to fight, killing 16 Arabs who are attacking her band of soldiers.

The novel captures both the idealism of the Jewish settlers in Palestine immediately after World War II and presents some of the range of opinion within the community about how best to secure a Jewish homeland. Young readers will need to look elsewhere to find the perspective of the Arabs living in Palestine. It is not difficult, however, to see the seeds of violence and conflict that plague Israel and Palestine to this day. **F • R**

111. MAYER, MARIANNA. *Women Warriors: Myths and Legends of Heroic Women*. Illustrated by Julek Heller. Morrow, 1999. Cloth 0-688-1522-7. Grades 4 to 8.

The author presents 12 profiles of legendary warrior women, both historical and literary, from many different traditions. There is Devi, the goddess who vanquished the evil Durga, and Rangada, whose exploits can be found in the Hindu classic tales of the Mahabarata. Semiramis and Boadicea were real-life warrior queens, while the Amazons' historical origins are murky. Arthurian legends tell of a woman who trained knights in weaponry, courage, and compassion; here she is called Lady Lochlyn. Morrigan and Gwendolen represent the Celtic tradition.

Winyan Ohitika and Aliquipso are Native American heroines. Mella, a figure from the oral history of the Buhera Ba Rowzi tribe in Zimbabwe, faces a feared python with courage and is rewarded by being named a leader of her tribe. The Japanese heroine Yakami slays a sea monster. Mayer points out that these stories do not glorify war; rather they celebrate the commitment and courage of each heroine and explore the power of women. **NF • R**

112. MORPURGO, MICHAEL. *Sir Gawain and the Green Knight*. Illustrated by Michael Foreman. Candlewick, 2004. Cloth 0-7636-2519-1. Grades 5 to 8.

In this retelling of a 14th-century Arthurian legend, the chivalrous Sir Gawain must live up to his vow to give the hideous Green Knight the opportunity to behead him in a single blow. At the end of his arduous journey to the chapel where he is due to face the Green Knight, he is welcomed by a knight and his beautiful—and very seductive—wife. He resists the temptation to sleep with his host's wife but succumbs to her gift of a green belt that she says will save his life. It develops that his host is the Green Knight himself, who spares his life because of his steadfast honesty. And from that day to this, English knights wear a green belt in his honor.

This handsome and well-written version of the legend highlights the code of chivalry that informed the behavior of medieval European knights. It was not enough to be brave and skilled at the art of war; one needed also to be honest and true. **F • R**

113. MORPURGO, MICHAEL. *War Horse*. Greenwillow, 1982. Cloth 0-688-02296-0. Grades 5 to 8.

The first-person narrator here is a horse named Joey, raised in England to work on a small farm where a teenage boy named Albert loved him and cared for him. To Albert's dismay, his father sells Joey, and the horse is sent to France to pull a cannon for Britain's soldiers fighting in the First World War. Joey's experiences parallel that of many of the humans in that war. He is wounded, captured by the enemy, rescued from no-man's land by a British soldier, comes down with a serious illness while recovering from his war wounds, and at last returns home to his farm to work once more with Albert. This is a heartrending look at war from the point of view of a heroic horse. **F • HR**

114. MURPHY, JIM. *Inside the Alamo*. Delacorte, 2003. Cloth 0-385-32574-6; LB 0-385-90092-0. Grades 6 to 8.

Murphy uses primary source materials and other historical accounts to sift through the facts and legends about the 1836 siege of the Alamo in San Antonio. Davy Crockett and Jim Bowie make their usual cameo appearances before dying with the rest of the Alamo defenders, and William Travis writes the "victory or death" letter that failed to bring the relief he had counted on. General Santa Anna is here, guaranteed a villain's place in American history with his policy to show no mercy. The author explains why the Texan stand at the Alamo resulted in no immediate military gain but provided a powerful symbol for the subsequent struggle for independence from Mexico. The illustrations from contemporary sources and sidebars add interest to this well-written history. **NF • HR**

115. O'BRIEN, PATRICK. *The Making of a Knight: How Sir James Earned His Armor*. Charlesbridge, 1998. Pap. 0-88106-355-X. Grades 3 to 5.

Any child reading this fictionalized account of one boy's progress from 7-year-old page to a full knight at the age of 21 will learn a lot about the institution of knighthood. Information about medieval life, arms and armor, chivalry, and tournaments are seamlessly integrated into the story. Color illustrations on every page add to the appeal. **F • R**

116. PAULSEN, GARY. *Soldier's Heart: A Novel of the Civil War*. Delacorte, 1998. Cloth 0-385-32498-7. Grades 6 to 8.

The author's foreword explains that "soldier's heart" was the term used after the American Civil War to describe the mental damage inflicted on its soldiers, much as today we talk about post-traumatic stress disorder. In this short novel, based on the real-life experiences of 15-year-old Charley Goddard, the boy lies about his age in order to become part of the First Minnesota Volunteers fighting on the Union side. He is excited about the opportunity to participate in a real "fighting war." Of course, the reality of battle is more frightening and horrific than exciting. Charley survives the Battle of Bull Run and many more minor skirmishes, only to be seriously wounded in Gettysburg. He returns home with a soldier's heart, damaged physically and emotionally, and dies at the age of 23.

In just 100 pages, Paulsen tells a story similar to Stephen Crane's *Red Badge of Courage*. The descriptions of battles and life in the soldiers' camps are vivid, and Charley's responses to these experiences seem authentic. A map and bibliography add value for young readers who want to learn more about this important event in American history and one teenager's participation in it. **F • R**

117. PIERCE, TAMORA. *Alanna: The First Adventure*. Simon & Schuster, 1983. Cloth 0-689-85323-8. Grades 5 to 8.

Eleven-year-old Alanna longs to be a knight, a career reserved for men in the kingdom of Tortall. She disguises herself as a boy and embarks on the training and apprenticeship as a royal page, the first step on the path to becoming a knight. Two years later, after proving herself to be adept in the martial arts, courageous, and loyal, her true identity as a girl is revealed and Prince Jon makes her his squire, the first female to achieve this status. Her adventures continue in three more volumes of the Song of the Lioness saga. **F • R**

118. PIERCE, TAMORA. *First Test*. Random House, 1999. Cloth 0-679-88914-0. Grades 4 to 6.

Ten-year-old Keladry of Mindalen is the first girl to apply for training as a knight in the kingdom of Tortall. The training master is skeptical that she can make the grade and requires an unusual probationary period. In spite of severe hazing and open prejudice, Kel survives her first year, acquits herself well in battle against the evil spidrens, and is allowed to return to begin her formal education as a page. This engaging fantasy is the first volume in the Protector of the Small series. **F • HR**

119. PIERCE, TAMORA. *In the Hand of the Goddess*. Simon & Schuster, 1984. Cloth 0-689-85324-6; Simon Pulse, 2005, pap. 0-689-87856-7. Grades 7 to 8.

In this second volume of the Song of the Lioness quartet, Alanna turns 18 and ultimately passes the Ordeal of Knighthood. She is still squire to Prince Jon and sworn to protect him. However, she also comes to realize the relationship between them is changing. What was mutual affection and respect is evolving into love. There is plenty of action and adventure here, as Alanna wards off the evil spells of Duke Richard, Jon's uncle and competitor for the throne; but the heart of the book is

Alanna's coming of age and discarding of the male identity that has enabled her to train for knighthood. **F • R**

120. PIERCE, TAMORA. *Lady Knight*. Random House, 2002. Cloth 0-375-81465-5. Grades 7 up.

In the final volume of the Protector of the Small series, 18-year-old Kel, now a knight of the realm, is asked to assume command of a refugee camp. Her leadership and battle skills are severely tested when all of the children in the camp are kidnapped by an evil mage who intends to take their souls in order to fuel his infernal killing machines. With some help—from a small band of comrades, some of the humble refugees who have escaped the mage's army, her bird and animal friends, and a little magic—she rescues the children and kills the mage. Kel is a reflective warrior who ponders the morality of war, the burden of honor, and the ambiguity of justice. At the story's end, she has earned the respect of her superiors, her peers, and the common people she has sworn to protect, those whose positions in life are too low to win the attention of most other noble knights. **F • HR**

121. PIERCE, TAMORA. *Page*. Random House, 2000. Cloth 0-679-88915-9. Grades 5 to 7.

In this second volume of the Protector of the Small series, Kel continues to prove herself as the only girl being trained to enter the knighthood in the kingdom of Tortall. She starts the book as an 11-year-old page still smarting from having to prove herself during a probationary period the year before and emerges three years later as a squire. During her three years as a page, she demonstrates unexpected leadership abilities, proves herself more than equal to the tasks of strength and skill required of the boys, and copes with the changes in her body and emotions caused by the onset of puberty. She also proves that girls can be as chivalrous as boys. **F • HR**

122. PIERCE, TAMORA. *Squire*. Random House, 2001. Cloth 0-679-88916-7. Grades 7 up.

Book Three in the Protector of the Small series follows Kel through her four years as squire and the terrifying Ordeal which allows her to finally enter the knighthood of her country. For the first time she experiences a true campaign of war against Tortall's traditional enemies, the Scanrans, and learns that war is dirty, uncomfortable, and sometimes boring. At the end, however, as she faces the final Ordeal before becoming a knight, in which she must face down her strongest fears, she wholeheartedly accepts the obligations of that post. Thoughtful young readers will find much to ponder as they join Kel in her moral deliberations. Kel is a genuine feminist heroine, but the issues she confronts should speak to any adolescent. **F • HR**

123. PIERCE, TAMORA. *The Woman Who Rides Like a Man*. Simon & Schuster, 1986. Cloth 0-689-85429-3; Simon Pulse, 2005, pap. 0-689-87858-3. Grades 7 to 8.

At the end of Book Two of the Song of the Lioness series, Alanna had been forced to kill the evil Count who threatened the life of Prince Jonathan. It seemed prudent to leave town for a while, and this third volume finds her searching for adventure in the desert lands to the south of Tortall. There she is captured by the ferocious Bazhir tribesmen. After proving herself in battle, she is slowly accepted by these people whose gender roles are even more strictly defined than those in her own kingdom. Alanna is forced to focus more on her own gifts of magic than on her warrior skills. She is also forced to confront her ambivalent feelings about both Jonathan and George, the dashing but disreputable prince of thieves who has been her admirer for many years. Be aware that Alanna feels free to express her sexuality, but these episodes are sufficiently veiled and non-graphic that younger readers may not even notice them. **F • RWR**

124. PINKNEY, ANDREA DAVIS. *Silent Thunder: A Civil War Story*. Jump at the Sun/Hyperion, 1999. Cloth 0-7868-0439-4; LB 0-7868-2388-7. Grades 5 to 8.

Eleven-year-old Summer and her older brother Rosco are slaves on a Virginia plantation in 1862. Each has a "silent thunder," a passionate desire. Summer wants to learn to read; Rosco wants to run away and join the Union Army. We see the Civil War through their eyes as their desires slowly become reality. **F • R**

125. SAN SOUCI, ROBERT. *Fa Mulan*. Illustrated by Jean Tseng and Mou-Sien Tseng. Hyperion, 1998. Cloth 0-7868-0346-0; LB 0-7868-2287-2. Grades 3 to 5.

Most American children know the story of Mulan, the girl who took her elderly father's place as a warrior for the Khan, from the Disney

movie. This book offers a more authentic version of the Chinese legend, taken from a 5th-century ballad. The illustrations, designed to mimic a traditional Chinese scroll, add another dimension to the story.
F • R

126. STANLEY, DIANE. *Joan of Arc*. Morrow, 1998. Cloth 0-688-14329-6. Grades 4 to 6.

Stanley frames this beautifully illustrated picture-book biography with an account of the Hundred Years War between France and England, helping the reader contextualize the life of the Maid of Orleans. Young readers who don't already know this story will be inspired by the conviction and courage of the young peasant girl who succeeded in defeating the English when more experienced men could not, and they will be appalled by her death at the hands of the Inquisition. **NF • HR**

127. STANLEY, DIANE. *Saladin: Noble Prince of Islam*. HarperCollins, 2002. Cloth 0-688-17135-4. Grades 4 to 6.

This brief illustrated biography presents the Islamic perspective on the Crusades, a historical event better known to American children from the European and Christian point of view. Saladin was the remarkable 12th-century warrior prince who united a divided people and retook Jerusalem from the Franks who had held it for 40 years. Saladin met his match at last in Richard the Lion-Hearted, but this narrative makes clear why this generous and chivalrous leader is remembered in the Muslim world as a hero. This story also contains the seeds of conflict that plague the Middle East today, nine centuries later. Stunning illustrations based on Islamic art, a postscript, glossary, and bibliography add to the value of this excellent informational book. **NF • HR**

128. STEELE, WILLIAM O. *Flaming Arrows*. Harcourt, 1957. Cloth 0-15-205212-7; 2004, pap. 0-15-205213-5. Grades 5 to 7.

Eleven-year-old Chad Rabun works nearly as hard as a grown man in the 18th-century Tennessee settlement where his father is respected as a leading member of the community of pioneers who have built cabins near the fort. The fort is there to protect them from Indian raids. On this occasion, the warning of an impending raid sends the families running for the fort. Chad is surprised to see a woman with her three children nearly turned away, but then he learns that this is the family of Traitor Logan, a white man who fights with the Indians. Chad's father speaks up for the Logans, and they are allowed to enter. The pioneer families are grudging with their welcome, however, and Chad finds himself shunned along with Traitor's family.

When the Indians attack, it is a brutal fight, described in much bloody detail. Chad does his share of killing. The pioneers run low on critical supplies as the siege of the fort continues. It is young Josiah Logan who finally makes the dangerous trip out of the fort to bring back the water that is so desperately needed inside. The Indians are eventually driven off, and Chad is forced to confront his own prejudices against the Logans as he learns that good men can do bad things and bad men can have good sons. He does not learn to see the Indians as anything other than savage enemies, however, and readers will have to look elsewhere for their side of the story. **F • R**

129. STEIN, R. CONRAD. *Emiliano Zapata: Revolutionary and Champion of Poor Farmers*. Child's World, 2004. Cloth 1-59296-166-5. Grades 4 to 6.

The author only partially succeeds in the daunting task of explaining the Mexican Revolution and Zapata's role in it to elementary school students in a book of less than 40 pages. Nevertheless, this well-illustrated, easy-to-read introduction to the life of the Mexican revolutionary hero covers the bases and creates a foundation on which students can build their knowledge. The publisher maintains a Web page (http://www.childsworld.com/links.html) with links to other resources about Zapata. **NF • RWR**

130. WELLS, ROSEMARY. *The Language of Doves*. Illustrated by Greg Shed. Dial, 1996. Trade 0-8037-1471-8; LB 0-8037-1472-6. Grades 2 to 4.

Julietta's grandfather gives her a homing pigeon on her 6th birthday and tells her the story of his own boyhood experiences caring for homing pigeons used during World War I in Italy. An author's note tells how these birds were used to carry coded messages during the Great War. **F • R**

131. WHITE, ELLEN EMERSON. *The Journal of Patrick Seamus Flaherty: United States Marine Corps*. Scholastic, 2002. Cloth 0-439-14890-1. Grades 6 to 8.

Patrick Flaherty keeps a journal during his time in Vietnam as a Marine, from 1967 to 1968. At first, it is a record of new experiences:

eating C-rations, meeting guys from other parts of the country, acquiring a nickname. Then his platoon is besieged at Khe Sanh, and Patrick sees the horrors of combat first-hand. Buddies are wounded and killed, and finally he himself takes a hit that sends him home and ruins his prospects of playing college football. Patrick is a likable young man, and boys especially will find his perspective on the war very accessible. Like other titles in the My Name Is America series, informational material at the back of the book provides historical background for this fictional but factual account. See the companion volume by the same author, *Where Have All the Flowers Gone*, for the parallel story of Patrick's sister Molly back home in Boston. **F • R**

132. WISLER, G. CLIFTON. *When Johnny Went Marching: Young Americans Fight the Civil War*. HarperCollins, 2001. Cloth 0-688-16537-0. Grades 5 to 8.

It is difficult for us to imagine a time when boys as young as 12 and 13 could enlist in the American Army. During the Civil War, they didn't even have to lie about their age if they signed up as drummer boys. Wisler has collected photos and profiles of some of these very young soldiers. They served in both the Union and Confederate Armies. Some even received the Congressional Medal of Honor. Their faces and their stories will haunt you. **NF • R**

133. WULFFSON, DON. *Soldier X*. Viking, 2001. Cloth 0-670-88863-X. Grades 6 to 8.

An elderly man, now living in Seattle, Washington, tells how he received his wounds in World War II while serving in the German Army. As a 16-year-old in 1943, Erik was called up with other boys his age. With very little training and inadequate equipment, these young soldiers were sent to augment the dwindling German troops. Because Erik's mother was Ukrainian, he spoke Russian, so he was sent to the Russian front as an interpreter. His unit was almost immediately subjected to the superior military force of the Russian Army. Wounded and lying among his fallen comrades, he remembers the advice of an experienced old soldier: play dead and use your brain. He is able to take the uniform from a dead Russian soldier and is sent to a Russian field hospital where he feigns amnesia. He and a Russian nurse make their way across various enemy lines, eventually to marry and emigrate to the United States.

While Erik's story begins with his adolescent dreams of hope and glory for the Fatherland, it quickly turns to the blood and gore and misery of war. In the end, the only hope is for survival. **F • R**

134. YOLEN, JANE, AND ROBERT J. HARRIS. *Prince Across the Water.* Philomel, 2004. Cloth 0-399-23897-2. Grades 6 to 8.

Thirteen-year-old Duncan has heard his Granda's tales about Scottish uprisings in the past, and he dreams of the day when his people will be liberated from English rule. When the clans are called to follow Prince Charlie to war, he is eager to don the MacDonald tartan and do his part. His father, worried about the family farm, heeds the call to arms reluctantly and makes Duncan stay home. He and his cousin Ewan practice with wooden swords and impatiently wait until they can join the battle. After a series of victories on Scottish soil, the clansmen push on to London where the tide of battle turns against them. Duncan's father returns home, more convinced than ever of the futility of this war, while Ewan's father is killed. Ewan convinces Duncan that they should run away and join the Scottish warriors. They catch up just in time for the dreadful Battle of Culloden, in which the English Army defeats the weary, hungry Scottish clans. Duncan sees Ewan die on the moor but remains loyal to the prince. In one last heroic deed, he helps Prince Charlie escape through the Highlands so he can return to France. The English impose even harsher laws upon the defeated Scottish clans, outlawing the wearing of the tartan. Duncan remains optimistic that his people will survive, with their songs and tales of courage to sustain them. An authors' note explains the historical background of the novel. **F • R**

WEB SITES

---

135. *Crazy Horse: Tashunca-uitco (1849–1877).* http://www.pbs.org/weta/thewest/people/a_c/crazyhorse.htm PBS, 2001. Grades 5 to 8.

A brief biographical overview of the visionary leader of the Lakota, noted for his role in defeating General Custer in the Battle of the Little

Big Horn and for his determination to preserve the traditional way of life of his people. **NF • R**

136. *George Armstrong Custer (1839–1876)*.
http://www.pbs.org/weta/thewest/people/a_c/custer.htm
PBS, 2001. Grades 5 to 8.

A brief profile of the flamboyant and complex Civil War general who went on to infamous defeat at the hands of Lakota and Cheyenne warriors at the Battle of the Little Big Horn. **NF • R**

137. *Medal of Honor Citations*.
http://www.army.mil/cmh-pg/moh1.htm
U.S. Army, n.d. Grades 5 to 8.

This site, maintained by the U.S. Army, contains a brief history of the Congressional Medal of Honor, which has been awarded to more than 3,400 members of the United States armed forces since it was created in 1861, as well as a table of statistics. The medal is given for acts of extraordinary heroism and bravery. Perhaps the most interesting information here is the full text of all the citations that have been awarded, from the Civil War to the Iraq War. **NF • R**

138. *Sitting Bull: Tatanka-Iyotanka (1831–1890)*.
http://www.pbs.org/weta/thewest/people/s_z/sittingbull.htm
PBS, 2001. Grades 5 to 8.

An excellent short overview of the Hunkpapa Lakota chief and holy man who led his people in a struggle to survive in the face of hostile U.S. policies. Many links lead searchers to other relevant sites. **NF • R**

139. *William Tecumseh Sherman (1820–1891)*.
http://www.pbs.org/weta/thewest/people/s_z/sherman.htm
PBS, 2001. Grades 5 to 8.

A brief biography of the Civil War general famous for his scorched-earth policies that contributed to the Union victory while devastating the South. This account also includes his role in subjugating the Indians of the Great Plains after the Civil War. **NF • R**

DVDs

140. *Quest for King Arthur*. A & E Television Networks. 2004. . Grades 6 to 8.

Patrick Stewart narrates this History Channel production that integrates historical reenactments with commentary by literary, archaeology, and history scholars. The quest is for the man behind the legends and myths about King Arthur. There are no definitive answers but many intriguing clues and possibilities that go back as far as the fall of the Roman Empire in the 5th century. Does the name Arthur derive from the Celtic word for Bear carried on the banners of British military heroes? Do the deeds of Ambrosius, the last Roman to lead the British against the invading Saxons, live on in the stories of King Arthur? Are the exploits of the British cavalry who defeated the Anglo-Saxons in the 6th-century battle of Baden Hill captured in the tales of the Knights of the Round Table? How did the ballads of the French poets such as Chretien de Troyes serve to create the code of chivalry? Middle school students will probably be most interested in the reenactments of the story as told by Sir Thomas Malory that are interspersed among the scholarly speculations. **NF • R**

THE CONSEQUENCES OF WAR

WHEN GOVERNMENTS DECLARE WAR and individuals choose to fight or are coerced into fighting that war, there are certain explicit consequences: victory or defeat, territorial expansion or loss, military casualties or survivors. However, there are always unintended or at least unvoiced consequences as well, and these are the themes and topics explored in this section of the resource list. Le Thi Diem Thuy writes in her novel about Vietnamese refugees, *The Gangster We Are All Looking For*: "War has no beginning and no end. It crosses oceans like a splintered boat filled with people singing a sad song" (2003, p. 87).

In this chapter, we will find books that demonstrate the truth of that quote. We will look at resources that make clear the unintended consequences of war. Some of the unintended consequences are positive, of course, usually scientific or medical breakthroughs resulting from military research. Walt Whitman's experiences as a nurse caring for wounded soldiers during the Civil War shaped his poetry in profound ways. The unique circumstances of war may throw together people who would otherwise not meet, leading to unexpected relationships and insights.

Most unintended consequences, however, tend to be negative: refugees, civilian deaths, erosion of human rights, the devastation of civil society and its institutions. Pediatrician Edward Goldson (1993) reminds us that war has both a direct and indirect effect on the health of children. The direct impacts are obvious: children are killed and maimed, and families are disrupted. The indirect impacts are also devastating. Data show that wars since World War II have caused serious nutritional problems for children. Wars cause a decrease in birth rates and increases in infant mortality. Health suffers as well because of the disruption to hospitals, clinics, and schools in a society at war.

One of the most devastating consequences of war is the creation of large numbers of refugees as civilian populations are forced from their homes. In a review of progress made since the 1996 United Nations Report on the Impact of Armed Conflict on Children, Graça Machel (2001) noted that 20 million children were currently refugees or displaced internally because of wars and political violence. This is a figure that is almost too large to comprehend. Just a quick dip into the Web site of the United Nations High Commissioner for Refugees gives a horrifying notion of the extent of the problem and the failure to find solutions. The lucky children are the ones who find a safe haven in a peaceful country, hopefully accompanied by family members. These few will still encounter the difficulties of assimilation into a new culture encountered by all immigrants, and they will often carry with them memories of war that no child should have. They are almost certainly better off, however, than those children left adrift in the limbo of refugee camps. Unfortunately, many young refugees have lost their parents in the chaos and violence of war. These are the ones the United Nations calls "unaccompanied and separated refugee children" ("Protection and Assistance . . . ," 2001). These children are not officially available for adoption, even if adoptive parents could be found, because there is a presumption that the birth parents are still alive somewhere. The UN aims to provide interim care for these children and ultimately to reunify them with their parents. The agency acknowledges, however, that it has nowhere near the financial and human resources to achieve those aims.

Refugees are not the only consequence of war, of course. One of the more disturbing new phenomena is the use of children as combatants, particularly in the violent guerrilla wars and civil wars being fought in Africa, Southeast Asia, and Latin America. It is difficult to estimate how many children under the age of 18 are serving as armed combatants, but most agencies concerned with the issue place the number at approximately 250,000 (Barnitz, 1999, p. 1). These child soldiers are not just killing other people in Third World countries. The first American casualty in Afghanistan was shot by a 14-year-old sniper (Singer, 2005, p. 25).

Of course, young boys served on both sides of the American Civil War, but the United Nations has formalized more progressive and humane policies about the use of young people as soldiers. (Such protocols and conventions are obviously ignored by unofficial insurgents and guerrillas.) And we prefer to think that child soldiers are coerced into playing that role; many children are indeed kidnapped or forced into service. Young girls are particularly vulnerable, and the practices used to socialize or brainwash unwilling children are horrific (Rubin, 1998; Singer, 2005, pp. 70ff.). However, many boys volunteer to be combatants. Rosen notes that the decision to take up arms is often the most rational option available to adolescents, who also are considered to be adults in many cultures. In some cases, military service is seen as essential to survival. There may also be family or other social pressures to serve. Other young people join for ideological or political reasons. There have been a number of studies, for example, documenting the ideological motivation of young Palestinian boys who have participated in the Intifada and other forms of resistance to the Israeli occupation (Rosen, 2005, pp. 91ff.).

The use of child soldiers has changed the nature of warfare. Singer (2005, pp. 95ff.) explains that the expanded pool of combatants represented by children has contributed to more and longer wars in some countries. He finds that child soldiers also tend to contribute to messier wars. The ways in which children are recruited, trained, and deployed tends to make atrocities such as mass killing, rape, and torture more prevalent tactics. The presence of child soldiers may also contribute to more violence against other civilian children, since it becomes difficult to identify who is a combatant and who is not. Perhaps the most devastating implication of the use of child soldiers, however, for those of us who champion peace is that it strengthens the cycle of violence. There are some interventions designed to rehabilitate child soldiers and to reintegrate them into civil society, but they are inadequate to the challenge. Children who have been socialized to fight are unlikely to shake off the effects of the experience and are very likely to retain their fear and hatred of whoever the enemy was determined to be.

TREATING THE CONSEQUENCES OF WAR IN LITERATURE FOR CHILDREN

The books in this section may at first appear to be chosen almost at random. This is more than a catch-all topic, however. The consequences of war themselves are somewhat random. Certain themes and patterns do reoccur. Refugees, for example, are a central focus of many books. Others deal with the aftermath of war or its lingering effects such as post-traumatic stress syndrome or haunting memories. However, many of these stories—and most of the books here are novels—are narratives about the experiences of children touched in unexpected ways by war. In *Trembling Earth* by Kim Siegelson, a poor white boy from Georgia's Okefenokee Swamp captures a runaway slave boy, hoping to collect the bounty. Instead, the two boys find themselves entangled in a mutual struggle to survive. In Gloria Whelan's *Angel on the Square*, an aristocratic Russian girl's life changes forever when the Russian Revolution takes away the privileges her family had enjoyed. The young Danish girl who is the protagonist of Lois Lowry's *Number the Stars* discovers hidden resources of courage and resourcefulness when she is called upon to help in the rescue of her Jewish friend.

A number of children's books deal with the aftermath of the Vietnam War. These are primarily stories of children who left Vietnam as refugees or as orphans adopted by American families. Adult characters often express a bittersweet longing for the homeland left behind. Sherry Garland's two picture books, *The Lotus Seed* and *My Father's Boat,* are good examples. Others depict the experience of returning to Vietnam in search of roots. *Going Home, Coming Home* by Truong Tran is notable for having a bilingual Vietnamese and English text, making it a good choice for children to share with grandparents who might be more comfortable in their mother tongue. Andrea Warren's *Escape from Saigon* and Lawrence McKay, Jr.'s *Journey Home* are both about adults who were taken from Vietnam as babies and returned later to reconnect with their homeland. Pegi Deitz Shea has written a picture book—*The Whispering Cloth*—and a novel—*Tangled Threads*—about the Hmong refugee experience. While *The Whispering Cloth* leaves the protagonist in the limbo of a Thai refugee camp, *Tangled Threads* takes her to America, with all of the cultural conflicts and misunderstandings that one might expect.

CHILDREN'S READING INTERESTS AND INFORMATION NEEDS

Why should children in the West know or care about the fate of refugee children or victims of land mines or child soldiers elsewhere in the world? We can hope that they will begin very young to develop both the compassion and the global awareness that will be needed for many years to come to try to address the consequences of war that we have left for them.

For Americans—who all arrived in the country as migrants, slaves, or refugees—the books in this section can create a frame of reference for children trying to understand their personal histories. The refugee stories here are also good choices for those homework assignments on immigrants. Whether they moved to escape war or to find political asylum or to ensure a better economic future, all immigrants share some universal experiences that are reflected in their stories.

The consequences of war are very real to many of the children we work with. The children who have fled civil unrest in the former Yugoslavia, the Middle East, Africa, and Latin America have terrible memories. They need stories that reassure them about the positive future that awaits them in their new land. They—and their classmates—also need stories that validate their past experiences and their cultural heritage.

Bibliography

BOOKS

141. ALMOND, DAVID. *The Fire-Eaters*. Delacorte, 2004. Cloth 0-385-73170-1; LB 0-385-90207-7. Grades 7 to 8.

Bobby has been happy with his life in the seaside coal-mining British town where his family has lived for generations. Now, however, as he starts secondary school, things are darker and more unsettled. His father may be seriously ill. The teachers at school seem to be abusing their power as they physically abuse the students. A vagrant shows up in town, performing strange acts of fire-eating and sword swallowing. His father tells him that the man, McNulty, saw things during the last war that unhinged his reason. Worst of all, it looks as if the world is inching toward a nuclear disaster as Russia and the United States face off in what we now know as the Cuban Missile Crisis. Against this background of approaching doom, Bobby and his family and friends search for hope and find it in their ties of love and friendship. Written in luminous prose, this is a challenging but rewarding novel for thoughtful young teens. **F • HR**

142. ALVAREZ, JULIA. *Before We Were Free*. Knopf, 2002. Cloth 0-375-81544-9; LB 0-375-91544-3. Grades 6 to 8.

Anita's life changes drastically during the year she is 12. It takes a while for her to become aware of the secrets the adults are keeping, but the tensions increase. Finally she realizes that her parents, uncles, and their friends are plotting to overthrow El Jefe, General Trujillo, the corrupt and cruel dictator of the Dominican Republic. The plot nearly succeeds. Trujillo is killed, but the revolutionaries fail to take control of the government. Instead, Trujillo's oldest son seizes power and takes revenge on those who opposed his father. Anita's father and uncle are arrested, and she and her mother go into hiding. They spend two months living secretly in the closet of friends before they are able to fly to the United States. Eventually they learn that the father and uncle have been killed and that their chances of returning to the Dominican Republic are remote. They can only remember and honor those who stayed behind.

There are echoes of *The Diary of Anne Frank* in this first-person account of the happy, middle-class girl who is caught up in the consequences of political violence. Like Anne, Anita keeps a diary and continues to have the normal concerns of any young teenager—clothes, a first kiss, small conflicts with her mother—while living under circumstances that are far from normal. **F • HR**

143. AMIS, NANCY. *The Orphans of Normandy*. Atheneum, 2003. Cloth 0-689-84143-4. Grades 3 to 5.

When the Allies invaded Normandy on June 6, 1944, that part of France became a dangerous battleground. This is the story of 100 girls who had to leave an orphanage there and make their way to safer ground. Carrying only a blanket, a white flag, and some bread, the girls managed to walk to Beaufort-en-Vallee, a town 150 miles to the south. The story itself is remarkable, but it gains immediacy and charm through the manner of its telling, in the words and drawings of the girls themselves. **NF • R**

144. ARMSTRONG, JENNIFER. *Shattered: Stories of Children and War*. Knopf, 2002. Cloth 0-375-81112-5; LB 0-375-91112-X. Grades 6 to 8.

Armstrong has edited a collection of stories about children and war. The well-known authors include Suzanne Fisher Staples, Joseph Bruchac, and M. E. Kerr. The topics and themes treated here are equally far-ranging: the Soviet invasion of Afghanistan, Native American soldiers in the Civil War, a conscientious objector to World War II, a

Palestinian family's flight during the Six-Day War, a coup in a Latin American country. While the contents of the stories vary, each highlights the effects of war on children and teenagers, whether they are direct witnesses and victims or not. **F • R**

145. BAUER, JOAN. *Stand Tall*. Putnam, 2002. Cloth 0-399-23473-X. Grades 5 to 8.

At 6 feet, 3 inches, 12-year-old Tree is the tallest student ever to attend his middle school. He struggles to cope with his parents' recent divorce and with his failure to be the star basketball player his coach expects him to be. The most positive influence in his life is his grandfather, a Vietnam vet whose war wound has finally resulted in having his leg amputated. His grandfather's stories about his war experiences and his gritty determination to walk with his new artificial leg provide wisdom and inspiration for this middle school boy on the brink of adolescence. **F • HR**

146. BOUDALIKA, LITSA. *If You Could Be My Friend: Letters of Mervet Akram Sha'ban and Galit Fink*. Orchard, 1998. Cloth 0-531-30113-3; LB 0-531-33113-X. Grades 5 to 8.

One of the tragic consequences of war, especially long-lasting conflicts, is the hatred for the enemy that it can instill in young people. This socialization to hate makes the prospects for peace in their lifetime as unlikely as it was for their parents' generation. This book is the result of the effort by a European journalist to facilitate a correspondence between an Israeli and a Palestinian girl in the hope of easing that hatred. These 12-year-olds began writing to each other at the height of the Intifada in 1988 and continued sporadically until they had a face-to-face meeting in 1991. The journalist/editor provides an introduction to each letter that explains what was happening in the conflict between the two communities at the time the letter was written. The girls are surprisingly honest with one another and grow to see that they could be friends, if only the situation were different. However, neither changes her mind about conflict between the Palestinians and the Israelis. The editor concludes, "Today I don't know if Galit has changed her anti-Palestinian opinions. Nor do I know what vengeance Mervet is planning against Israel. Hundreds of miles away, the peace discussions between the Israelis and the Palestinians continue. So does the war." (p. 81) There is a useful historical overview of the conflict at the back of the book. **NF • R**

147. BRUCHAC, JOSEPH. *The Winter People*. Dial, 2002. Cloth 0-8037-2694-5. Grades 6 to 8.

Bruchac tells a good adventure story here. Fourteen-year-old Saxso, an Abenaki boy living in what is now Canada, single-handedly rescues his mother and two sisters who have been taken hostage by English rangers. With its representation of the Indian perspective on the French and Indian Wars, this is a good corrective to the bias in books such as the Newbery-winning *The Matchlock Gun*. It also offers an authentic glimpse into Abenaki culture and the Abenaki people's relationship with their environment. **F • R**

148. CARMI, DANIELLA. *Samir and Yonatan*. Arthur Levine/Scholastic, 2000. Cloth 0-439-13504-4. Grades 5 to 8.

When Samir, a young Palestinian boy, smashes his kneecap in a bicycle accident, he is sent to an Israeli hospital for the operation that will enable him to walk again. There, in a ward with four Israeli children, he deals with his fear and hatred of the people who are his enemy. We learn a great deal about his family's difficult life under Israeli occupation and about his little brother's death when he got in the way of Israeli bullets. Little by little, Samir bonds with the children in the ward, united by their illness and by their universal experience of childhood. His special friend is Yonatan, who takes him to Mars via computer software. In the perfect, virtual world that the two friends explore together, he finally finds some peace with his brother's death.

This is a beautifully written story about the damaging consequences of armed conflict for one Arab boy. His reconciliation with the Israeli children and their acceptance of him may be overly optimistic, but it is a story that can give other young readers some hope for peace. **F • R**

149. CLINTON, CATHRYN. *A Stone in My Hand*. Candlewick, 2002. Cloth 0-7636-1388-6. Grades 5 to 8.

Eleven-year-old Malaak is a Palestinian girl living in the Gaza Strip. Her life is difficult enough before her father disappears and is presumed dead and her brother Hamid becomes drawn to a radical group advocating violent resistance to the Israeli occupation. She finds a haven and some solace on the roof of her house with a bird she has tamed. When Hamid is shot and critically wounded by an Israeli soldier, she nearly loses hope. She finds a way, however, to give moral support to her brother as he lies in a coma, and she takes sustenance from a rare desert rain. Her father had told her that in Palestine when it rains it means that God is smiling. **F • R**

150. COLLIER, JAMES LINCOLN, AND CHRISTOPHER COLLIER. *With Every Drop of Blood: A Novel of the Civil War*. Delacorte, 1994. Cloth 0-385-32928-0. Grades 6 to 8.

Pa was wounded while fighting for the South in the Civil War. On his deathbed, he makes his son promise that he will stay home and help his Ma on their little Virginia farm. Johnny can't resist, however, when he is asked to use his mule team and wagon to deliver supplies for the Rebel troops. On the way to Petersburg, he is captured by a Union soldier, a black boy just his age. Thrown together by desperate circumstances in the chaos of the last two weeks of the war, the two boys become allies and then friends.

The uneasy relationship between these two boys, caught in a role reversal that is new and uncomfortable for each of them, is presented in ways that seem both historically and psychologically plausible. It is Johnny, the poor white southern boy, who learns the most from the situation, finally coming to understand that he and Cush see the world—and the war—in fundamentally different ways. **F • R**

151. CORMIER, ROBERT. *Heroes*. Delacorte, 1998. Cloth 0-385-32590-8. Grades 7 to 8.

Francis enlisted in the army with forged identity papers at the age of 15. He has a Silver Star for bravery, received when a grenade blew up in his face. So disfigured that he must wear a scarf to cover what is left of his face, he haunts the streets of his hometown, looking to take revenge on the childhood hero who betrayed his ideals. This is a dark story, full of ambiguity about the nature of heroism. Thoughtful young teens will ponder its message and debate what happens to Francis in the end. **F • R**

152. DICKINSON, PETER. *AK*. Delacorte, 1992. Cloth 0-385-30608-3. Grades 6 to 8.

Paul is a child soldier, living in a fictional African nation. He can't remember his family or his village. All he has is Michael, his "uncle," the commando who trained him to use his AK-47 and fight in the guerrilla war against a corrupt government. The war is his only mother. When peace comes to the country, Michael goes to the capital to join the new government. Paul buries his gun, hoping to find a new way of life. Soon, however, there is another coup, and a new regime takes power. Paul uncovers his gun and sets out to free Michael. The author provides two epilogues for the story, both set 20 years in the future. In the first scenario, Paul has become a deputy minister in charge of national parks in his nation, which seems to be recovering from its years of civil war. His AK is buried under a great concrete monument that is dedicated to Michael, who had lived to see the first elephant herds return to the land. In the alternate scenario, the land continues to be torn apart by the civil war, and Paul has continued to be a warrior. Now, reaching for his gun, he is killed by other guerrillas. A small boy picks up the gun; he will carry on the war. **F • R**

153. ELLIS, DEBORAH. *The Breadwinner*. Groundwood, 2000. Cloth 0-88899-419-2; pap. 0-88899-416-8. Grades 5 to 8.

Eleven-year-old Parvana has never known a time of peace and security. Her country of Afghanistan was fighting Soviet invaders when she was a baby. Now it is the ultra-religious Taliban who rule her country. Women and girls are not allowed to go to school or even leave their homes without a man. When her father is arrested for political crimes, their all-female family is left with no means of support. The ingenious solution is for Parvana to dress like a boy and earn the family's living as a scribe in the marketplace. There is a strong feminist subtext to this story of survival in hard times. Its primary value for young American readers, however, is that it gives a human face to the faraway land with which the United States has become so entangled since September 11, 2001. **F • R**

154. ELLIS, DEBORAH. *Mud City*. Groundwood, 2003. Cloth 0-88899-518-0; pap. 0-88899-542-3. Grades 5 to 8.

At the end of *The Breadwinner*, Parvana's friend Shauzia left Afghanistan, determined to make her way to France where she will see the lavender fields pictured in a treasured photo torn from a magazine. In this book, we learn that she has only made it as far as a refugee camp in Peshawar, Pakistan. After a brief period in which she tries to earn a living as one of the street children in that city, she realizes that her chances of making it to France any time soon are remote. She returns to the refugee camp to help the indomitable Mrs. Weera improve the lives of the Afghan women and children made homeless by the wars in their country. She still plans to meet her friend Parvana at the Eiffel Tower in 20 years, however, and the reader suspects that she will keep that appointment. Like the other two books in the Breadwinner trilogy by Ellis, *Mud City* dramatizes the devastating economic consequences of war in developing countries. **F • R**

155. ELLIS, DEBORAH. *Parvana's Journey*. Groundwood, 2002. Cloth 0-88899-514-8; pap. 0-88899-519-9. Grades 5 to 8.

In this sequel to *The Breadwinner*, Parvana and her father have left Kabul in a search for her mother, sisters, and baby brother, all of whom had gone to Mazar-e-Sharif for her sister's wedding. The Americans have begun to attack the country in their effort to find Osama bin Laden and to rid the country of the Taliban. The father dies, and Parvana is now alone in a devastated landscape. She continues her journey with little direction or hope. Along the way, she finds a baby abandoned in a bombed-out village, an angry little boy with only one leg, and a little girl who has survived on her own by salvaging the remains of animals and the meager possessions of people who die in the field of land mines next to her hut. All four children eventually reach an internal refugee camp where Parvana accidentally meets up with her mother and sisters.

This is a sobering look at the unintended consequences of war for the noncombatants in a battle-worn land. In Afghanistan, land mines have rendered the fields useless for growing food; and the limited water supply is polluted. Malnutrition and disease are the inevitable result. There are no soldiers in this book, but there are many civilian casualties of the war. A baby is orphaned, and a grandmother is killed when bombs fall on their mud homes. A boy loses a leg, and a little girl loses her life when land mines explode. There is no glory and little hope in this war story, but Parvana struggles to live in spite of these horrendous circumstances. **F • R**

156. ELLIS, DEBORAH. *Three Wishes: Palestinian and Israeli Children Speak*. Groundwood, 2004. Cloth 0-88899-554-7; pap. 0-88899-645-4. Grades 6 to 8.

Ellis interviewed children and teens living in Israel and in the occupied Palestinian territories of Gaza and the West Bank. The interviews with several of these young people are captured here, along with brief introductions that give some context. Adult readers will be heartbroken by what appears to be intractable hatred and distrust for the people who happen to be on the other side of the Arab-Israeli conflict. It is instructive that none of the children appear to know a child from the other side of the border. All of their values and opinions are formed with no firsthand knowledge of their traditional enemies. While the conflict has taken its toll in deaths and hardships on both sides, Ellis makes obvious that the Palestinian children are living in drastically more severe hardship and deprivation than the Israelis. No false comfort or hope is given here. One can only hope that American children will feel compassion and concern for these children caught up in the most terrible consequences of war. **NF • HR**

157. FILIPOVIC, ZLATA. *Zlata's Diary: A Child's Life in Sarajevo.* Viking, 1994. Cloth 0-679-85724-6. Grades 5 to 8.

When Zlata begins keeping her diary in the fall of 1991, her concerns are similar to those of any privileged 11-year-old living in Sarajevo: friends, popular music, fashion models, music and tennis lessons, the start of a new school term. In the spring of 1992, however, her life— and her diary entries—change dramatically. Serbian soldiers take up positions in the mountains surrounding the city and begin shelling its residents. It is the start of a siege that will last nearly four years. Life becomes very dangerous and very harsh. Zlata reports the deaths of friends and family members. There is often no electricity or heat. School is closed for months on end. Food becomes scarce. Her responses to the war are authentic. She is most often angry. Sometimes she is sad and depressed. She frequently feels helpless.

In 1993, Zlata showed her diary to her teacher, who arranged to have parts of it published with the assistance of UNICEF. After this, Zlata became a minor celebrity, besieged by journalists looking for a good story. She records these encounters with the same matter-of-fact voice in which she writes about the continuous shelling. The introduction by journalist Janine di Giovanni tells us that Zlata and her family were able to escape to Paris in December of 1993. At one point, Zlata compares her diary to that of Anne Frank; luckily, young readers will be relieved to learn that she escaped Anne's fate. **NF • R**

158. FLEMING, CANDACE. *Boxes for Katje.* Illustrated by Stacey Dressen-McQueen. Melanie Kroupa/Farrar, Straus and Giroux, 2003. Cloth 0-374-30922-1. Grades 2 to 4.

Conditions were very bad in Holland for several years after World War II ended. Food, clothing, and basic necessities like soap were in desperately short supply. Many American charitable organizations sent care packages to families in Holland and other European countries. This is a picture-book account of what happened when a little Dutch girl receives a box of soap, socks, and chocolate from an American girl named Rosie. **F • R**

159. FRENCH, JACKIE. *Hitler's Daughter*. HarperCollins, 2003. Cloth 0-06-008652-1; LB 0-06-008653-X. Grades 5 to 8.

What if Adolf Hitler had a daughter, one with a disfiguring birthmark on her face and one leg shorter than the other? What if he kept her identity secret? What if she escaped from the bunker at the very end of the war and ended up in Australia where she grew up, married, and had children of her own? What if she finally told her story to one of her granddaughters who shares it with a group of school friends? That is the premise of this provocative novel. Intriguing as that idea is, the focus of this story is on Mark, one of the boys who hears the story and is fascinated by it. It raises questions for him about family, the nature of evil, and the ability of individuals to escape their genetic destinies and make choices of their own. **F • R**

160. GARLAND, SHERRY. *The Lotus Seed*. Illustrated by Tatsuro Kiuchi. Harcourt Brace, 1993. Cloth 0-15-249465-0; Voyager/Harcourt Brace, 1997, pap. 0-15-201483-7. Grades 3 to 5.

A Vietnamese American child tells how her grandmother took a lotus seed from the Imperial garden on the day that the Emperor gave up his throne. Thirty years later, when she fled her country during the Vietnam War, she brought the lotus seed with her to America. Later still, a grandson plants the seed. When it blooms, the old woman tells the children that this flower of life and hope represents their home-land, and she gives each of them a seed to keep as she did. An author's note gives a brief history of Vietnam. **F • R**

161. GARLAND, SHERRY. *My Father's Boat*. Illustrated by Ted Rand. Scholastic, 1998. Cloth 0-590-47867-2. Grades 2 to 4.

A young Vietnamese American boy spends the day on his father's fishing boat, learning the craft and hearing about his grandfather's fishing boat in Vietnam. The war that forced his father to leave his country—and his grandfather to stay behind—is only alluded to in passing, but the tone is bittersweet. The man is making a life in the United States but will always miss the land and the father he left behind. It is a story about the refugee experience that has been told over and over again but remains relevant and true. **F • R**

162. GREENFELD, HOWARD. *After the Holocaust*. Greenwillow, 2001. Cloth 0-688-17752-2; LB 0-06-029420-5. Grades 5 to 8.

Greenfeld repeats the approach he used in *The Hidden Children*, here profiling the lives of eight representative Jewish children who survived the Holocaust. He traces their experiences from liberation to the search for missing families and life as displaced persons, usually in camps, to eventual resettlement in the United States. The stories are not as dramatic as those of the camps and hiding places in which the children spent the war years, but they provide links to significant postwar events and the continuity of human experience. **NF • R**

163. HAHN, MARY DOWNING. *Promises to the Dead*. Clarion, 2000. Cloth 0-395-96394-X. Grades 5 to 7.

Twelve-year-old Jesse is hunting for a turtle in the bog near his great-uncle's plantation on Maryland's Eastern Shore when he encounters a dying runaway slave and her young son Perry. She extracts his promise to take Perry to Baltimore to live with his white father's sister. Reluctantly, Jesse, whose great-uncle is a slave-owner, decides that he must keep the promise and begins an arduous odyssey to bring Perry to safety. Their journey coincides with the opening days of the Civil War, as the Confederates fire on Fort Sumter and people in the state of Maryland begin to take sides in the conflict. By the time Jesse has finally found a safe haven for Perry, he has had many narrow escapes from a menacing bounty hunter and has gained a new understanding of the plight of slaves and his own status as a relatively poor but still privileged white boy. The plot is overly complex and contrived, and some of the characters in this novel are stereotypical and one-dimensional. Still, it reflects many of the issues individuals faced during the events leading up to the Civil War. **F • RWR**

164. HAUTMAN, PETE. *Mr. Was*. Simon & Schuster, 1996. Cloth 0-689-81068-7. Grades 6 to 8.

It is difficult to classify or summarize this novel that uses time travel as a central device. The story begins when the teenaged Jack journeys with his mother to the bedside of his dying grandfather. Although Jack has never seen his grandfather before, the old man seems to recognize him, and tries to strangle the boy in his last living moments. A strange metal door in his grandfather's home in Memory, Minnesota, leads Jack into the past and the jungles of Guadalcanal where he and another young man, who turns out to be his grandfather, fight the Japanese and finally each other. **F • R**

165. HERTENSTEIN, JANE. *Beyond Paradise*. Morrow, 1999. Cloth 0-688-16381-5. Grades 6 to 8.

Thirteen-year-old Louise is looking forward to the changes that a move to the Philippines with her missionary family will bring. However, those changes become less positive when the Japanese bomb Pearl Harbor and then invade the island of Panay, where the family has settled. Her father is stranded in Manila, and her mother has slipped into a profound depression. Louise learns a lot about her own strengths and beliefs when the missionaries are captured by the Japanese and moved into an internment camp. Neither the harsh conditions in the camp nor the cruelty of the Japanese soldiers are sugarcoated, but the author does a good job of presenting these elements through the eyes of Louise, who comes to understand some of the cultural differences involved and to value peace more deeply. **F • R**

166. HESSE, KAREN. *Letters from Rifka*. Holt, 1992. Cloth 0-8050-1964-2. Grades 5 to 8.

In 1919, life has been difficult for Rifka's family for some time. As poor Jews in a small Russian village, they have worked hard for very little return. Now, Nathan has deserted the Russian Army to warn them that they are coming for his younger brother Saul as well. Rather than leave his sons to the harsh fate that would await them in the army, the father moves quickly to take the family to America. Only Rifka, the 12-year-old daughter, is left behind in Belgium, quarantined by a case of ringworm. What happens to her is told through the letters she writes to her cousin Tovah, back in Russia. Her resourcefulness and gift for languages help her during the months that she waits in Belgium for her ringworm to be cured, her sometimes stormy voyage across the Atlantic, and yet another wait at Ellis Island. This is a refugee story with a happy ending. **F • R**

167. HOWARD, ELLEN. *A Different Kind of Courage*. Jean Karl/Atheneum, 1996. Cloth 0-689-80774-0. Grades 4 to 6.

There were several private initiatives to take European and English children away from the dangers of World War II. This is a fictionalized account of one such effort, organized by an American woman named Martha Sharp. The two children who are the focus here are a French boy and a French girl of Russian parentage. Their story does not involve the horrors faced by Jewish children and others who were sent to concentration camps. Rather, these are ordinary children whose parents went to extraordinary efforts to send them to a safer environment. They suffer some physical discomfort and the anxiety and fear caused by separation from their parents. In the end, however, they realize that their parents sent them away because they loved them. **F • R**

168. KAY, VERLA. *Broken Feather*. Illustrated by Stephen Alcorn. Putnam, 2002. Cloth 0-399-233550-7. Grades 3 to 5.

A simple, poetic text and stunning block prints tell the story of the coming of the white man to Native American lands and the years of war that resulted when those lands were forcibly taken. An author's note explains that the story is based on real events surrounding the Nez Perce War of 1877. **F • R**

169. KERLEY, BARBARA. *Walt Whitman: Words for America*. Illustrated by Brian Selznick. Scholastic, 2004. Cloth 0-439-35791-8. Grades 4 to 8.

This brief picture-book biography of Walt Whitman explains how the Civil War shaped the man and his poetry. The text and illustrations work together beautifully to bring that historical time to life for young readers today. End matter includes notes by both the author and the illustrator and a sampling of Whitman's poetry. **NF • HR**

170. KUCHUKOV, HRISTO. *My Name Was Hussein*. Illustrated by Allan Eitzen. Boyds Mill, 2004. Cloth 1-56397-964-0. Grades 2 to 4.

A young boy tells about life in his village in Bulgaria. His Roma family is Muslim. Their life is good, filled with rich family ties and a religion that sustains them. This life is shattered, however, when Communist soldiers take over the land. The mosque is closed, and everyone is forced to give up their Muslim names for Christian ones in order to get required identity cards. Illustrations and text hint at the devastation to personal identity and culture of such policies. An author's note explains the background of the story and discloses that the story is based on events in his own life. **F • R**

171. LISLE, JANET TAYLOR. *The Art of Keeping Cool.* Richard Jackson Book/Simon & Schuster, 2000. Cloth 0-689-83787-0; Aladdin/Simon & Schuster, 2002, pap. 0-689-83788-7. Grades 6 to 8.

Robert's father had enlisted with the Canadian Royal Air Force even before the Japanese bombed Pearl Harbor, and his mother finds it impossible to keep up their farm in Kansas. She and Robert move to the small town on the coast of Rhode Island where her husband's family lives. She is able to find work in a factory there, and Robert has his eccentric cousin Elliott to hang out with. He soon learns, however, that his grandfather is a tyrannical bully and that a dark secret surrounds his father's earlier life there. Elliott is distracted by his friendship with a German painter who has fled persecution as a "degenerate" artist only to be persecuted as a possible Nazi spy by his paranoid American neighbors. In a dreadful incident, the painter is burned in the shed where he has stored his latest work; and Robert learns why his father has never returned to his hometown. **F • R**

172. LORBIECKI, MARYBETH. *My Palace of Leaves in Sarajevo.* Illustrated by Herbert Tauss. Dial, 1997. Cloth 0-8037-2033-5; LB 0-8137-2034-3. Grades 4 to 6.

Ten-year-old Nadja begins to write to her cousin in Minnesota just before war comes to Sarajevo, where she lives. Their correspondence continues through the four years in which the city is under attack from the Serbian army. Nadja's letters effectively communicate the fear, anger, hope, confusion, and uncertainty that children experience and the courage they must demonstrate while living in a war zone. There are other real physical consequences as well: hunger, death, and injury. The author's introduction and afterword provide some historical background, and a glossary of Yugoslavian words used in the letters is included. **F • HR**

173. LOWRY, LOIS. *Number the Stars.* Houghton Mifflin, 1989. Cloth 0-395-51060-0. Grades 4 to 6.

This Newbery Medal-winning novel tells the story of Annemarie Johansen, a "righteous Gentile," who shelters her Jewish friend Ellen Rosen when the Nazis come to round up the Danish Jews. Annemarie and her family are exemplars of the ordinary Danish citizens who succeeded in smuggling 7,000 people, nearly the entire Jewish population of their country, to safety in Sweden. It is an inspirational story of quiet courage and human decency in the face of massive force and injustice. **F • HR**

174. McKay, Lawrence, Jr. *Journey Home*. Illustrated by Dom Lee and Keunhee Lee. Lee & Low, 1998. Cloth 1-880000-65-6; pap. 1-58430-005-2. Grades 3 to 5.

Mai's mother Lin was left in an orphanage in Saigon during the Vietnam War. Lin doesn't know anything about how she got there; all she has is a photograph of herself as a toddler, holding a kite. Now Mai and her mother are going to Vietnam to try to learn more about her past. They troop from one Vietnamese orphanage to another, showing the photo, but nobody has any helpful information. Finally, at an outdoor market, they see a kite just like the one in their photo. The merchant writes down the name of a place and the name of a person. It is a clue. Mai and her mother go to the remote village of Sa Dec and ask for Tran Quang Tai. They find the old man, who says that he is indeed the kite maker, but that he had learned the art from Lin's father. He tells her that her father and mother died in the bombing. When the village was destroyed, he had found the baby Lin under the kite that her father had made for her. He took her to the orphanage where she would be safe. He tells Lin that her name is Le Duc Lan.

The story is about homecoming on many levels, about recovered heritage and the experience of belonging to two cultures. **F • R**

175. Maguire, Gregory. *The Good Liar*. Clarion, 1999. Cloth 0-395-0967-0. Grades 4 to 6.

When three girls doing a homework project ask a famous painter to tell them about his boyhood experiences in France during World War II, he sends them a long, reflective narrative. It is a story about lies—the tall tales and exaggerations of the painter and his two brothers and the more serious deceptions practiced by their mother to protect the Jewish woman and her daughter hiding out in their attic. It is ultimately a story about the effects of war on children who have little understanding of the larger issues but who nevertheless are called upon to play small parts in the adult dramas taking place around them. **F • HR**

176. MARX, TRISH. *One Boy from Kosovo*. Illustrated by Cindy Karp. HarperCollins, 2000. Cloth 0-688-17732-8. Grades 4 to 6.

Photographs and a brief text portray a 12-year-old boy who is much like the American children who will read this book. This good-looking fair-haired boy wears a baseball cap backwards on the title page, plays pick-up basketball games, misses his school friends, and longs to have his own computer. But Edi Fejzullahu is an ethnic Albanian whose family was forced from its home in Kosovo by the policy of ethnic cleansing set in motion by the Serbian government of Slobodan Milosevic. Now in a Macedonian refugee camp with 30,000 people living in tents, he and his family have nothing but their memories and their hope of returning to their home. An introductory chapter explains the ethnic and religious conflicts that led to the civil war in Kosovo. **NF • R**

177. MATAS, CAROL. *After the War*. Simon & Schuster, 1996. Cloth 0-689-80350-8; Simon Pulse, 1997, pap. 0-689-80722-8. Grades 7 to 8.

Ruth is a 15-year-old survivor of the Buchenwald concentration camp, alone and severely depressed as she searches Poland for any living family members. She is recruited by *Brichah*, the underground organization that is smuggling illegal immigrants into Palestine. The journey that she makes from Poland to Italy and then by ship to Palestine is arduous and dangerous, but successful in the end. Along the way, she learns to laugh again and to find some measure of joy in the struggle to reach Eretz Israel and in her first romantic relationship. **F • R**

178. MATTHEWS, L. S. *Fish*. Delacorte, 2004. Cloth 0-385-73180-9. Grades 5 to 8.

Young Tiger has grown up in an unnamed foreign country where his parents are aid workers. Severe drought, followed by flooding, has made the environment a harsh one. People are starving, and now civil war is also threatening their village. With the assistance of a wise and competent guide who has lost his family to the war, the family undertakes an arduous trek to a neighboring country where they hope to be safe. Through all of the hardships of their journey, Tiger carries a fish that he has caught in the mud near his home. The fish becomes a symbol of hope, perseverance, and ultimately, survival. The book hints at the complex interaction between hunger and civil war in countries that have been devastated by both phenomena. **F • R**

179. MEAD, ALICE. *Adem's Cross*. Farrar Straus Giroux, 1996. o.p. Grades 6 to 8.

This novel tells the story of a young Albanian Muslim boy living under Serbian rule in Kosovo in 1993. The Serbian oppression has become increasingly brutal, but the Albanian people are committed to nonviolent resistance. His older sister is killed while she reads a poem at a peaceful protest. Her funeral becomes a rally for the Albanian people, precipitating harsh reprisals from the Serbs. Adem's father is jailed and beaten; the family home is occupied. At last Adem has no choice but to try to flee Kosovo for Albania. It is a treacherous journey, and the gypsy who leads him to the border is killed by Serbian sentries. Adem continues on alone, and the reader can only hope that he makes it to safety and an uncertain future. The author's foreword gives the history of the war in the former Yugoslavia up to 1995. **F • R**

180. MIKAELSEN, BEN. *Red Midnight*. HarperCollins, 2002. Cloth 0-380-97745-1; LB 0-06-001228-5. Grades 6 to 8.

The Guatemalan civil war comes to 12-year-old Santiago's remote village, where the inhabitants—all indigenous people of Mayan heritage—have no political stake in the outcome. However, the guerrillas kill all of the residents and burn their homes. Santiago escapes with his 4-year-old sister Angelina. He is a resourceful boy who makes his way to his uncle's home where there is a crude wooden boat, a *cayuco*. His uncle's neighbor gives him some elementary sailing and navigation lessons, a machete, and a little food. Now Santiago and Angelina begin a harrowing voyage up the coast of Central America and across the Gulf of Mexico to refuge in the United States. It is an inspiring survival story. However, Santiago and Angelina's story is extraordinary, and it is fiction. In real life, few children escaped when soldiers or guerrillas targeted the villages occupied by peasants in the Central American countries ravaged by civil unrest. Some were forced to be soldiers; others were killed. An author's note provides some of this important background information. **F • R**

181. MORPURGO, MICHAEL. *Private Peaceful*. Scholastic, 2004. Cloth 0-439-63648-5; pap. 0-439-63652-1. Grades 7 up.

Although Thomas is under age when World War I begins, he signs up to join the British Army at the same time as his beloved older brother Charlie. They find themselves in the trenches of Belgium, doing their best to survive. The story is told in flashbacks as Thomas tries to stay awake during a long night's vigil. He remembers his father's death when he was just a small boy, his mother's love and courage as she raised her boys in circumstances of poverty, his brain-damaged brother Joe, his childhood love for Molly, and the cruelty and arrogance of the local squire. It is only at the end of the long night—and the end of the novel—that we learn that Charlie has been court-martialed for refusing an order to leave his wounded brother behind in no-man's land. He will be shot at dawn. Thomas—and the reader—are shattered by grief and shaken by the consequences of a brother's loyalty. An author's note explains that more than 290 British and Commonwealth soldiers were executed for cowardice or desertion during World War I, many of them unjustly. **F • HR**

182. MOSHER, RICHARD. *Zazoo*. Clarion, 2001. Cloth 0-618-13534-0. Grades 7 to 8.

Zazoo was a baby in Vietnam when her parents were killed by a land mine. An old man, "Grand-Pierre," adopted her and took her to France, where he lives a solitary life as a lock keeper on a canal. Zazoo is 13 years old when she meets a boy who has come to their rural village by train and bicycle on a mysterious mission. As Zazoo and Marius begin to share a first crush, Grand-Pierre's health begins to deteriorate. Little by little, Zazoo learns about the secrets in Grand-Pierre's past, dating back to the awful time when he was a resistance fighter in World War II. In its quiet way, this lyrical, reflective novel shows the deep wounds caused by two different wars, as well as the power of forgiveness. **F • R**

183. NAPOLI, DONNA JO. *Stones in Water*. Dutton, 1997. Cloth 0-525-45842-5. Grades 6 to 8.

Roberto and his friend Samuele are taken from a movie theater in their town just outside Venice and forced to work for the German war effort in the Ukraine. The conditions are harsh and made particularly perilous by the fact that Samuele is Jewish. The boys' friendship and loyalty to each other enable them to survive until one night when Samuele is badly beaten while trying to keep some thugs from stealing Roberto's boots. Samuele dies, and Roberto decides to escape from the labor camp and make his way back to Venice. It is a terrible odyssey, but he finally returns home, aided in the end by a deserting Italian soldier. The book ends with Roberto's decision to join the *partigiani*, Italian partisans fighting to sabotage the war effort and fascism in their country. **F • R**

184. PARK, LINDA SUE. *When My Name Was Keoko.* Clarion, 2002. Cloth 0-618-13335-6; Dell, 2004, pap. 0-440-41944-1. Grades 5 to 8.

In 1940, Korea had already been under Japanese occupation for more than 30 years. Much of Korea's own culture and traditions had been under systematic attack during this period; but after Japan attacked Pearl Harbor in 1941, its stranglehold on Korea intensified. We see those war years through the eyes of two Korean children, Sun-hee and her older brother Tae-yul. Things begin to change dramatically when the Japanese government orders all Koreans to take Japanese names, and Sun-hee becomes Keoko for the duration of the war. Each member of their family responds differently to the privations and humiliations during the period that follows, but all remain true to their Korean heritage.

The novel has much to offer to young American readers. Through the actions of the characters, abstract concepts such as collaboration, patriotism, injustice, and courage are made concrete. The presentation of the Korean perspective on World War II is also an illuminating correction to the overwhelmingly American and European point of view that dominates much of children's literature. **F • HR**

185. PECK, RICHARD. *The River Between Us.* Dial, 2003. Cloth 0-8037-2735-6; Puffin, 2005, pap. 0-14-240310-5. Grades 7 to 8.

The Civil War comes to a small southern Illinois town on the banks of the Mississippi River in this story within a story. At its end, the lives of the Pruitt family have changed forever. Tilly travels to a military hospital in search of her twin, Noah, who is convalescing there. Accompanying her is the mysterious and glamorous Delphine, who has fled the war in New Orleans for a somewhat more certain fate to the North. Noah eventually loses an arm but finds true love with Delphine. Tilly will marry the doctor who cared for Noah in the hospital camp. Their mother will go mad from grief, thinking that Noah has died in the war. And 50 years later, as America is on the verge of entering World War I, a teenage boy will return with his father to that same small town and discover family secrets that have their origin in the Civil War.

Peck's rendering of the time and place is masterful, and his treatment of race relations in a border town is poignant. All of the adolescent characters in this novel deal with issues of identity in ways that will resonate for young readers. **F • HR**

186. POLACCO, PATRICIA. *Pink and Say*. Illustrated by the author.
Philomel, 1994. Cloth 0-399-22671-0. Grades 3 to 5.

Polacco tells a family story in this picture book for older readers. Say
was a young Union soldier from Ohio, wounded and left for dead in a
Georgia pasture. Pink was a young black man serving in the Forty-
Eighth Colored regiment. Pink finds Say and carries him home to his
mother, who cares for Say and shelters the two men until Confederate
marauders arrive. When Pink's mother tries to lead the Confederate
soldiers away from the house where the boys are hiding, they shoot
her. The two young men try to find their way back to the Union lines
but are captured and sent to Andersonville. Say survives his stay in
that notorious prison, but Pink is hanged. Polacco concludes the book
by saying that this story was a memorial to Pink, who saved her ances-
tor's life. It is also a vivid reminder of the consequences of war. **F • R**

187. PROPP, VERA W. *When the Soldiers Were Gone*. Putnam, 1999.
Trade 0-399-23325-3. Grades 4 to 6.

Henk has no other memories but the farm where he lives with his
Papa and Mama. Now Papa tells him that the strangers sitting in the
living room are his real parents and that he must go live with them in
the city. This little boy must grow accustomed to his new name—
Benjamin—these new parents, and his new identity as a Jewish child.
The author does not sugarcoat the difficulties of such a transition; but
she does show how Benjamin, like so many hidden children during
World War II, learns to assume his new identity and his new life. **F • HR**

188. PRYOR, BONNIE. *Thomas*. Illustrated by Bert Dodson. Morrow,
1998. Cloth 0-688-15669-X. Grades 4 to 6.

Eleven-year-old Thomas Bowden lives with his mother, younger sister,
and baby brother on the western frontier of Pennsylvania. His father
has gone to join General Washington's army fighting the British. The
Bowdens are forced from their home when a band of Tories and their
Iroquois allies burn them out. They flee to a nearby fort, but that refuge
proves to be unsafe as well when the soldiers defending them are outnumbered by the British forces. Thomas and his family decide to take
their chances on a harrowing escape over treacherous terrain, facing

swamps, mosquitoes, copperhead snakes, bears, and a rocky mountain range. They reach safety at last in the home of a friendly mountain man and his family. Their next stop will be Philadelphia, where they hope they will be reunited with Mr. Bowden sometime soon. This is one of many novels that depict the consequences of war for women and children, who face many of the same dangers as soldiers on the front line. A sequel, *Thomas in Danger* (Morrow, 1999), finds Thomas kidnapped and turned over to Mohawk fighters, Tory allies in the early days of the Revolution. **F • R**

189. RECORVITS, HELEN. *Where Heroes Hide*. Frances Foster/Farrar Straus and Giroux, 2002. Cloth 0-374-33057-3. Grades 4 to 6.

Eleven years after the end of World War II, Junior Webster's father is still haunted by his experiences. Ten-year-old Junior loves his father, especially when they're hanging out together, but the man's sudden explosions of anger frighten him. Things come to a crisis when Mr. Webster lashes out at Junior's long-time friend Lennie, in a leg brace because of polio. When a house fire threatens the life of another friend who is trapped inside, the decorated veteran proves that he is still a hero when he risks his life to save the boy. This event seems to trigger a resolution to the tensions between Lennie's family and the Websters and to provide a kind of healing for all involved. **F • R**

190. REEDER, CAROLYN. *Across the Lines*. Atheneum, 1997. Cloth 0-689-81133-0. Grades 4 to 6.

Twelve-year-old Edward and Simon grew up on the same Virginia plantation. When the Yankees take it over, their lives veer in different directions. Edward, the young master, goes with his mother to stay with relatives in nearby Petersburg, which is soon under siege. Simon, Edward's slave, runs away to find work and freedom with the Union Army. Each boy gains new awareness of his own identity and a more nuanced understanding of their former relationship. **F • R**

191. ROSENBERG, LIZ. *The Silence in the Mountains*. Illustrated by Chris K. Soentpiet. Orchard, 1999. Cloth 0-531-30084-6; LB 0-531-33084-2. Grades 2 to 4.

Iskander loves his beautiful country, where he lives on a farm with his extended family. War comes, however, and the family must flee to America. Life is good there, especially when they move from the city to a farm, but Iskander continues to miss the country they left behind. His wise grandfather helps him to find the beautiful mountain silence that is the same in both the old home and his new one.

This is a story of contemporary refugees, torn from an unnamed war-ravaged country, a place like Bosnia. Simply written, it should be comforting for children who have been displaced by wars and civil unrest and should provide a bridge to understanding for their American classmates. **F • R**

192. SHEA, PEGI DEITZ. *Tangled Threads: A Hmong Girl's Story.* Clarion, 2003. Cloth 0-618-24748-3. Grades 6 to 8.

With her grandmother, Mai Yang has been in a Thai refugee camp for ten years, among the many Hmong people forced to flee their Laotian homelands because of their cooperation with American forces during the Vietnam War. The camp is primitive, with unsanitary conditions and few educational opportunities for girls like Mai. The Thai soldiers who keep order in the camp are also known to rape and brutalize the powerless residents. At last, however, Mai and her grandmother are released to join relatives in the United States. The rest of the story deals with issues of adjustment and socialization that are part of every refugee story. After some predictable mishaps, Mai begins to find a way to integrate her traditional Hmong culture and values with those of the American middle school milieu in which she finds herself. Like many older immigrants, however, Grandmother finds it more difficult to adapt and dies before very much time has passed in the new world. At the back of the book are glossaries of Hmong and Thai words, information about Hmong names, suggestions for further reading, and an author's note giving some historical background. **F • R**

193. SHEA, PEGI DEITZ. *The Whispering Cloth: A Refugee's Story.* Illustrated by Anita Riggio and You Yang. Boyds Mill, 1995. Cloth 1-56397-134-8; 1996, pap. 1-56397-623-4. Grades 2 to 4.

Mai and her grandmother have been living in a Thai refugee camp ever since the Communist government drove them out of Laos, killing her parents. Mai is learning how to make the traditional Pa'ndau, or story cloths. At first, she is only allowed to stitch the borders of the embroidered tapestries that will be sold to traders. Finally she creates her own story, showing how she slept between her mother and father while the blood dripped from their bodies, how she and her grandmother escaped to the river with bullets whistling over their heads, and how soldiers in different uniforms took them to the refugee camp. Her grandmother tells her that the story seems unfinished, so Mai creates a picture of the life she hopes to live in America, making snowmen with her cousins. **F • R**

194. SIEGELSON, KIM. *Trembling Earth*. Philomel, 2004. Cloth 0-399-24021-7. Grades 6 to 8.

Young Hamp is a proud swamper, born and raised in Georgia's Okefenokee Swamp. His father has taught him the lore of the swamp and the means to wrest a living from this beautiful but tough environment. It is 1864, and Pap has returned from the battle of Shiloh a broken man who is wounded in body and spirit. Hamp resents the stranger his father has become and longs to escape their island in the swamp. When he hears about a bounty on a runaway slave boy, he seizes this opportunity to track him down. The two boys—white and black—find themselves entangled in a mutual struggle to survive in which each must confront his prejudices and stereotypes. We see the Civil War from the different perspectives of the boy who has suffered under slavery and the boy whose father was much too poor ever to own slaves himself but nonetheless fought to maintain the South's right to perpetuate that institution. **F • R**

195. SORENSEN, VIRGINIA. *Miracles on Maple Hill*. Illustrated by Beth Krush and Joe Krush. Harcourt Young Classics, 2003. Cloth 0-15-204719-0. Grades 4 to 6.

Marly's father has returned from World War II with no apparent physical wounds, but he has not recovered emotionally from his experiences in a prisoner-of-war camp. The family decides to move to Grandma's old house in the country, where the pace of life will be slower and less stressful than in Pittsburgh. Marly loves the life on Maple Hill from the beginning; she expects miracles to happen there. She learns to appreciate each of the seasons, but spring is the best when the sap rises in the maple sugar trees. Her father begins to bloom again in this rural setting where he can see the results of his labor in his garden crops and his first batch of maple syrup. The gender roles in this 1956 Newbery Medal winner may seem very constricting to readers today, but the message of hope and renewal after a traumatic war experience remains as relevant as it was 50 years ago. **F • R**

196. STOLZ, MARY. *A Ballad of the Civil War*. Illustrated by Sergio Martinez. HarperCollins, 1997. Cloth 0-06-027362-3. Grades 4 to 6.

Stolz spins a moving novella out of a ballad her mother and aunt sang when she was a girl. It is a common story from the Civil War, two brothers torn apart as they choose to fight on different sides. Here the story is especially wrenching because the brothers are twins. It is possible to trace the origins of the different choices they make as adults in their boyhood expressions of values and preferences. Tom feels sympathy for the slaves his father owns, especially the children, while Jack accepts his position of superiority and ownership without question. **F • R**

197. TRAN, TRUONG. *Going Home, Coming Home*. Illustrated by Ann Phong. Children's Book Press, 2003. Cloth 0-89239-179-0. Grades 2 to 4.

A young girl accompanies her parents to their family home in Vietnam, where her grandmother lives. Her parents haven't returned since they left the country during the Vietnam War. It all seems very strange and very foreign to Ami Chi. It is hot. The food is strange. She can't understand what people are saying. At last, however, she comes to feel that she has two homes, one in Vietnam and one in America.

The text is bilingual, Vietnamese and English, making this a good choice for children to share with older adults who read Vietnamese. **F • R**

198. WARREN, ANDREA. *Escape from Saigon: How a Vietnam War Orphan Became an American Boy*. Melanie Kroupa Books/Farrar Straus and Giroux, 2004. Cloth 0-374-32224-4. Grades 5 to 8.

The author does a good job of explaining the complex circumstances in wartime Vietnam that resulted in Amerasian Long's being placed in an orphanage in Saigon by his grandmother, who was no longer able to care for him. The narrative follows his flight through Operation Babylift at the end of the war to the American family in Ohio that adopted him. His adjustment to life in America—as Matt Steiner—was relatively easy, and he went on to finish medical school, marry, and have two children. In 1994, Matt was able to return to Vietnam and rekindle his memories and connections with his birth country. An afterword gives more information about Operation Babylift and international adoption. Resources for more information are included. **NF • HR**

199. WHELAN, GLORIA. *Angel on the Square*. HarperCollins, 2001. Cloth 0-06-029030-7; HarperTrophy, 2003, pap. 0-06-440879-5. Grades 6 to 8.

Twelve-year-old Katya has been raised in luxury, the daughter of a Russian aristocrat. In 1913, she and her mother leave their home in Saint Petersburg to join the household of Tsar Nicholas II. Katya enjoys her friendship with the Duchess Anastasia but misses her older cousin Misha, who has been sent to military school. Everything changes dramatically with the outbreak of World War I and the subsequent Russian Revolution. Misha survives the war and joins those who are supporting Kerensky for a democratic government in Russia. When Lenin's radical movement takes power instead, the Tsar and his family are executed. Katya and her mother escape to their former estate in the country, where the peasants have burned the house and taken everything of value. Katya works hard alongside two former servants, planting crops and making a humble home out of a smithy. Misha shows up in time for her 18th birthday, and the two young people return to St. Petersburg to try to build a life together.

Whelan depicts both the causes and unintended consequences of war in this insightful novel. Young readers will be drawn into Katya's life, as she develops from a spoiled, selfish girl to a more sensitive and aware young woman who must do hard physical labor in order to survive. They will also see how ordinary people are impacted by the sweep of historical events. **F • HR**

200. WHELAN, GLORIA. *Burying the Sun*. HarperCollins, 2004. Cloth 0-06-054112-1; LB 0-06-054113-X. Grades 5 to 8.

This companion to *Angel on the Square* and *The Impossible Journey* is told from the point of view of Georgi, nearly 15 years old and living in Leningrad with his sister Marya and his mother. The story begins in a glorious springtime in 1941 and soon darkens when Germany declares war on Russia. By the following winter, Leningrad is under siege, and conditions for the people living there are becoming desperate. Shortages of food and fuel are critical; people eat bark from the trees and burn books to keep warm. Georgi is too young to volunteer to fight with the Russian Army, but he does help with the truck brigade that makes risky trips across the frozen Lake Ladoga to bring back food for the starving people of Leningrad. We see both the most admirable aspects of human nature and civic culture and some of the most reprehensible as individuals and government bodies try to survive under the most trying circumstances. The great Russian composer

Dmitri Shostokovich makes a cameo appearance, first helping with the manual labor needed to protect the city and then composing a magnificent symphony to honor it. **F • R**

201. WHELAN, GLORIA. *The Impossible Journey*. HarperCollins, 2003. Cloth 0-06-623811-0; LB 0-06-623812-9. Grades 5 to 8.

While *The Impossible Journey* does not deal with war directly, it is an important bridge between the earlier *Angel on the Square*, set during the time of the Russian Revolution, and *Burying the Sun*, with its backdrop of the Siege of Leningrad that began in 1941. All three novels deal with generations of a Russian family, beginning with privileged aristocrats who suffer reverses in fortune after the Revolution of 1917. The events of *The Impossible Journey* revolve around the arrest of two adult offspring of that first generation, now married and working as laborers in Leningrad while quietly resisting the Stalinist regime. Their children, 13-year-old Marya and her little brother Georgi, set off on an impossible journey to Siberia to find them. They meet a sympathetic doctor and a band of resourceful Samoyeds who help them along the way. They find their mother in a small town far to the north, and the doctor eventually reunites them with their father. Unfortunately, his health has been so battered by his experiences in a labor camp that he dies shortly after their reunion. As the book ends, Marya is already planning a return to her beloved home, which she still calls St. Petersburg in her mind. **F • R**

DVDs

202. *Grave of the Fireflies*. Central Park Media Corporation. 1992, 1998. 88 minutes. Grades 6 to 8.

Toward the end of World War II, two orphaned children—teenage Seita and his little sister Setsuko—struggle to survive in the Japanese countryside. Continual air raids by American bombers have taken the life of their mother and destroyed their home. A relative gives them grudging help at first, but they soon find themselves on their own, scrounging for food and hope in a hostile environment. A tin container of candy fruit drops, a symbol of happier times, ultimately becomes the receptacle for Setsuko's ashes when she dies from malnutrition. This anime masterpiece is a lyrical testimonial to the resilience of children in extreme conditions and also a deeply moving reminder of the innocent victims of any war. **F • R**

THE HORRORS
OF WAR

THERE IS ONLY A MATTER OF DEGREE BETWEEN many of the more horrific consequences of war and what I am calling here the horrors of war. I have decided, however, to reserve the label "horror" for the most awesome and horrendous acts of war: the nuclear bombs used in Japan to end World War II and the Holocaust perpetrated by Nazi Germany against the Jewish people of Europe and millions of other souls considered undesirable by that regime. These are very difficult matters for most of us to contemplate and particularly difficult to contemplate sharing these events with children.

Nevertheless, nearly every educator and caring parent agrees that children should know about these episodes in the recent history of humankind. As the authors of a guide to teaching the Holocaust to young people explain, we continue to live in violent times in which acts of genocide and "ethnic cleansing" occur with disturbing frequency. They urge us to awaken in young people revulsion for the atrocities being committed against peoples around the world and compassion for the victims (Stephens, Brown, and Rubin, 1995, pp. 7ff.).

The National Council of Teachers of English adopted a position statement, "On Teaching About Intolerance and Genocide" (1993), because they were alarmed by a Roper survey showing that 22 percent of students and 20 percent of adults believed there was a possibility that the Holocaust did not happen. In its statement, the organization affirmed that "students should read and discuss literature on genocide and intolerance within an historically accurate framework with special

123

emphasis on primary source material." Fortunately, there is now no dearth of materials for teachers to use as they tackle these tough topics.

Whenever I talk to parents about their children's information needs, they tell me how difficult it is to talk about injustice and evil. Some families have a religious framework that enables them to accommodate these issues. For many, however, there is an understandable reluctance to tamper with a child's innocence by introducing such disturbing topics. And there is no way to talk about the Jewish Holocaust without talking about injustice and evil. There are special sensitivities for Jewish families who must balance the important cultural and religious imperative "never to forget" with the need to explain why Jewish children were killed simply because they were Jewish.

Many adults are also troubled by the issue of the American bombing of Hiroshima and Nagasaki. This seems to be one of those areas in which values conflict. On the one hand, we want to believe that our government's decision ended a war that would otherwise have gone on to claim even more lives. On the other hand, we look with horror at the casualties and the hideous suffering inflicted on civilian survivors of the blasts. How can we justify the costs?

There is little doubt that our use of a nuclear weapon also led to the escalation of arms development and the paranoia of the Cold War. I was one of those children in the 1950s who was led through "duck and cover" drills and marches to the cold halls of our school basement as practice for a possible Soviet attack. I can remember feeling a frisson of fear when I saw a plane fly overhead. While the threat of a global nuclear holocaust seems to have eased along with the thawing of the Cold War, current concerns about the nuclear capabilities of North Korea and Iran may resurrect the old fears.

CHILDREN AND THE HORRORS OF WAR

For the past three years, I have taught a freshman seminar at UCLA on the topic of children's literature about war and peace. These 18-year-old students are still close enough to their own childhoods to remember the books they read and how they felt about them, especially when reminded of certain titles. Many of them read Lois Lowry's *Number the Stars* when they were younger, and it was often their first exposure to the Holocaust. Of course, that book focuses on the Gentile girl and her discovery that she had the capacity for courage as well as compassion. It does not take the reader into the degradation of the concentration camps. Many of these students, however, talk about their growing awareness that a government had perpetrated evil almost beyond imagining. Many find it difficult to believe that other governments stood by and let it happen, especially the United States. Then we talk about other, more recent genocides in Cambodia, Rwanda, and Bosnia. It is a sobering discussion but an essential one as young people prepare to take their places as citizens of the world and formulate their own positions regarding the injustice that still exists.

In that same seminar, several Jewish students have talked about going through a phase when they were in middle school in which they read everything they could get their hands on about the Holocaust. One girl described it as being obsessed. One can speculate that it was important for these Jewish children to somehow reconcile the events of the Holocaust with their own deepening awareness of their Jewish identity.

While I can sympathize with adults who want to spare their children from knowledge about evil in the world—the horrors of war being only one aspect—I do not see how they can succeed in doing so. It is there on the nightly news and on the front page of the paper. My own preference has always been to provide the children in my care with weapons to fight the evil. Those weapons are ethics and values and information.

CHILDREN'S LITERATURE AND INFORMATION RESOURCES ABOUT THE HORRORS OF WAR

There has been surprisingly little published for children about the bombing of Hiroshima and Nagasaki since I did my last research in 1992. However, there are some titles that should be highlighted here:

- The classic graphic novel by Keiji Nakazawa, *Barefoot Gen*
- Laurence Yep's compelling novella *Hiroshima*
- Clive A. Lawton's nonfiction account of the development and use of the atomic bomb, *Hiroshima*

The literature on the Jewish Holocaust of World War II, however, has burgeoned. There are enough titles now to develop a kind of typology or classification of sub-genres. Perhaps the best general treatment of the Holocaust is Barbara Rogasky's masterful *Smoke and Ashes*, now available in a second edition.

As recently as 10 or 15 years ago, it was rare to find a children's book that took the reader inside the concentration camps. That has changed dramatically. Many survivor accounts deal dramatically with time spent in the camps. These include:

- *Four Perfect Pebbles* by Lila Perl
- *I Have Lived a Thousand Years* by Livia Bitton-Jackson
- *No Pretty Pictures* by Anita Lobel

Some commentators praise the survivor stories as communicating to children the message of the triumph of the human spirit under the worst of conditions. This is true, of course. The best and most honest of these, however, also convey the capriciousness of fate and the accidents of luck that enabled some to survive while others died.

There are even picture books now that present the concentration camps in pictures as well as words. Unlike *Let the Celebrations Begin* by Margaret Wild with illustrations by Julie Vivas (1991), which was controversial for its somewhat sentimental and even positive message about the experience of children in a camp, these newer titles are more realistic without being morbid. *Luba, the Angel of Bergen-Belsen* by Michelle R. McCann and *The Harmonica* by Tony Johnston are both picture books that could be read by children in a broad age range.

I would also call attention to *Brundibar*, with its text by Tony Kushner and illustrations by Maurice Sendak. This is the opera that was produced and performed by the children at the Terezin concentration camp and has recently been presented at various venues in the United States. Since this picture book has little content to explain the circumstances under which it was originally created, it is good to know that there are books about Terezin. In *Fireflies in the Dark*, Susan Goldman Rubin writes about a gifted art therapist who worked with children in the camp. She also describes the production of the opera. Another book by Rubin and Ela Weissberger, *The Cat With the Yellow Star: Coming of Age in Terezin* (Holiday House, 2006), highlights the experiences of one of the children who sang in a production of *Brundibar* and who was one of the few survivors.

I was impressed by two books that contrasted the lives of Jewish and Gentile young people in Nazi Germany. One is the novel *Daniel Half Human and the Good Nazi* by David Chotjewitz. It focuses on the ways in which the lives of two boys, one Jewish and one Aryan, friends since their early school days in Hamburg, are intertwined and interdependent. It does much to explain how even "good" Germans were coopted to accept and implement the policies designed to dehumanize and demonize the Jewish people during Hitler's regime. Another book that uses the device of "compare and contrast" to good effect is *Parallel Journeys* by Eleanor Ayer. This nonfiction book follows the lives of two young people who were born a few miles from each other in the German Rhineland. Helen, a Jewish girl, escaped to Amsterdam and lived in hiding for a year before being sent to Auschwitz. Alfons, on the other hand, rose to a position of leadership in the Hitler Youth. Both survived the war and eventually immigrated to the United States where they told the stories of their parallel lives on the lecture circuit. Both of these books lend themselves to discussion and to consideration of the parallel lives of people around us.

Anne Frank has become something of a publishing cottage industry. We have not only seen a new "definitive" edition of her famous diary; there are also books by her childhood friends, such as *A Friend Called Anne* by Jacqueline Van Maarsen and Carol Ann Lee. Susan Goldman Rubin has crafted a well-researched book based on Anne's correspondence with an American pen pal. Yona Zeldis McDonough and Malcah Zeldis have created a picture-book biography. Ruud Van der Rol and Rian Verhoeven have put together a moving photoessay about Anne's life and its remarkable impact after her death. With all of this publishing attention surrounding the most famous victim of the Holocaust, it is a sobering corrective to read Cynthia Ozick's 1997 *New Yorker* essay in which she questions the value of Anne Frank's diary as the definitive message about that event. She worries about the young people who have responded to its universal theme of adolescent angst, missing the very real and important fact that Anne died miserably of typhus in Auschwitz just days before the camp was liberated. Anne Frank's story is not about the triumph of the human spirit; it is about a promising life hideously truncated in its youth through government policies and practices of great evil.

It is not easy to read the books in the section that follows. I frequently found myself weeping in sorrow and despair or clenching my jaw in anger as I read and then thought and wrote about them. These are important responses, however. Good writing about tough subjects enables us to generate authentic emotional and cognitive responses. Children should not be denied the opportunity to feel and to think about the issues that have shaped their world, no matter how horrific. Hopefully, feeling and thinking about the horrors of war will lead to appropriate actions. James E. Young (1988, p. 191) urges a critical thinking approach to reading the texts about the Holocaust, keeping in mind that the texts frame our understanding of the event.

There is an important ethical component to reading and writing about the horrors of war. Susan Sontag (2003, p. 115) has written that remembering is an ethical act but one that needs to be tempered with compassion and reason. Too much remembering, she points out, can also embitter. Think of the consequences of remembering ancient grievances in Northern Ireland, Bosnia, and the Middle East. Sometimes it is necessary to forget, or at least to reconcile, in order to make peace or at least to move on.

Bibliography

✜

BOOKS

203. ADLER, DAVID A. *A Hero and the Holocaust: The Story of Janusz Korczak and His Children*. Illustrated by Bill Farnsworth. Holiday House, 2002. Cloth 0-8234-1548-1. Grades 3 to 5.

This eloquent picture-book biography tells the story of Janusz Korczak, the Polish doctor who accompanied the orphans in his care into the Warsaw Ghetto and then to the Treblinka concentration camp, where they all died. This is a clear introduction to the horrors of the Holocaust for younger children as well as a glimpse into the life of one very good man. **NF • HR**

204. ADLER, DAVID A. *Hiding from the Nazis*. Illustrated by Karen Ritz. Holiday House, 1997. Cloth 0-8234-1288-1. Grades 3 to 5.

Lore Baer's family fled from the Nazi regime in Germany to Holland, where they thought they would be safe; and for a while, they were. However, by 1943, the situation had become critical for Jews in Holland as well. Lore's parents entrust their 4-year-old daughter's safety to a Gentile family living on a farm. There Lore grows to love the adult daughter of the family like a mother. Even though there are dangers, and Lore must sometimes hide in the barn, she is alive and well at the end of the war. Like many hidden children, Lore had trouble being reconciled with her parents, and her mother was always afraid of losing her child again.

This picture-book account, based on a true story, personalizes the experience of hidden Jewish children in ways that some of the longer narratives fail to do. The illustrations make it clear how very young Lore was when her parents sent her away. An author's note gives a few more details about Lore's life and about the family that kept her safe. **F • R**

205. ADLER, DAVID A. *Hilde and Eli: Children of the Holocaust.*
Illustrated by Karen Ritz. Holiday House, 1994. Cloth 0-8234-1091-9.
Grades 4 to 5.

Moving illustrations and simple text tell the stories of two Jewish children who were killed in the Holocaust. Hilde had a happy early childhood in Frankfurt am Main, Germany; Eli was the son of a rabbi in rural Czechoslovakia. Both families tried unsuccessfully to emigrate; both families were swept up in Nazi pogroms. Hilde and her mother were gassed in a freight car on its way to Riga, Latvia. Eli died at Auschwitz. Adler tells their stories unflinchingly and unforgettably. An author's note gives the sources used to document these two representative lives lost. **NF • R**

206. ADLER, DAVID A. *One Yellow Daffodil: A Hanukkah Story.*
Illustrated by Lloyd Bloom. Gulliver Books/Harcourt Brace, 1995. Cloth 0-15-200537-4. Grades 2 to 5.

Morris Kaplan is an old man who has a flower shop. Ilana and Jonathan buy flowers from him every Friday for the Sabbath, but one day they come in on Tuesday. They want flowers for the first night of Hanukkah. When they learn that he doesn't observe the holiday, they invite him to celebrate with their family. Mr. Kaplan is forced to remember his childhood in Poland when he did celebrate the holiday and the terrible years in the concentration camp where the sudden miraculous appearance of a yellow daffodil in the mud had convinced him that he, too, could survive. Remembering, he is able to acknowledge his heritage and celebrate the holiday again. The brooding acrylic illustrations capture the story's mood of painful remembrance. **F • R**

207. *Anne Frank in the World.* Knopf, 2001. Cloth 0-375-81177-X; LB 0-375-91177-4. Grades 7 to 8.

Compiled by staff of the Anne Frank House in Amsterdam, this is a collection of 225 photos depicting the life of the Frank family before going into hiding in 1942, the places they lived in Germany and in the Netherlands, and the terrible political events happening around them. A foreword by Rabbi Julia Neuberger helps to contextualize the photos, but the captions and brief introductory text for each of the subsequent chapters is often too truncated to provide the background that children would need to fully understand them. The quality of these black-and-white photo reproductions varies a great deal as well. It is the school pictures of Anne and Margot as well as their family snapshots that will draw the attention of most children. **NF • RWR**

208. AYER, ELEANOR. *Parallel Journeys*. Atheneum, 1995. Cloth 0-689-31830-8; Aladdin, 2000, pap. 0-689-83236-2. Grades 5 to 8.

Helen and Alfons were young people who were born a few miles from each other in the German Rhineland. Their experiences during World War II, however, could hardly have been more different. After escaping to Amsterdam and living in hiding for a year, Helen was sent to Auschwitz. Alfons, on the other hand, rose to a position of leadership in the Hitler Youth. Both survived the war and eventually immigrated to the United States. Both wrote about their wartime experiences. They joined forces as adults to tell the stories of their parallel lives on the lecture circuit. The narrative presented here, in parallel chapters, is a powerful testament both to the power of socialization and propaganda used to create fanatic believers in Hitler's ideology of a "master race" and to the triumph of the human spirit under the most excruciating conditions of degradation. **NF • HR**

209. BITTON-JACKSON, LIVIA. *I Have Lived a Thousand Years: Growing Up in the Holocaust*. Simon & Schuster, 1997. Cloth 0-689-81022-9. Grades 6 to 8.

One of the chief values of the best of the Holocaust survivor memoirs is that they go inside the concentration camps and tell the young reader not only what happened but how an individual could adapt to the horrors of that existence. This is one of the better examples, written by a woman who was a normal 13-year-old when the Nazis invaded Hungary in 1944, changing her life forever. She and her family were moved to a crowded ghetto and then to Auschwitz. As one of the few teenager inmates in the death camp, she has insights that will resonate for young readers as she describes her life and the various twists of fate that allowed her to survive. **NF • R**

210. CHOTJEWITZ, DAVID. *Daniel Half Human and the Good Nazi*. Richard Jackson Book/Atheneum, 2004. Cloth 0-689-85747-0. Grades Grades 7 to 8.

Daniel and Armin had been friends since their early school days in Hamburg, in spite of the gap between their social classes. Daniel's father is a successful attorney; Armin's is a frequently unemployed laborer. In 1933, as the boys prepare to join the Hitler Youth, Daniel learns that his mother is Jewish. His life changes dramatically at this point, as the anti-Jewish policies of the Nazi regime begin to affect the family's fortunes, his friendship with Armin, and his own sense of identity. Armin goes on to become a leader in the Hitler Youth and then a soldier in the Third Reich. In the end, Daniel and his mother are able to escape the ultimate terrors of the Holocaust; and Daniel becomes an interpreter for the British Army. The novel focuses on the ways in which the lives of the two boys, one Aryan and one Jewish, are intertwined and interdependent. Armin carries on a dangerous romance with Daniel's Jewish cousin and alerts her to the need to escape before the family is sent to the deadly concentration camps. Still, he follows the orders of his commander and beats Daniel's parents in a raid on their apartment.

In 1945, Daniel finds himself again in Hamburg, this time helping the Allies as they round up war criminals. Armin is one of the Germans whose status as a member of the dreaded SS and Nazi Party is in question. Daniel checks for the SS tattoo on his former friend's arm and sees that it has been scratched out. He thinks that Armin had merely done his job; now he has his own job to do. He takes the form and confirms Armin's membership in both the SS and the Nazi Party.

This book does not take the reader into the horrors of the concentration camp. Instead, it chronicles the steady escalation of policies designed to dehumanize and demonize the Jewish people under Hitler's regime and the ways in which even "good" Germans were co-opted to accept and implement those policies. F • HR

211. FRANK, ANNE. *The Diary of a Young Girl: The Definitive Edition*. Doubleday, 1995. Cloth 0-385-47378-8. Grades 6 to 8.

Anne Frank's wartime diary, kept while in hiding from the Nazis in Amsterdam, is now considered a classic. Many adults are aware of the controversy surrounding her father's editing of the original diary. This definitive edition begins with a foreword that explains the various versions. Based primarily on version "b," which Anne herself edited in 1944 with an eye for future publication, it adds 30 percent more material to the original edited version that was published in 1947 and presents a more authentic picture of Anne's developing sense of self and of the growing dangers of the war outside the walls of the secret annex. **NF • HR**

212. GREENFELD, HOWARD. *The Hidden Children*. Ticknor & Fields, 1993. Cloth 0-395-66074-2. Grades 5 to 8.

Very few Jewish children living in Europe during World War II survived the Holocaust. The best estimates are that only 11 percent of the approximately 1.7 million European Jews under the age of 16 who were alive in 1939 survived. Many of those were hidden in convents or other religions institutions, orphanages, boarding schools, and with private families. Greenfeld describes the experiences of some of these hidden children, from the chaotic moments in which they were sent into hiding to their liberation at the end of the war. Some were treated well; others were abused or neglected in various ways. What they all shared was the loss of their childhood and the loss of their Jewish identity. These are poignant stories that should cause young readers of today to think about their own lives and the lives of less fortunate children in new ways. **NF • HR**

213. HESSE, KAREN. *The Cats in Krasinski Square*. Illustrated by Wendy Watson. Scholastic, 2004. Cloth 0-439-43540-4. Grades 3 to 4.

The horrors of the Warsaw Ghetto are only hinted at in this picture book for young readers. Instead, we see the quiet heroism and clever thinking of a Jewish girl who is passing as an Aryan Pole and doing what she can to help those who are confined behind the wall of the ghetto. When her older sister learns that a plan to smuggle in food by train has been detected, she comes up with an ingenious solution. The conspirators gather up dozens of stray cats and carry them to the train station in baskets and bags. When the train pulls in, they release the cats who distract the Nazi soldiers and their dogs long enough for the food to be successfully moved through cracks in the wall to the Jews waiting there. An author's note gives the historical source for the story and some basic information about the German efforts first to confine the Warsaw Jews in the overcrowded ghetto and then to relocate them to death camps. Wendy Watson's pencil, ink, and watercolor illustrations complement the story perfectly. **F • HR**

214. INNOCENTI, ROBERTO, AND CHRISTOPHE GALLAZ. *Rose Blanche*.
Illustrated by the author. Stewart, Tabori & Chang, 1999. Cloth 1-55670-207-8. Grades 4 to 8.

A young German girl watches the comings and goings of soldiers and tanks in her village. One day a little boy jumps from the back of a truck but is stopped by a soldier and herded back on board. Curious, she follows the truck far out of town into a clearing in a forest where she finds a concentration camp filled with people in striped uniforms branded with yellow stars. They say they are hungry, so she gives them some bread and returns day after day to share what little food she has with the people behind the barbed wire fence. Then one day the soldiers all leave town in a rush. Rose Blanche runs to the concentration camp and finds it empty. In the fog, there is a shot. The little girl's mother waits a long time, but she does not return. On the last page of the book, we see a bit of the hair ribbon Rose Blanche always wore, snagged in the barbed wire.

This is a moving account in the tradition of "the righteous Gentile," the non-Jewish person who acts with courage and decency to help Jewish people in times of trouble. It is also one of the few books for children to take the reader right up to the gates of the concentration camps and to hint at the fate of those imprisoned within. While most children will understand that Rose Blanche has died in the chaotic cross-fire of war, there is enough ambiguity to allow others to select a happier ending if they wish. **F • R**

215. JOHNSTON, TONY. *The Harmonica*. Illustrated by Ron Mazellan. Charlesbridge, 2004. LB 1-57091-547-4. Grades 3 to 5.

A young Jewish boy is separated from his parents when the Nazis invade Poland. Alone in a concentration camp, the boy has only a harmonica as a tangible reminder of his family and their love of music. One night, he wakens suddenly, convinced that his parents are dead. He pours his grief into the harmonica, playing Schubert. The commandant hears him and summons him night after night to play the harmonica for him. He rewards him with a bit of bread. The boy feels guilty for these rewards until one of his fellow prisoners thanks him for the Schubert. Then he knows that they, like the commandant, have been soothed by his music. **F • R**

216. KUSHNER, TONY. *Brundibar*. Illustrated by Maurice Sendak. Michael Di Capua/Hyperion, 2003. Cloth 0-7868-0904-3. Grades 4 to 8.

No foreword or author's note explains the background of this book, an opera composed by Czech musicians and performed by Jewish children at the Terezin concentration camp during World War II. One paragraph on the front jacket flap gives this basic information. The opera's libretto is retold here by the American playwright Tony Kushner, and it is innocuous enough. When two children discover that their mother is sick, they try to earn money for milk to make her better by singing in the town square. They are bullied by a menacing hurdy-gurdy player but are finally helped by three talking animals and 300 schoolchildren. It is Sendak's subversive illustrations that provide some of the cultural and historical clues to the opera's origins. Susan Goldman Rubin's *Fireflies in the Dark* is an excellent nonfiction accompaniment to this book. It includes an account of the staging of the opera at Terezin and photos of the children who performed in it. **F • R**

217. LAWTON, CLIVE A. *Auschwitz: The Story of a Nazi Death Camp*. Candlewick, 2002. Cloth 0-7636-1595-1. Grades 5 to 8.

Telling the story of the Nazi death camps for young readers is a daunting endeavor. Lawton gets it right. With eloquent photos and primary source documents and a clear, unflinching text, he explains why the German government felt it necessary to build institutions for killing people they felt were undesirable and how they went about it. He describes life in Auschwitz as well as the deaths that awaited most of the people who were sent there. A particularly useful chapter tells how historians have been able to determine what happened during the Holocaust, using such evidence as Nazi documents, witness accounts, survivor stories, photos, and the possessions of the victims that were accumulated in the camps. It is a chilling story but one that children have the right to know. **NF • HR**

218. LAWTON, CLIVE A. *Hiroshima: The Story of the First Atom Bomb*. Candlewick, 2004. Cloth 0-7636-2271-0. Grades 5 to 8.

Using a variety of documentary sources including many photos, the author chronicles the scientific work that led to the creation of the first atom bomb, the decision to use it as a means to end the war, its consequences for the civilian population of Japan, and the prognosis for nuclear deterrence today. **NF • R**

219. LOBEL, ANITA. *No Pretty Pictures: A Child of War*. Greenwillow, 1998. Cloth 0-688-15935-4. Grades 5 to 8.

The accomplished children's book illustrator explains at the end of the prologue to this memoir that she had long resisted writing down this story of a time from which she has few pretty pictures to remember. Indeed, her narrative of a childhood spent hiding and running from the Nazis in Poland until she and her brother were finally captured and sent to a series of concentration camps is full of ugly pictures. Perhaps because she is an artist, her memories are visual and full of telling graphic details. Young readers will be able to see and smell and feel the people and places in the nightmare world she inhabited during the war years and the comparative paradise of a Swedish sanitarium where she recovered from tuberculosis and regained her sense of well-being. **NF • R**

220. MCCANN, MICHELLE R. *Luba: The Angel of Bergen-Belsen*. Illustrated by Ann Marshall. Tricycle Press, 2003. Cloth 1-58246-098-1. Grades 3 to 5.

This is an eloquent picture-book biography of a Polish woman who has lost her small son to Nazi soldiers. Imprisoned at the Bergen-Belsen concentration camp, she is in despair, feeling that her life has no meaning or purpose until the December evening when she hears children crying. She finds 54 Jewish children who have been abandoned in the cold by a truck driver who could not bear to take them to be killed as he had been ordered to do. She determines to save them and manages to keep all but two of them alive until the allies liberate the camp the following April. The beautiful oil and collage illustrations enhance this story of courage, heroism, and the triumph of the human spirit in the most daunting of circumstances. **NF • HR**

221. MCDONOUGH, YONA ZELDIS. *Anne Frank*. Illustrated by Malcah Zeldis. Henry Holt, 1997. Cloth 0-8050-4924-X. Grades 3 to 5.

In simple, unsparing language, the author tells the story of Anne Frank's life—from her birth and happy childhood in Germany to the family's move to Amsterdam to avoid Nazi persecution, the years in hiding, and death in Auschwitz. An author's note gives a rationale for sharing the story with younger readers in a picture-book biography. At first the colorful gouache illustrations in a folk art style seem out of place for such a sad story, but they ultimately convey the hope and

optimism that so many readers have found in Anne Frank's diaries.
NF • R

222. MARUKI, TOSHI. *Hiroshima No Pika*. Illustrated by the author.
Lothrop, Lee & Shepard, 1980. Cloth 0-688-01297-3. Grades 6 to 8.

In Japan, they call it the Flash, the atomic bomb that devastated
Hiroshima on August 6, 1945. This is a graphic picture-book representation of the event and its horrific aftermath, as experienced by one
family. Strong visual images depict the suffering of men, women, and
children caught in the blast. The narrative ends with the ceremony
held on August 6 every year in Hiroshima in which people light
lanterns in memory of those who died and set them in the rivers that
run to the sea. **F • HR**

223. MATAS, CAROL. *In My Enemy's House*. Simon & Schuster, 1999.
Cloth 0-689-81354-6. Grades 6 to 8.

With her blond hair and blue eyes, Marisa is able to escape the
roundup of Jews in her Polish town. She takes the identity papers of a
Polish girl and goes to work as a servant for a wealthy family in
Germany. Herr Reymann is a high-ranking Nazi official, and his
daughter attends the League of German Maidens. Marisa, now known
as Maria, struggles with her hatred of the Nazi regime and her fear of
discovery while hanging on to her father's teaching that everything she
needs to know to live her life well is found in the Torah. The book
ends with the defeat of the Germans. Marisa fears that she is the only
Jew left alive. Indeed, most of her family have died; but she is reunited
with her childhood sweetheart Shmuel in a camp for displaced persons. **F • R**

224. MAZER, NORMA FOX. *Good Night, Maman*. Harcourt Brace, 1999.
Cloth 0-15-201468-3. Grades 6 to 8.

First their father is arrested in a roundup of Jews in Paris. Then 12-
year-old Karin, her older brother Marc, and their mother go into hiding
in a small town in France. They spend a year there until the woman
who has sheltered them feels it is no longer safe. They try to make their
way to Italy, where Jews are said to be safer, and at last to a boat that
will take them to America. Unfortunately, Maman becomes too sick to
make the journey with them so Karin and Marc go alone to the camp
in Oswego, New York, where they live with nearly 1,000 other European

refugees. Karin makes friends with an American girl and her family, but she misses her mother dreadfully and writes letters to her that she cannot mail because there is no address. Finally, her brother tells her that their mother died before they left Europe but he had wanted to spare her the terrible news.

A historical note explains that the novel is based on a true incident, the one small effort made by the American government at the end of the war to bring a boatload of refugees to the United States. These refugees were housed in an unused fort in Oswego, where the 22,000 residents of the town did what they could to make them welcome. The book manages to balance many competing points of view: the survival of two Jewish teenagers with the deaths of both of their parents; the humanitarian effort that saved their life with the failure of the American government to take action earlier. **F • R**

225. MOCHIZUKI, KEN. *Passage to Freedom: The Sugihara Story.*
Illustrated by Dom Lee. Lee & Low, 1997. Cloth 1-880000-49-0. Grades 3 to 5.

Chiune Sugihara was a Japanese diplomat stationed in a small town in Lithuania in 1940. When he was besieged by Polish Jews desperate for visas to leave the country, he defied the direct orders of his country and issued hundreds of visas on his own personal authority. This picture-book account is told from the point of view of his young son, who has contributed an afterword telling what happened after his father's courageous act. The family was imprisoned for 18 months in a Soviet internment camp, and his father was asked to resign from diplomatic service when they finally returned to Japan. In 1985, he received the "Righteous Among Nations" Award from the Yad Vashem Holocaust Memorial in Israel, the first and only Asian to have received his honor. This is an inspiring story of a man who listened to his conscience rather than his government and saved hundreds of lives by doing so. **NF • HR**

226. NAKAZAWA, KEIJI. *Barefoot Gen: A Cartoon Story of Hiroshima.*
Last Gasp, 2003. Pap. 0-86719-450-2. Grades 7 to 8.

This early graphic novel, published originally in Japan in 1972, is now considered a classic of the manga genre. Based on the author/illustrator's own experiences, it tells the story of the bombing of Hiroshima through the eyes of a young boy whose family opposes Japan's militaristic government and its involvement in World War II. The family

members are persecuted by their Japanese neighbors for their unpopular political views and then suffer alongside them when the atom
bomb is dropped on their city. The horrors of the bombing are presented in the graphic detail that is traditional in manga comics. The ultimate message is a plea for peace, as Gen's mother holds up her newborn baby girl to see the devastation caused by the bomb. "Remember
this, Tomoko!" she says. "This is what took your father, brother, and sister from us . . . This is war—when you grow up you must never let this
happen again!" **F • R**

227. NIEUWSMA, MILTON J. *Kinderlager: An Oral History of Young
Holocaust Survivors*. Holiday House, 1998. Cloth 0-8234-1358-6.
Grades 6 to 8.

The author provides oral histories from three women who survived the
Kinderlager, a section of Auschwitz created near the end of the war for
children. While the stories of these three women, all Jewish children
from the town of Tomaszow Mazowiecki, Poland, are poignant, the
overall value of the book is lessened by a lack of context or background. It is only the entry in the glossary at the back of the book that
gives a little information, mostly speculative, about the *Kinderlager*.
These children were, after all, anomalies, among the very few who survived Auschwitz. **NF • RWR**

228. ORLEV, URI. *Run, Boy, Run*. Houghton Mifflin, 2003. Cloth 0-618-
16465-0. Grades 5 to 8.

Srulik is 8 years old and on the run from the Germans. His father's last
words are to learn how to behave like a Christian—but never to forget
that he is Jewish. For the next two years, he survives in the Polish
forests that harbor partisans, in fields, and in farming households
where he works for his keep. He meets with astonishing kindness from
Christians—even several German soldiers—who shelter him in spite
of their suspicion that he is Jewish. He also encounters cruelty and
harsh discrimination, losing an arm when a doctor refuses to operate
on a Jewish boy. Perhaps the most touching part of his story is the
ending, when the war is over and Jewish social workers win over his
resistance to accept his true identity. An epilogue explains how Srulik
ended up in Israel, where Orlev heard his story and used it as the
inspiration for this novel. **F • HR**

229. PERL, LILA, AND MARION BLUMENTHAL LAZAN. *Four Perfect Pebbles: A Holocaust Story.* Greenwillow, 1996. Cloth 0-688-114294-X. Grades 5 to 8.

This is the memoir of one Jewish child's horrendous odyssey through the refugee, transit, and prison camps of the Nazi regime. It is a story of dashed hopes and resilience, as Marion's family nearly escapes to America and then to Palestine, only to be deterred and sent into still more brutal environments. Marion keeps hope alive by collecting groups of four perfect pebbles wherever she goes, as alike as possible, representing her family, alive and intact. Astonishingly, the mother, father, brother, and sister do remain together as they are moved from camp to camp only to have Mr. Blumenthal die of typhus after being liberated by the Russians at the end of the war. An epilogue traces the remaining family's eventual move to new and happier lives in the United States. **NF • R**

230. PRESSLER, MIRJAM. *Malka.* Philomel, 2003. Cloth 0-399-23984-7; Puffin, 2005, Pap. 0-14-240269-9. Grades 6 to 8.

In 1943, Doctor Hannah Mai realizes that it is no longer safe for Jews like her and her daughters to stay in Poland. They have begun an arduous journey to Hungary when 7-year-old Malka becomes very sick. Hannah finds a kind family to care for Malka and travels on without her, arranging for her younger daughter to join her when she is well enough. Things do not work out as planned, however, and Malka finds herself on her own in Poland, a Jewish child trying to survive under the worst possible circumstances. The book alternates between the child's ordeal and her mother's trek to dubious safety, only to learn that Malka has not been able to escape. Ultimately, the two are reunited, but the scars remain due to the hardships each has suffered, complicated by the mother's guilt and the child's experience of abandonment. The story never takes the reader to the concentration camps, but the repeated German "operations" in which Jews are forcibly removed from the ghettos in Polish cities and towns foreshadow their fate. **F • R**

231. RADIN, RUTH YAFFE. *Escape to the Forest: Based on a True Story of the Holocaust.* Illustrated by Janet Hamlin. HarperCollins, 2000. Cloth 0-06-028520-6; LB 0-06-02851-4. Grades 3 to 5.

Sarah is 10 years old at the beginning of the war, living in Russian-occupied Eastern Poland. Life is difficult for her Jewish family, but it becomes desperate when the Germans succeed in replacing the Russians in their territory. At first it seems that the family might be able to survive as a unit in the ghetto to which they are confined; but when they are evacuated for the last journey to the death camps, Sarah's parents make a difficult decision. They send Sarah away to join the Jewish partisans in the forest, where the legendary Tuvia Bielski has managed to save many of his people with the support of the Russians. Endnotes tell what happened to the real child and to the Bielski partisans whose experiences were the basis for this short novel. Simple black-and-white drawings add to the accessibility of the story. **F • R**

232. ROGASKY, BARBARA. *Smoke and Ashes: The Story of the Holocaust*. Holiday House, 2002. Cloth 0-8234-1612-7; pap. 0-8234-1677-1. Grades 6 to 8.

This revised and expanded edition of the 1988 title remains the best overall account of the Holocaust for young people. Unflinching and respectful of its young readers' intelligence, it provides historical background, political analysis, and careful descriptions of the steps taken by the Nazi government to carry out the Final Solution. It covers topics such as resistance by the Jews, the lack of response by the United States and Great Britain, and the acts of the few Gentiles who saved and rescued Jewish people imperiled by the Nazi regime. Final chapters include discussions of other genocides, the justice meted out by the War Crimes tribunal in Nuremberg after the war, contemporary neo-Nazism, and the work of those who deny that the Holocaust took place. This is essential reading for young people who want to try to understand what happened and why. **NF • HR**

233. ROSENBERG, MAXINE B. *Hiding to Survive: Stories of Jewish Children Rescued from the Holocaust*. Clarion, 1994. Cloth 0-395-65014-3; pap. 0-395-90020-4. Grades 5 to 8.

A well-written, concise introduction gives children the context for the survivor narratives that follow, explaining the circumstances under which some Jewish children were hidden to avoid death at the hand of the Nazis. Fourteen people who were hidden as children tell their stories. Their experiences varied. Some had to learn to pass as Gentiles; others were hidden away in secret attics and closets. Many came to love the families who took them in. Some of these rescuers were members of resistance movements who were devoted to helping Jews. Others were actually anti-Semitic but were motivated by nationalistic hatred of the Germans. At least one woman just needed the money. A glossary and bibliography of books for further reading are included. **NF • R**

234. RUBIN, SUSAN GOLDMAN. *Fireflies in the Dark: Friedl Dicker-Brandeis and the Children of Terezin*. Holiday House, 2000. Cloth 0-8234-1461-2. Grades 5 to 8.

Rubin uses the story of Friedl Dicker-Brandeis, an artist and art educator, to tell the larger story of Terezin. This was the concentration camp established by the Nazis as a "model Jewish settlement," intended to mask their actual genocidal policies. Initially, many artists, writers, and children were settled there; and some educational and cultural activities were allowed. This is where the children's opera *Brundibar* was staged. The actual conditions were brutal, and only 100 of the 15,000 children who passed through the camp survived the war. Because of the efforts of people like Dicker-Brandeis, however, much of the children's extraordinary art and writing remains as a testimony. **NF • HR**

235. RUBIN, SUSAN GOLDMAN. *Searching for Anne: Letters from Amsterdam to Iowa*. Abrams, 2003. Cloth 0-8109-4514-2. Grades 5 to 8.

In 1939, a 10-year-old Iowa school girl picked a name from a list of pen pals and wrote to her. Juanita Wagner received one letter from her pen pal, Anne Frank, before the tragic events of World War II interrupted their correspondence. Susan Goldman Rubin has used that letter, on display at the Museum of Tolerance in Los Angeles, as a basis for a book that compares and contrasts the lives of the two girls. She uses primary sources, first-hand reports, and interviews to piece together what was happening in Iowa and in Amsterdam. The whole world knows the fate of Anne, dead of typhus at the Bergen-Belsen just weeks before the camp was liberated. Juanita and her older sister worked for the war effort, watched friends and neighbors join the armed forces, and wondered why Anne didn't write back. Illustrated with carefully chosen photos and other documents, the book gives a uniquely child-oriented view of the Holocaust and other aspects of World War II. **NF • R**

236. SCHNUR, STEVEN. *The Shadow Children*. Illustrated by Herbert Tauss. Morrow, 1994. Cloth 0-688-13281-2; LB 0-688-13831-4. Grades 5 to 8.

Eleven-year-old Etienne is spending the summer on his grandfather's farm in the French countryside. He encounters ghosts of Jewish children who were killed by the Nazis during World War II and learns the terrible secret his grandfather and other villagers have been keeping. The supernatural element gives this fictional narrative about the Holocaust a different tone than more factual accounts, and some children who prefer fiction to nonfiction may find this a more approachable way to read about this period of history. However, children who lack any previous knowledge of the Holocaust may find that the book raises more questions than it answers. **F • RWR**

237. SMITH, FRANK DABBA. *My Secret Camera: Life in the Lodz Ghetto*. Illustrated by Mendel Grossman. Gulliver/Harcourt, 2000. Cloth 0-15-202306-2. Grades 4 to 8.

Mendel Grossman was one of the Polish Jews who was forced into the ghetto in the city of Lodz by the Nazis. He found a job in the photo laboratory of the ghetto administration and used that position to take secret photos of the daily life there, creating a visual testimony of the tragedy taking place. Like most of the residents of the ghetto, Grossman was sent to a prison camp where he died. However, some of the negatives and prints that he had hidden survived. Sixteen of those photos are included in this slim volume, along with an interpretive narrative supplied by a rabbi and photographer. The text is simple enough for young children, but the content is strong enough to engage older children as well. This is an excellent companion to novels that take place in the Polish ghettos established by the Nazis. **NF • R**

238. SPINELLI, JERRY. *Milkweed*. Knopf, 2003. Cloth 0-375-81374-8; LB 0-375-91374-2. Grades 6 to 8.

We meet the anti-hero of this story as a little boy living by his wits on the streets of Warsaw just before the Nazis march in. He doesn't know his name, his age, his parents, or his history. Another boy takes him under his wing and gives him a name—Misha—and a back story to explain his origins. The other boys are all Jews, but Uri decrees that

Misha is a gypsy, kidnapped and left on his own. Running from danger one night, Misha meets a little girl, Janina, in a fine home; and they become friends. Soon they will find themselves in the Warsaw Ghetto, where her father treats him like a son. The situation becomes ever more desperate in the ghetto; and at last, the Nazis begin to move the Jews by train to concentration camps. Misha has been warned and tries to prevent Janina from getting on the train, but he fails. He is left with nothing but her broken shoe; she loses her life.

Against all odds, Misha survives and emigrates to America. He makes his living as a small-time salesman but cannot keep himself from ranting on street corners, telling whoever will listen what happened to him in Warsaw. He marries, but it does not last. He is too broken in spirit to be a husband to anyone. Twenty-five years later, working as a stockboy in a grocery store, he is found by the daughter he never knew he had, hand in hand with her own small daughter. Living with his daughter's family, his heart and soul finally healed, Misha at last knows who he is—a grandfather, Poppynoodle.

Some adult readers have criticized this book for its portrayal of Jews who steal and betray one another in the desperate circumstances of the ghetto. But there are admirable characters here as well: Janina's kind father and the infinitely good Dr. Korczak who stays with his band of Jewish orphans until the very end, marching off to his own death with the children he has tended. Some readers have also found the sudden shift to Misha's life as an adult in America to be jarring. The ending can be understood, however, as the only possible happy ending for the story of one extremely unfortunate boy, caught up in the horrors of the Holocaust. **F • RWR**

239. TAKAYUKI, ISHII. *One Thousand Paper Cranes: The Story of Sadako and the Children's Peace Statue*. Dell Laurel-Leaf, 1997. Pap. 0-440-22843-3. Grades 4 to 6.

This is a straightforward account of the bombing of Hiroshima by the Americans at the end of World War II, its immediate and long-term consequences, and the role played by Sadako, the young girl who died as a result of radiation sickness, as a symbol of peace in the atomic age. Young readers will find useful background information about the meaning of the thousand paper cranes and the Children's Peace Statue. Directions for folding an origami crane are included. **NF • R**

240. VAN DER ROL, RUUD, AND RIAN VERHOEVEN. *Anne Frank, Beyond the Diary: A Photographic Remembrance*. Viking, 1993. Cloth 0-670-84932-4. Grades 6 to 8.

A moving introduction by Anna Quindlen establishes the context for this scrapbook of photos, historical documentation, and explanatory text that adds a great deal to one's appreciation for the diary kept by Anne Frank from 1942 until she and her family were taken from their hiding place in Amsterdam to the concentration camps where all but her father died. Quindlen reminds us that most young teenagers who read Anne's diary do not find it a tragic document. Instead, they read about a girl who shares many of their own thoughts and emotions about everyday matters: one's appearance, conflicts with parents, a first kiss, movie stars and other elements of popular culture, hopes and dreams for the future. There are many poignant images in this book, but I was particularly moved by the page that simply shows the red and white diary itself, with its broken lock. **NF • HR**

241. VANDER ZEE, RUTH. *Erika's Story*. Illustrated by Roberto Innocenti. Creative Editions, 2003. Cloth 1-56846-176-3. Grades 4 to 8.

A German woman, Erika, tells her story. She doesn't know exactly when she was born or where. All she knows is that her Jewish parents, on a train bound for a concentration camp, threw her from the train in the hope that she would be found and raised in safety. Their hope was realized. The baby landed in a patch of grass, and a German woman raised her as her own. She married and had children of her own, and those children had children. While she never forgets the terrible fate that must have come to her parents, she is grateful to have survived.

The story is told in simple, elegant prose; and Innocenti's haunting illustrations contribute to the poignancy of the story. Both adults and children will find much to think about and discuss: could they have made the choice that Erika's parents did? **F • R**

242. VAN MAARSEN, JACQUELINE, AND CAROL ANN LEE. *A Friend Called Anne*. Viking, 2004. Cloth 0-670-05958-7. Grades 6 to 8.

Jacqueline became Anne's best friend when she was 12. Anne called her "Jopie" in her diary. This is Jacqueline's memoir of that childhood friendship, her own wartime experiences, and her evolving relationship with the famous diary. Jacqueline's mother was a French Catholic who was able to convince the German authorities in Amsterdam to reclassify her daughters as non-Jews. This enabled Jacqueline to escape the deportations that many of her friends—and members of her father's family—suffered. This gives her a unique perspective on life in Holland as the Nazis set out to eliminate its Jewish population. Young readers, however, will be more interested in her portrait of Anne and her account of their friendship. **NF • R**

243. WARREN, ANDREA. *Surviving Hitler: A Boy in the Nazi Death Camps*. HarperCollins, 2001. Cloth 0-688-17497-3; LB 0-06-029218-0. Grades 6 to 8.

Jack Mandelbaum was separated from his mother, brother, and sister in Poland and sent to the Blechhammer concentration camp. He was 15 and strong, and he vowed to work hard and do whatever it took to survive. This is his story, but there are also some memorable cameo appearances—the fat *kapo* whose red triangle labeled him as a criminal, the irrepressible Moniek who encouraged Jack to laugh, and the world-weary older prisoner who told him to think of the experience as a game in which the object was to outlast the Nazis. An epilogue tells of Jack's resettlement in the United States and the productive, rewarding life he has led here. **NF • R**

244. YEP, LAURENCE. *Hiroshima*. Scholastic, 1995. Cloth 0-590-20832-2. Grades 5 to 8.

On August 6, 1945, two teenage sisters go about their wartime activities in the city of Hiroshima. When the *Enola Gay* drops its bomb, Riko is killed immediately. Twelve-year-old Sachi is severely burned, and for years she covers her face with a surgical mask when she goes outdoors, fearing the looks of revulsion that her scars produce. In 1949, she becomes one of the 25 Hiroshima Maidens who are brought to the United States for reconstructive surgery. Back in Hiroshima, every year on August 6, she joins those who put lighted candles in paper boxes floating on the river as a remembrance of the horrors that the bomb brought and as a prayer for peace.

In this novella, Yep evokes the destruction caused by the atom bomb on Japanese civilians and makes an impassioned plea for peace. **F • R**

245. YOLEN, JANE. *The Devil's Arithmetic*. Viking, 1988. Cloth 0-67-081027-4; Puffin, 1990, pap. 0-14-034535-3. Grades 6 to 8.

Teenage Hannah Stern is tired of the family Passover Seders, with all of her relatives talking about the need to remember the past. This year, however, when she is sent to open the door for Elijah, she finds herself in a Polish shtetl in 1942. Soon she and the other Jewish villagers are rounded up and sent to a concentration camp. Hannah, with her knowledge of the future, is aware of their fate; but she is unable to convince the others. She grows close to another girl in the camp, Rivka, and almost impulsively takes her friend's place when she is arbitrarily selected for the gas chamber. When the door to the gas chamber opens, Hannah is transported back in time to her family's Seder. She realizes then that her Aunt Eva is Rivka. Her time travel has enabled her to understand a part of her family history and to appreciate her Jewish heritage. **F • HR**

246. ZINDEL, PAUL. *The Gadget*. HarperCollins, 2001. Cloth 0-06-027812-9; LB 0-06-028255-X. Grades 6 to 8.

Thirteen-year-old Stephen joins his father, a physicist working on a secret project at Los Alamos in 1945. The base is obsessed with security. Children like Stephen are warned to be alert to spies and kidnappers who might want to use them as hostages. His father's Native American housekeeper is even suspicious of his new friend Alexei whose father looks after the guard dogs. The two boys try to learn the secret that is at the core of Los Alamos, and one night in the middle of July they sneak out of the house and follow a caravan to a desert location where they see the first atom bomb exploded. Three weeks later, similar bombs will be dropped on Hiroshima and Nagasaki. In the end, Alexei and his father do turn out to be spies; and Stephen has a frank conversation with his father about the morality of creating such a weapon. The book only hints at the consequences for civilians and for future foreign policy. Zindel based this book on real events and real people. Appendices give profiles of the major people involved in developing the atom bomb and a chronology of events leading up to its use by the United States on the two Japanese cities, thus ending the war. **F • R**

WEB SITES

247. *United States Holocaust Memorial Museum*.
http://www.ushmm.org/main.php
United States Holocaust Memorial Museum. Grades 5 to 8.

The focus of this Web site is the World War II Holocaust perpetrated by Nazi Germany. The resources supporting this mission are excellent, including an online encyclopedia, online exhibitions, and special educational links for both students and teachers. However, there are also significant resources pertaining to other genocides, including those in the Congo and in Darfur. Visitors to the Web site are encouraged to reflect on the civic values—or lack of them—and other circumstances that make such horrors possible in today's world. **NF • R**

DVDs

248. *The Devil's Arithmetic*. Punch and Millbrook Farm/Showtime. 2002. 97 minutes. Grades 7 up.

Kirsten Dunst stars as Hannah Stern in this made-for-television movie of Jane Yolen's novel. Some of the details have been changed for the movie, but the basic plot and theme have been left intact. When Hannah is transported back in time to a Jewish village in 1942, she is caught up in the horrors of the Holocaust, ending up in a brutal concentration camp where she ultimately gives up her life to save her cousin Rivka, who will survive to become the modern Hannah's Aunt Eva. Waking back in the present, surrounded by her relatives at the family Seder (who think she has drunk too much of the Passover wine), she has finally accepted her Jewish heritage and the need to remember the past. The movie is even more emotionally wrenching than the novel, and it is rated PD-M, Parental Discretion for mature children 13 and over. As Dustin Hoffman eloquently explains in his introduction, however, this is content to which children must be exposed in order for them to do their part to ensure that these horrific events are never repeated. **F • HR**

THE AMERICAN HOME FRONT

THERE ARE THE FRONT LINES OF BATTLE, where soldiers engage the enemy. Then there is the home front, where civilians—traditionally women, children, and men too old to fight—support the fighting men however they can. For most American children, the home front has been far from the front lines. Their wartime experiences have been shaped by battles fought in distant lands.

World War II generated a distinctive American home front. The war produced profound changes in everyday life as fathers and brothers went to war and women went to work, and as food, gasoline, and other critical resources became scarce. American children were enlisted as young soldiers on the home front. Two scholars who have studied the impact of that war on childhood in America (Kirk, 1994; Tuttle, 1993) note that the involvement of children as active supporters of the American war effort was a conscious government policy. Children were actually mobilized to participate in such activities as collecting scrap metal and paper as well as buying and selling war bonds. They were the target of propaganda disseminated in the Saturday afternoon movie programs and comic books of the day.

Of course, some American children had a particularly harsh experience during World War II. On February 19, 1942, President Franklin D. Roosevelt signed Executive Order 9066, effectively depriving 112,000 Japanese Americans on the West Coast of their rights as citizens and of their freedom. Japanese American children were removed from their homes along with their parents and sent to remote internment camps where their education and community ties were severely

149

disrupted. A prevailing climate of racism and ethnic prejudice was reinforced by government propaganda, and few Americans protested the
policy. Children received messages of fear and racism through movies,
comic books, and the words and actions of adults around them. There
are stories of parents smashing any toys that were made in Japan. The
enemy was referred to with racist epithets such as "dirty Japs" or "little
yellow bastards." Signs on restaurant windows read: "No Dogs or Japs
Allowed." Chinese Americans and Filipino Americans did what they
could to distance themselves and distinguish themselves from the
Japanese American targets of racial hatred. Anti-Japanese messages
were so ubiquitous and so effective that many who were children during World War II retained their fear and hatred well into adulthood
(Tuttle, 1993, pp. 167 ff.).

A few people, usually those with strong personal relationships
with individual Japanese Americans, did what they could to ease the
circumstances of their interned friends and neighbors. Clara Breed, a
children's librarian who served a Japanese American community in San
Diego, corresponded with her young patrons who were interned and
sent them books and other personal objects to make their lives in the
camps a little more bearable. Joanne Oppenheim has written about her
activities in a remarkable book for young people, *Dear Miss Breed: True
Stories of the Japanese American Incarceration During World War II and a
Librarian Who Made a Difference* (Scholastic, 2006), published too late
to be included in the resource lists of this volume. We can also find
Clara Breed's words to her fellow librarians in an article that she wrote
for *The Horn Book* at the time. Her opening words make her position
clear: "A little more than a year ago, libraries in California, Oregon, and
Washington were swept clean of some of their most enthusiastic bor-
rowers—Americans whose parents, grandparents, or great-grandpar-
ents happened to emigrate from the wrong country, Japan" (Breed, 1943,
p. 253). Her voice of reason and tolerance is rare among the more jingo-
istic writings of the time.

During World War II, American parents worried about how best
to prepare children for the dramatically changed conditions of their
lives. Child psychologists and educators responded in the pages of
women's and parenting magazines and in popular books and pamphlets. The content and question-and-answer format of a brochure
published by the Child Study Association (*Children in Wartime*, 1943)
seem eerily contemporary. Parents are advised that babies are frightened by sudden noise—such as an air raid siren—but that they can
get used to a noisy environment and learn to ignore it. They are told to

be sensible and matter-of-fact when they talk to their children about possible dangers. Parents are reminded that preschool children cannot understand what the war is about or where it is; their lives should reflect "business-as-usual" as much as possible. A mother who worries that her 11-year-old son is "bloodthirsty" in his eagerness for news about the war and enthusiasm for war play is reassured that her son is a normal boy.

Anna Wolf takes a slightly different approach in her 1942 book, *Our Children Face War*. Her message is that the best thing parents can do is "to help them day by day, not to forget, but to understand, and to find a place for themselves, too, in America at war" (p. 3). She reminds parents that their children will take their cues from these most significant adults in their lives. If mothers are nervous, their children will feel insecure. Strong family ties are the best defense against an uncertain and dangerous world. With calm confidence, she advises parents about what to say and how to say it in order to maximize the chances that children will not only survive their home front experiences but go on to become good adults. She encourages parents to build values and moral frameworks that will help to prevent future wars.

While Anna Wolf may have unintentionally terrified parents with her high expectations for parental responsibility, Dorothy Baruch (1942) is a little more gentle and understanding. She tells her readers that she will share the latest understanding from the world of child psychology in an effort to help them with the burden of parenting in difficult times. Her "Pointers Toward Perspective" outlines her approach:

1. On the shoulders of to-day's children lies the hope of America's future.
2. To-day's children are dependent on to-day's parents for their fear and their courage.
3. Parents can help children to take the war years in stride. But to do so, they themselves must take them in stride.
4. It isn't alone what happens to you; it's the way you can take it.

The final line—presented in all capital letters in the book—sums it up: Parents can raise their own morale through psychological understandings (p. 7).

The attack on the World Trade Center on September 11, 2001, brought what would soon come to be known as the war on terrorism to our shores. The home front didn't seem so safe any longer. Much as Pearl Harbor had propelled complacent or isolationist Americans into World War II, this attack on our own soil generated calls for revenge and a new kind of patriotism. Only a few months later, President George W. Bush invaded Afghanistan, the country that had sheltered Osama bin Laden and the other leaders and architects of the 9/11 attack. Soon we were also at war with Iraq, in a quest for weapons of mass destruction that were probably never there at all. All of these events brought new concerns for American parents, and again experts responded with advice. The World Wide Web was now the primary information source. In Part III, Resources for Adults, you will find selected examples.

Of course, America has been very fortunate to escape the first-hand consequences of war. For European children, on the other hand, World War II was fought in their own neighborhoods. The home front and the front lines often merged. There are a number of books that capture both the sense of adventure that the war engendered in some child witnesses and the devastation it wreaked in other children's lives. Some of the more horrific stories are found in the chapters on the consequences and the horrors of war; those that focus on more positive aspects are in the section titled "Hope and Glory." This resource list is devoted to books about the American home front.

THE AMERICAN HOME FRONT IN BOOKS AND INFORMATION RESOURCES FOR CHILDREN

Most of the books in this section are set in World War II. As noted above, this is the only war in which the American government recruited children in the war effort as a matter of policy. Children were the targets of wartime propaganda disseminated in the popular culture of the time. They were encouraged to be on the lookout for spies, to plant victory gardens, and to collect newspaper and scrap metal. They did without favorite foods and new shoes as rationing went into effect. This was also a war in which almost all fathers were drafted, so nearly every child had a personal stake in the outcome.

Sixteen titles in the resource list that follows deal with the World War II home front as experienced by non-Japanese Americans. One nonfiction book and one Web site are devoted to Rosie the Riveter, the iconic woman working at a nontraditional job in support of the war effort. The 14 novels are overwhelmingly set in white, middle-class families. The two notable exceptions are picture books for older readers. Jacqueline Woodson's poignant *Coming on Home Soon* is about an African American girl waiting for her mother to return from her war job in the North. *Nim and the War Effort* by Milly Lee is the story of a Chinese American girl living in San Francisco who does her best to collect the most newspapers for the war effort. Clearly there are many stories that still need to be told about the experiences of other American children during World War II.

The consequences for Japanese Americans of Executive Order 9066 are told in three fictional accounts, four nonfiction treatments, and one Web site. The nonfiction titles make excellent use of primary source materials. Allen Say's surrealistic picture book, *Home of the Brave*, is an experimental approach to the topic, linking the experiences of Japanese Americans during World War II with those of Native Americans who were also removed from their homes earlier in our history.

The Vietnam War and the Persian Gulf War of 1991 are each represented by two fiction titles. Ellen Emerson White's *Where Have All the Flowers Gone*, part of Scholastic's Dear America series, gives some good insights into the home front during a time of conflicting values. Maria Testa's *Almost Forever*, is a novel in verse, portraying the experiences and emotions of a young girl whose father is serving as a doctor in Vietnam. Here, too, there are glimpses of the anti-war movement that was such a major part of life in the United States while we were at war in Vietnam. The distinguished author of young adult novels M. E. Kerr tackled the Persian Gulf War in *Linger*. She returns to themes she has explored elsewhere—class differences, the nature of adolescent popularity, and the weakness of some adults—but set this time during Operation Desert Storm. Alice Mead's *Soldier Mom* introduces for the first time the issue of a single mother whose reserve unit is called up for active duty. The young protagonist's response to her mother's going away is realistic and will make many readers wonder how they would feel in the same situation.

Bibliography

✂

BOOKS

249. AVI. *Don't You Know There's a War On?* HarperCollins, 2001. Cloth 0-380-97863-6. Grades 5 to 8.

Sixteen-year-old Howie Crispers looks back to 1943, when he was 11 years old and mounted a campaign to save his favorite teacher from being fired. The fact that it was wartime is integral to the reasons for Miss Gossim's termination; a whirlwind romance with a soldier led to a secret wedding and has left her pregnant with no idea where her husband is stationed. School rules of the time prevent pregnant women from teaching. The impact of the war is everywhere. Children collect scrap, buy war stamps, and look for spies. Fathers are serving as soldiers; some of them die. Mothers are working. Food is in short supply. Even shoes are rationed. The first-person voice of a working-class Brooklyn boy is pitch-perfect, and his earnest effort to retain his teacher is touching. **F • HR**

250. BANKS, SARA HARRELL. *Under the Shadow of Wings.* Anne Schwartz/Atheneum, 1997. Cloth 0-689-81307-8. Grades 4 to 6.

This story of Tattnall, an 11-year-old girl, and her brain-damaged cousin Obie plays out against the backdrop of a small southern town during World War II. As Obie's behavior becomes more troublesome and more dangerous, Tattnall feels complex emotions of love, obligation, and resentment for the cousin she has looked after for most of her life. The denouement, motivated to some degree by Obie's fascination with the warplanes that pass overhead, is tragic and inevitable. **F • R**

251. BUCHANAN, JANE. *Goodbye, Charley.* Farrar Straus & Giroux, 2004. Cloth 0-374-35020. Grades 4 to 6.

Everything seems to be changing in twelve-year-old Celie's coastal Massachusetts town. It is 1943, and war is on everyone's mind. The unexpected arrivals of a pet monkey and the grandson of her crabby neighbor generate the twists and turns of the plot. The author has made good use of details about life on the home front—food and gas rationing, worries about a father at war in the Pacific, an older brother's desire to enlist, mothers going to work in the shipyards—to create a sense of that time and place. **F • R**

252. CAREY, JANET LEE. *Molly's Fire.* Atheneum, 2000. Cloth 0-689-82612-5. Grades 6 to 8.

Molly refuses to believe the official telegram that says that her father was shot down and presumed dead. Months pass, and her mother is even seeing another man, the father of a boy in her class who bullies her. She sees a POW who is working at a camp outside of town, and he seems to have her father's watch. Could this be a sign from her father that he is really alive? It turns out that Molly's father does return, one of the few soldiers presumed dead who managed to survive; but the POW's watch was not his. Molly was right, but for the wrong reason.

There are many other subplots here—a first romance, a classmate whose Japanese ancestry makes her the subject of cruel teasing, the ruins of a stained glass window that Molly reassembles. It doesn't quite hang together, but some young readers will be pleased that Molly's belief in her father's return leads to a happy ending after all. **F • RWR**

253. COLMAN, PENNY. *Rosie the Riveter: Women Working on the Home Front in World War II*. Crown, 1995. Cloth 0-517-59790-X; LB 0-517-59791-8. Grades 6 to 8.

Colman uses real-life examples to tell the story of the great mobilization of women for nontraditional jobs during World War II. The result was an astonishing record of productivity that supported the military efforts of the fighting men. Colman does not whitewash the racism that made it impossible for Japanese American women and difficult for African American women to find the same employment opportunities as white women. She also tells the bittersweet ending to the story of Rosie the Riveter and her sisters; almost all were laid off after the war ended and the men came home to reclaim their jobs. A backlash against working women in the 1950s laid the blame on them for social problems ranging from juvenile delinquency to divorce. As Colman points out, however, the experience of earning good wages, being independent, and doing important work was something the women war workers never forgot. **NF • HR**

254. COOPER, MICHAEL L. *Remembering Manzanar: Life in a Japanese Relocation Camp*. Clarion, 2002. Cloth 0-618-06778-7. Grades 5 to 8.

Archival photos, including some by Dorothea Lange and Ansel Adams, add to the power of this story of dignity and survival in the face of injustice and hardship. Cooper makes clear that traditional Japanese heritage combined with more newly acquired American values made it possible for these people who were forcibly removed from their homes to this barren site in the California high desert to create a semblance of civilized community there. He also makes clear the devastating consequences—emotional, economic, and social—that this experience created for most of those who lived through it. **NF • HR**

255. GIFF, PATRICIA REILLY. *Lily's Crossing*. Delacorte, 1997. Cloth 0-385-32142-2. Grades 4 to 6.

In the summer of 1944, the war changes many things in Lily's life. She and her Gram go to the family home in Rockaway Beach as usual, but her father joins the army and is sent to Europe. Her best friend's father moves his family to another town where he can work in a weapons factory; and she meets Albert, a Hungarian boy who is a refugee staying with neighbors. Lily knows that she needs to curb her tendency to exaggerate, but the consequences of her lies become dire when she convinces Albert that they could swim out and join one of the troop ships sailing from the East Coast to Europe. Then he could find his sister Ruth who was left behind in France, and she could find her father. A tragedy is narrowly averted, and the next summer when Lily goes to Rockaway, Albert is still there—and so is his sister Ruth. **F • R**

256. HARLOW, JOAN HIATT. *Shadows on the Sea*. Margaret K. McElderry/Atheneum, 2003. Cloth 0-689-84926-5. Grades 5 to 8.

In the summer of 1942, 14-year-old Jill is sent to stay with her grandmother on the coast of Maine while her mother travels to Newfoundland to care for a sick brother, and her father, a well-known popular singer, tours on the West Coast. She encounters a very insular small-town culture and stumbles into an espionage plot. The author skillfully incorporates many details about the home front at the beginning of the United States' involvement in World War II with the elements of a mystery story. **F • R**

257. KERR, M. E. *Linger*. HarperCollins, 1993. Cloth 0-06-022879-2. Grades 7 up.

Sixteen-year-old Gary is surprised when Lynn Dunlinger, the pretty, popular daughter of the owner of the restaurant where his entire family is employed, tells him that she has had a letter from his brother. Bobby had left school suddenly, enlisted in the army, and been sent to the Middle East to serve in Operation Desert Storm. The story that unfolds is told through Gary's narrative and through the ongoing letters that Bobby writes to Lynn and the journal he keeps. It is a story of class differences, a kind of false patriotism that is whipped up by Lynn's father, the conflicts generated by anti-war sentiments, and the very human consequences of combat. The denouement occurs at a big event at the restaurant that Mr. Dunlinger has planned to celebrate Bobby's return as a decorated war veteran. When Bobby shows up with his best

buddy who was horribly burned by friendly fire in Iraq, the restaura-
teur asks Bobby to keep his friend out of sight of the guests, saying his
wounds would make everyone feel nervous and depressed. This story
should trigger some questions about the facile display of flags and yellow ribbons by Americans whose true commitment to our foreign
engagements may be more self-serving than patriotic. **F • R**

258. KOCHENDERFER, LEE. *The Victory Garden.* Delacorte, 2002. Cloth
0-385-32788-9. Grades 4 to 6.

For the past two summers, 11-year-old Theresa and her father have
worked hard to produce the best tomatoes in their small Kansas town,
even waging a friendly competition with their elderly neighbor. This
year, 1943, things are different. Theresa's brother Jeff, a big fan of ripe
tomatoes, has enlisted and is flying bomber planes somewhere in
Europe. When the elderly neighbor has a serious accident and is no
longer able to take care of his large vegetable garden, Theresa convinces
her classmates to take on the garden as a special project to help the
war effort. The Young Sprouts are successful with their Victory Garden
and learn a lot about group dynamics and cooperation in the process.
The author provides many telling details about life in a small midwest-
ern town during World War II, and an end note gives more information about the role that Victory Gardens played in ensuring an ample
food supply during the war years. **F • R**

259. LEE, MILLY. *Nim and the War Effort.* Illustrated by Yangsook
Choi. Farrar Straus & Giroux, 1997. Cloth 0-374-35523-1; Sunburst,
2002, pap. 0-374-45506-6. Grades 3 to 5.

Living in San Francisco's Chinatown in 1943, Nim is determined to win
her school's prize for collecting the most newspapers for the war effort.
Her effort to win leads to a conflict with her traditional grandfather. In
the end, she succeeds in collecting the most papers and also reaches an
understanding with her grandfather, who is revealed as a patriotic
American as well as a concerned elder. There are glimpses of racism in
the reaction of a white classmate to Nim's efforts. **F • HR**

260. MEAD, ALICE. *Soldier Mom.* Farrar Straus & Giroux, 1999. Cloth
0-374-37124-5. Grades 5 to 8.

Jasmyn is excited about starting 7th grade and being captain of her
basketball team. Then her single mother's reserve unit is called up to

serve in the Persian Gulf War, and there are just a few days to arrange for the care of Jasmyn and her baby brother. The mother's boyfriend Jake, the father of her baby, is pressed into service, but he is ill-prepared for the demands of managing a household, much less the responsibilities of parenting. After a rocky beginning, however, both Jasmyn and Jake grow into their new roles and adapt to the difficult situation.

While the theme and plot are a little didactic, the characterization of the young teen's reaction to her mother's leave-taking and the mother's own ambivalence about her military service are well drawn. With more and more women serving in the volunteer army and with more of the burden for American military action falling on the Reserves, this story continues to be relevant. **F • R**

261. MOCHIZUKI, KEN. *Baseball Saved Us*. Illustrated by Dom Lee. Lee and Low, 1993. Cloth 1-880000-01-6. Grades 2 to 4.

A young boy nicknamed Shorty tells how his Japanese American family came to live in a harsh desert internment camp during World War II. Shorty's father decides that morale and short tempers would be eased if they could play baseball, so the grownups create a field and equip the players using the few resources they have at hand. Shorty is not one of the better players; but in the final game of the season, he has a breakthrough. Looking up at the guard who stands in his tower with the sunlight glinting off his sunglasses, he is suddenly filled with anger. He puts all of his pent-up emotions into a mighty swing and hits a home run. After the war, when he returns home and still faces prejudice from his schoolmates, he calls on his memory of that moment and again hits a home run. Baseball saved him. **F • R**

262. OUGHTON, JERRIE. *The War in Georgia*. Houghton Mifflin, 1997. Cloth 0-395-81568-1. Grades 6 to 8.

Thirteen-year-old Shanta lives in Atlanta with her grandmother and her beloved Uncle Louie, bedridden with rheumatoid arthritis. It is 1945, and the war is winding down with a series of events that are difficult to understand—the liberation of the concentration camps, the bombing of Dresden, Hiroshima, and Nagasaki. It is Louie who tries to put these things in perspective and to help Shanta see that even a righteous war has terrible consequences. In the meantime, a more domestic battle is happening on her own block. The two men who have moved in across the street seem to be waging war on their weaker family members, especially the simple-minded son. Shanta is the one to uncover the depth of the cruelty being practiced there and to bring the abusive men to justice. The evil across the street is balanced by the compassion, love, and generosity of friends and neighbors. Luminous writing and fully realized characters make this a story to remember. **F • HR**

263. PATERSON, KATHERINE. *Jacob Have I Loved*. HarperCollins, 1980. Cloth 0-690-04078-4; LB 0-690-04079-2. Grades 7 to 8.

This is not a story about the World War II home front. It is a story about a young girl struggling to find her own identity while living in the shadow of her beautiful, talented twin sister. It is also a story about life in a Chesapeake Bay crabbing community. Paterson is such a careful writer, however, that the time frame of the novel—beginning with the bombing of Pearl Harbor and ending with the immediate postwar period—is integral to both the action and the character development. It is the war that sends Call off the island to join the navy and become the man whom Caroline will marry. It is the war that takes the men away and makes it possible for Louise to work on the boats with her father. It is the bombing of Hiroshima that shifts Grandma's preoccupation from the whore of Babylon to Armageddon. The war is always there, shifting from foreground to background, but always affecting the way that people live out their lives. **F • HR**

264. PAULSEN, GARY. *The Quilt*. Wendy Lamb Books/Random House, 2004. Cloth 0-385-72950-2; LB 0-385-90886-5. Grades 6 to 8.

In this novella, based on the author's own childhood experience during World War II, a young boy is sent to live with his grandmother in a small, close-knit Norwegian American community in Minnesota. The men are gone—either dead or off fighting the war—so this is a woman's world. Women do all the work usually done by men as well as their traditional household chores. When a young woman goes into labor, the women gather to see her through, and the little boy watches with that sense of knowing and not knowing simultaneously that is the essence of childhood. He also begins to see where he fits in this community when the women take out the quilt that contains a square for all of the relatives who have died. The baby is born, and everyone returns to their own homes except for the boy and his grandmother. They are there when two men come and tell Kristina that her husband has been killed in the fighting in the Pacific. Olaf, the new baby's father, will now have a square in the quilt. **F • R**

265. RINALDI, ANN. *Keep Smiling Through*. Harcourt, 1996. Cloth 0-15-200768-7; 2005, pap. 0-15-205399-9. Grades 4 to 6.

Ten-year-old Kay is having a rough time. Her stepmother treats her with calculating hostility, and her father is too busy trying to make ends meet to notice. She doesn't fit in at the new school she must attend. The rationing and other sacrifices required of Americans on the home front during World War II have taken away the few small pleasures left. Still, she struggles to be a good girl and a good patriotic citizen, doing what she can to avoid angering her stepmother and to support the war effort. She faces a crisis of conscience when she unwittingly witnesses an incident that seems to place her stepmother's father, a man of German descent, in the middle of a Nazi plot. She does what she thinks is right and then must face the consequences as her stepmother loses a baby and sinks into depression.

The book is rich in details about life on the World War II home front, taken from the author's own childhood experiences. Today's children may need some historical background in order to contextualize the references to "Japs," an expression that they will correctly understand to be derogatory. **F • R**

266. SAY, ALLEN. *Home of the Brave*. Illustrated by the author. Houghton Mifflin, 2002. Cloth 0-618-21223-X. Grades 5 to 8.

After a kayaking accident, a man finds himself in a dreamlike desert environment inhabited by Native American and Japanese American children from the World War II internment camps. With haunting illustrations and a minimal text, this book evokes and links the enduring legacy of two unjust policies in American history—the removal and isolation of Indians to reservation lands and the forced evacuation of Japanese Americans during World War II. Children will need to look elsewhere for the historical facts, but this book will generate thought and discussion about the meaning of history. **F • R**

267. STANLEY, JERRY. *I Am an American: A True Story of Japanese Internment*. Crown, 1994. Cloth 0-517-59786-1; LB 0-517-59787-X. Grades 5 to 8.

Stanley focuses on the experiences of one boy, Shiro Nomura, to tell the story of the evacuation and internment of Japanese Americans from the West Coast of the United States during World War II. Shiro was a senior in high school when he and his family were sent to Manzanar. Like other families, they lost their home and livelihood. The author does a good job of documenting the tremendous contributions Japanese Americans made to the agricultural and fishing industries before the war as well as the devastating effects of the internment on their own financial situations. **NF • R**

268. TESTA, MARIA. *Almost Forever*. Candlewick, 2003. Cloth 0-7637-1996-5. Grades 4 to 6.

A series of short poems convey the experiences and emotions of a young girl whose father has been called up to serve as a doctor in Vietnam. He is only away for a year, but to his children at home, it is "almost forever." There are some hints here about the beginnings of anti-war protests that characterized the home front during the war in Vietnam. However, this could be the story of any family whose life is disrupted when a parent is suddenly called away for wartime military service. **F • R**

269. TRIPP, VALERIE. *Meet Molly*. Illustrated by Nick Backes. Pleasant Company Publications, 1986, 1989, 2000. Cloth 0-037295-81-7; pap. 0-937295-07-8. Grades 3 to 5.

Molly is one of the American Girls Collection historical dolls. Her back story is that she is a girl "who schemes and dreams on the home front during World War Two." She is also the heroine of her own series of books, of which this is the first entry. These are slight, but appealing stories with enough details about life in a middle-class American home during World War II to give a child some understanding of the times. In the first chapter, Molly is faced with a plate of disgusting turnips that she must eat for the war effort. Her understanding mother adds a bit of their rationed butter and sugar and makes the despised vegetables more appealing. An appendix, "Looking Back at America in 1944," gives some basic information about the war and about life for Americans during that time. **F • R**

270. TUNNELL, MICHAEL O., AND GEORGE W. CHILCOAT. *The Children of Topaz: The Story of a Japanese-American Internment Camp: Based on a Classroom Diary.* Holiday House, 1996. Cloth 0-8234-1239-3. Grades 5 to 8.

What is perhaps most touching about this account of life at the Topaz internment camps, based on the diary of a 3rd-grade class in 1943, is the patriotism of the children and the high level of civic culture maintained by the adults in their lives. The Japanese American children, uprooted from their homes on the West Coast to this barb wire-enclosed camp in the desert of Utah, collected scrap metal for the war effort and bought war bonds, just as elementary school children did all across America. The authors fill in the gaps left by the children's accounts of the highlights of their days with necessary background about the political and social circumstances that resulted in their internment. It is an evenhanded presentation, as honest about the loyalty of some Japanese-born residents to their emperor as it is about the virulent racism behind the internment order itself. **NF • HR**

271. UCHIDA, YOSHIKO. *The Bracelet.* Illustrated by Joanna Yardley. Philomel, 1993. Cloth 0-399-22503-X. Grades 2 to 4.

When Emi, a 7-year-old Japanese American girl, is sent away with her mother to an internment camp, her best friend Laurie gives her a bracelet to remember her by. Somewhere in the confusion at the Tanforan Racetrack, where Emi and her mother are housed temporarily in a horse stall, Emi loses the bracelet. Devastated at first, her mother helps her realize that she doesn't need the bracelet to keep her friend's memory alive; memories live on in the heart. An afterword explains the circumstances during World War II that led to the imprisonment of Japanese Americans. This is a good introduction to the topic for younger children. **F • R**

272. UCHIDA, YOSHIKO. *The Invisible Thread.* Beech Tree, 1994. Pap. 0-688-13703-2. Grades 5 to 8.

Uchida has written moving novels for young people about the experience of growing up Nisei in California in the 1930s and being forcibly relocated to the Topaz internment camp after the bombing of Pearl Harbor in 1943. This is her autobiographical memoir of those same events. We read here about the real-life occurrences that became telling details in her novels. We learn about the invisible thread that tied her parents to Japan and about her own growing awareness of her

Japanese heritage and culture. Uchida's own story, told with honest self-reflection, will help young readers understand a shameful period in our country's history in which racism and injustice were perpetrated by the national government against its own citizens. **NF • HR**

273. WHITE, ELLEN EMERSON. *Where Have All the Flowers Gone? The Diary of Molly Mackenzie Flaherty.* Scholastic, 2002. Cloth 0-439-14889-8. Grades 6 to 8.

This companion volume to *The Journal of Patrick Seamus Flaherty* chronicles Molly's experiences as a high school student in Boston while her beloved older brother serves as a Marine in Vietnam. It is a good look at the home front during that time of conflicting values. Molly, a good student, nevertheless gets in trouble when she confronts her history teacher with questions about communism. She opposes the war but supports her brother. Wanting to do some good when there is so much around her that seems bad, she finds satisfaction volunteering in the orthopedic ward of a VA Hospital where soldiers wounded in Vietnam are being rehabilitated. **F • R**

274. WOODSON, JACQUELINE. *Coming on Home Soon.* Illustrated by E. B. Lewis. Putnam, 2004. Cloth 0-399-23748-8. Grades 2 to 5.

With most adult men off fighting in World War II, jobs opened up for African American women. This is the story of a young girl who stays with her Grandma while her mother travels north to Chicago to work on the railroad. The lyrical text and watercolor illustrations evoke the time and place, as well as the child's emotional state as she waits for letters and for her mother's homecoming. It is a story that should resonate for all children who have a parent who must leave home because of war. **F • HR**

WEB SITES

275. *Dear Miss Breed: Letters from Camp.*
http://www.janm.org/exhibits/breed/title.htm
Japanese American National Museum, n.d. Grades 5 to 8.

Clara Breed was a children's librarian at the San Diego Public Library from 1929 to 1945. When the Japanese American children she served were forced from their homes to live in internment camps during

World War II, she gave them stamped postcards addressed to her. She asked them to write and tell her about life in camp. A sample of the letters can be found on this web site as well as more information about Clara Breed. Joanne Oppenheim has written an excellent book based on this correspondence. *Dear Miss Breed: True Stories of the Japanese American Incarceration During World War II and a Librarian Who Made a Difference* (Scholastic, 2006) was published too late to be included in this bibliography, but it is highly recommended. The Web site for the Japanese American National Museum includes many other links to useful information about the wartime experiences of Japanese Americans as well as their difficult resettlement after the war. **NF • R**

276. *Rosie the Riveter*.
http://www.rosietheriveter.org
Rosie the Riveter Trust, n.d. Grades 6 to 8.

The Rosie the Riveter Trust is a nonprofit organization supporting the Rosie the Riveter National Park site in Richmond, California, and other related historical sites. Atchison Village, for example, was the development built to house the women workers and their families. It has now been named a National Historic Site and may be available for visits soon. The Web site includes a lot of information about the National Park, located near the Richmond shipyards where so many women worked during World War II. There are links to other interesting resources, including sheet music for a song about Rosie. **NF • R**

PEACE AND ALTERNATIVES TO WAR

PEACE IS MORE THAN THE FLIP SIDE OF WAR. It is a state of mind as well as a desired but often unobtainable condition for communities and nations. It often seems more abstract than war and therefore difficult to grasp. Is peace merely the absence of war? War presents itself with vivid, concrete images: soldiers, guns, bombs, blood, destruction, medals. What are the images of peace? Doves and olive branches? I have recently seen the iconic peace sign embroidered on the pockets of expensive jeans and printed on tie-dyed t-shirts, a statement of retro chic rather than a point of view.

Do the young teens wearing the symbolic peace sign even know what it is? Designed in 1958 for the British Direct Action Committee Against Nuclear War, it was originally made into ceramic buttons that were worn by demonstrators on the first major anti-nuclear march from London to Aldermaston. Marchers were informed that in the event of a nuclear war, these pottery badges would be among the few human artifacts to survive ("A History . . .", n.d.).

Writing about the ethics of peace for a volume on the history of ideas, Elizabeth Flower points out that human beings have always behaved with aggression and hostility and that history can be read as the "progressively successful pursuit of the technology and waging of war" (1973, p. 440). By contrast, it was relatively late in the history of civilization before a notion of peace was even formulated. Certainly the

165

Homeric Greeks glorified war and the warrior tradition, as exemplified in *The Iliad*. It is only in the later classical period of Greek thought that dramatists such as Euripides and Aristophanes expressed a general anti-war sentiment.

We can find visions of peace in both the Jewish and Christian traditions, although countless wars have been fought in the name of religion as well. The Sermon on the Mount may be Christianity's most powerful statement of a pacifist ideology. Both Leo Tolstoy and Mahatma Gandhi were influenced by its message. Both developed the concept of nonviolence as a peaceful way to resist violence and as a strategy for provoking the opponent to moral reflection (Flower, 1973, pp. 445–446). In the United States, of course, Dr. Martin Luther King, Jr. was perhaps our most eloquent spokesperson for nonviolence as a means to generate social change.

Still another way of thinking about peace and its relationship to war can be found in one Native American tradition. In his book about Native Americans who served in Vietnam, Tom Holm (1996) writes about the Going to the Water ceremony performed for Cherokee soldiers returning from that war. They believe that the evil of war must be washed away in order for men to be returned to the White Path of Peace. The author describes the White Path of Peace as much more than the absence of war. Rather, it is an ordered state of being in which an individual—and indeed an entire society—attempts to live harmoniously within a particular environment. This ordered state of peace is thought to be divine, and warfare is seen as a terrible and yet fairly common disruption to the normal functioning of everyday life. The Going to the Water ceremony not only restores the individual soldier's balance and harmony; it also shares his war-induced stress and guilt with his community and confirms the society's belief that war is an abnormal human activity.

Pacifism is generally understood to be the ideology that stands for the moral renunciation of war (Coates, 1997, p. 77). There are, of course, varying shades of beliefs and varying underlying motivations for people who consider themselves pacifists. The British scholar Martin Ceadel (1987) has developed a complex classification scheme to tease out these variations. We need not consider them in detail here, but it is useful to recognize the differences, for example, between those with deeply held religious beliefs opposing war—such as Quakers—and those who argue simply that aggression only generates more aggression—the pragmatists—and those who believe that it is always wrong to take a human life—the ethicists.

Warren Kuehl (1973) traces the origin of organized peace movements to the early 19th century in the United States and England. Ironically, there was a surge of activity in the period just prior to the First World War. It was an optimistic time in which armed conflict between nations seemed to be declining. Pacifists were encouraged by the spread of representative democracies, believing that "the people" would be less likely than authoritarian rulers to support wars. Efforts after World War I were directed at the establishment of a League of Nations, and after World War II, pacifists supported the United Nations. World War II had stimulated a change of thinking in many mainstream peace organizations. It had been widely perceived as a just and perhaps even a necessary war. Therefore, many peace activists now turned their attention to the encouragement of constructive means—diplomacy, arbitration, mediation, and so forth—by which nations could settle differences without resorting to armed conflict.

CHILDREN AND PEACE

Many children—especially boys—play soldier and delight in toy weapons of all kinds. They do not necessarily learn these games from their parents. Peace-loving mothers often talk about the ways in which their sons, forbidden to play with toy guns, manufacture them out of twigs and blocks and even pieces of bread. I have yet to hear of a child playing at peace.

Most of the books that counsel parents on these matters are aimed at the raising of preschool children. By the time children reach 4th grade and are ready for the books and information resources in this book, they have usually put aside their military action figures and other contemporary war toys. Concerns of parents and caregivers tend to shift to issues of peer pressure that may lead to emotional or physical violence through bullying, gangs, and fighting.

By the time children are 9 or 10, they can begin to learn about efforts to avoid war by individuals and organizations. Parents, caregivers, and teachers can present alternative heroes to the warriors who often loom larger in popular culture and in children's imaginations: people like Nelson Mandela, Rosa Parks, Gandhi, Muhammad Ali, and Dr. Martin Luther King, Jr. They can point out the unintended consequences of war and call attention to innocent victims. Children should also learn that patriotism does not always require them to support their government's policies.

Perhaps even more important, adults can try to give children a global perspective. It is more important than ever for children to see themselves as citizens of an interconnected world. The ninth thematic strand in the Curriculum Standards for Social Studies, Global Connections, recognizes the importance of teaching our children their place in an interdependent world. The performance expectations for this theme are explicit:

> a. Explore ways that language, art, music, belief systems, and other cultural elements may facilitate global understanding or lead to misunderstanding;
> b. Give examples of conflict, cooperation, and interdependence among individuals, groups, and nations;
> c. Examine the effects of changing technologies on the global community;
> d. Explore causes, consequences, and possible solutions to persistent, contemporary, and emerging global issues, such as pollution and endangered species;
> e. Examine the relationships and tensions between personal wants and needs and various global concerns, such as use of imported oil, land use, and environmental protection;
> f. Investigate concerns, issues, standards, and conflicts related to universal human rights, such as the treatment of children, religious groups, and effects of war (*Expectations of Excellence*, 1994, p. 70).

This sobering list of expectations gives a realistic picture of the competencies, skills, and knowledge today's children will need as they take their places as the parents, leaders, and citizens of tomorrow.

PEACE AND NONVIOLENCE IN BOOKS AND INFORMATION RESOURCES FOR CHILDREN

Peace is rarely the focus of a children's book. However, the few books in this section do present a nuanced picture of peace and nonviolence and include some of the most beautifully written and illustrated titles in the contemporary canon of children's literature. There are several picture-book biographies of significant peacemakers, including two about Mahatma Gandhi, one by Demi and one by Leonard Everett Fisher. Other titles to consider are:

- Tonya Bolden. *The Champ: The Story of Muhammad Ali*
- Yona Zeldis McDonough. *Peaceful Protest: The Life of Nelson Mandela*
- Doreen Rappaport. *Martin's Big Words: The Life of Dr. Martin Luther King, Jr.*

There is a splendid novel about a young Jewish girl in 11th-century France who courageously aids a deserter from the Crusades— Sylvie Weil's *My Guardian Angel*. Children also serve the cause of peace in the nonfiction titles *Out of War: Stories from the Front Lines of the Children's Movement for Peace in Colombia* by Sara Cameron and *Six Million Paper Clips: The Making of a Children's Holocaust Memorial* by Peter W. Schroeder and Dagmar Schroeder-Hildebrand. The children's Holocaust memorial project is also featured in a documentary film called *Paper Clips*. In Florence Parry Heide's *Sami and the Time of the Troubles* we enter the world of a child living in a war-torn Middle Eastern city and see his desire for peace.

Opposition to war is treated in several novels. Cynthia Rylant's *I Have Seen Castles* and M. E. Kerr's *Slap Your Sides* are both set in World War II. *Lighting Time* by Douglas Rees explores a Quaker boy's moral dilemma during the Civil War.

Two picture books take an allegorical approach as they present an anti-war message: Anita Lobel's *Potatoes, Potatoes* and Vladimir Radunsky's *Mannekin Pis*. Both of these titles can be used with a wide range of children, from the 5- to 8-year-olds who are the traditional audience for read-alouds to middle school students who will see beyond the obvious to a more sophisticated reading of the text and pictures. *Patrol* by Walter Dean Myers is a classic picture book for older readers as it depicts a moment of epiphany for an American soldier in Vietnam.

Older boys and girls will also appreciate the CD *Ceasefire* by Emmanuel Jal and Abdel Gadir Salim. Recorded during a time of fragile peace in Sudan, it is a collaboration between a Christian rapper from the Darfur region and a Muslim master of traditional music from northern Sudan. Adults old enough to remember the protest movements of the 1960s will enjoy sharing Pete Seeger's *Turn! Turn! Turn!* The picture book, illustrated by Wendy Anderson Halperin, includes a CD with performances of the song by Seeger and The Byrds.

Perhaps the most eloquent testament to peace is the collection of poetry edited by Neil Philip, *War and the Pity of War.* The well-chosen poems and somber scratchboard drawings evoke a profound yearning for peace in the face of war. Finally, of course, readers may need to be reminded that many of the books about war, especially those in the segment of the resource list that deals with the horrors of war, are at least implicitly pleas for peace.

Bibliography

❈

BOOKS

---

277. BOLDEN, TONYA. *The Champ: The Story of Muhammad Ali.*
Illustrated by R. Gregory Christie. Knopf, 2004. Cloth 0-375-82401-4.
Grades 3 to 5.

The picture-book format makes this biography of Muhammad Ali attractive and accessible to young readers. The author presents the boxing champion's refusal to be drafted in 1967 as a principled stand based on his religious beliefs and his conviction that he could not support the war in Vietnam. Threatened with a prison sentence, his passport revoked, and his boxing career in ruins, he spent three years on the lecture circuit in the United States, talking about his own life, the struggles of African Americans, and his opposition to the war. It wasn't until 1971 that the U.S. Supreme Court ruled that he could not be jailed for his resistance to the draft on religious grounds. **NF • R**

278. CAMERON, SARA. *Out of War: True Stories from the Front Lines of the Children's Movement for Peace in Colombia.* Scholastic/UNICEF, 2001. Cloth 0-439-29721-4. Grades 6 to 8.

Colombia has been beset with civil war and with violence associated with the production of cocaine for more than 40 years. This book, commissioned by UNICEF, looks at Colombia's culture of violence through the eyes of nine young people who have become involved with the Children's Movement for Peace. This organization came into being through the auspices of UNICEF, but it is now a relatively autonomous association that is organized and run almost entirely by young people. Adults serve only in advisory capacities. The young people who are profiled here have all been touched personally by the violence in their country. All of them have chosen to stop the cycle of violence by working for peace. They recognize that the struggle for peace is not easy, but their sense of efficacy is inspiring. A list of resources for further information is included. **NF • R**

279. DEEDY, CARMEN AGRA. *The Yellow Star: The Legend of King Christian X of Denmark.* Illustrated by Henri Sorenson. Peachtree, 2000. Cloth 1-56145-208-4. Grades 3 to 5.

It is inspirational to learn about how the Danes quietly and effectively resisted German efforts to deport their Jewish citizens. This picture book tells a legend associated with the Danish King Christian. It is said that when the Nazis ordered all Danish Jews to wear the six-pointed yellow star, King Christian wore a star on his own uniform when he went out on his daily horse ride. While there is no evidence that this really happened, the legend does much to explain the kind of leadership King Christian practiced and the culture of civility and tolerance that enabled the Danes to save most of the Jews in their country from the fate that awaited them elsewhere in Europe. **F • R**

280. DEMI. *Gandhi.* Margaret K. McElderry/Simon & Schuster, 2001. Cloth 0-689-84149-3. Grades 3 to 6.

Demi deftly captures the life and teachings of Mahatma Gandhi in this picture-book biography. She explains how he developed his theory of *satyagraha*, the force of love, after being thrown off a train by a racist steward. In simple words and illustrations, she portrays how this theory developed into a powerful force for nonviolent resistance to injustice and tyranny. While on his way to a prayer meeting, Gandhi was killed by a Hindu fanatic. His last words were "Rama, rama, rama": "I forgive you, I love you, I bless you." **NF • HR**

281. FISHER, LEONARD EVERETT. *Gandhi.* Atheneum, 1995. Cloth 0-689-80337-0. Grades 4 to 6.

The life of Mohandas Gandhi illustrates many of the issues and themes we want children to think about as they develop into thinking adults. This picture-book biography outlines that life, describing how a boy born into privilege in an Indian family during the rule of the British Empire became a crusader for justice and the independence of his people as well as a practitioner of nonviolent civil disobedience. The book ends with the hard-won independence for India after World War II, while an afterword tells the bitter story of Gandhi's death at the hands of Hindu militants angered at his reconciliation with their Muslim countrymen. This brief introduction may stimulate some young readers to learn more about the principles of *satyagraha*, nonviolent resistance based on love for one's enemy. **NF • R**

282. HEIDE, FLORENCE PARRY, AND JUDITH HEIDE GILLILAND. *Sami and the Time of the Troubles.* Illustrated by Ted Lewin. Clarion, 1992. Cloth 0-395-55964-2. Grades 2 to 4.

Sami tells his own story, that of a 10-year-old Lebanese boy who lives in a country that has been at war for his entire life. His father was killed by a bomb in the market, and now he and his mother and little sister live with his uncle and grandfather. Sometimes, on a beautiful day, it almost seems like the times when there was no war. The family might have a picnic on the beach, or Sami and his friend Amir might build a fort from the rubble left by the bombing. But most days, the family must stay in the basement in order to be safe from the guns and fighting. The grandfather likes to tell about the day of the children, a day when children appeared on the streets with banners, flags, and signs that said, "Stop the fighting." Now on a day when the fighting is bad again, Sami tells his grandfather that it may be time for another day in which the children march for peace. The grandfather answers that this time maybe the ones who fight will listen. This is an eloquent picture book that communicates the desire that all children have for peace and also empowers them to express it. **F • HR**

283. KERR, M. E. *Slap Your Sides.* HarperCollins, 2001. Cloth 0-06-029481-7; LB 0-06-029482-5. Grades 6 to 8.

There is a strong Quaker community in the small Pennsylvania town where this novel takes place. Still there is little support for Ben Shoemaker when he witnesses to his Quaker beliefs by becoming a conscientious objector during World War II. This story, told from the point of view of Ben's younger brother Jubal, tells how the Shoemaker family suffers as the townspeople turn against them. The consequences for Ben are even more dire; he loses hearing in one ear after being badly beaten by local men in the town where he is serving as an aide in a mental hospital. Jubal is torn between his crush on a local girl who has been among the fiercest critics of Ben's stand and his own desire to register as a conscientious objector himself when he is old enough. In a tragic denouement, he kills a crazed man who appears to be attacking that girl. This book should help young readers clarify their own values and think about courage in a new way. **F • R**

284. LOBEL, ANITA. *Potatoes, Potatoes*. Greenwillow, 2004. Cloth 0-06-023927-1. Grades 2 to 5.

This is a welcome reissue of a 1967 picture book that is an allegory about war and peace. A woman builds a wall around her cottage to keep out the winds of war that blow from both the East and the West. She peacefully plants her potatoes and raises her sons until the day when one young man marches off to join the army of the East and the other joins the army of the West. What starts out in hope and glory ends predictably for both sons, now the commanders of their respective forces. Tired and hungry, each remembers his mother's potatoes; and they order their armies to the cottage. The armies tear down the walls and battle each other for the precious food until the mother is found lying still on the ground. Her sons begin to weep and so do all the other soldiers as they remember their own mothers. The woman is not dead, however, and she announces that she has potatoes enough for everyone in their cellars—if they promise to end the fighting and clean up the mess. Everyone lives happily ever after. **F • HR**

285. MCDONOUGH, YONA ZELDIS. *Peaceful Protest: The Life of Nelson Mandela*. Illustrated by Malcah Zeldis. Walker, 2002. Cloth 0-8027-8821-1. Grades 3 to 5.

This picture-book biography of the great South African leader covers his life from childhood to his later years. It tells how he finally emerged from his confinement as a prisoner of conscience from 1963 to 1990 determined to find a peaceful solution to the tremendous social problems created by apartheid. His nonviolent stance brought nations of the world to support bringing down the oppressive apartheid government and led to his becoming the first black president of the democratic Republic of South Africa. The folk art paintings that illustrate the book have a childlike quality that is sometimes at odds with their serious content. **NF • R**

286. MYERS, WALTER DEAN. *Patrol: An American Soldier in Vietnam*. Illustrated by Ann Grifalconi. HarperCollins, 2002. Cloth 0-06-028364-5. Grades 6 to 8.

A young soldier moves through the jungle, both searching and waiting for a sight of his enemy, hidden by the beautiful terrain. The soldier fights his fear. His squad is ordered to secure a village, where the enemies are elderly men and children and babies, "little enemies crying on the mud roads. Little enemies with tears running down dusty cheeks."

Outside the village, in the tall grass, the soldier finally sees the real enemy, a young man who is as surprised and shocked as he is. They lift their rifles and then lower them again without shooting. Back at his base, the soldier writes a letter home and wonders if his enemy is doing the same thing. He is so tired, so tired of this war.

The eloquent, simple text and stunning illustrations make this the perfect picture book to share with older children. Like so many books about war, it is ultimately a plea for peace. **F • HR**

287. PHILIP, NEIL, ED. *War and the Pity of War*. Illustrated by Michael McCurdy. Clarion, 1998. Cloth 0-395-84982-9. Grades 6 to 8.

The anthologist points out in his introduction that until World War I, poetry about war tended to express the sentiment that war was a natural manifestation of manly virtues. World War I was so horrific in its toll of human life that a new breed of war poet emerged. Their message can be summed up in the words of Wilfred Owen, "My subject is War, and the Pity of War. The poetry is in the pity." These well-chosen poems from many wars and many countries are mostly about the pity of war. A few, from earlier centuries, seem at first read to trumpet the earlier messages of honor and glory. A second reading reveals that those poets too were aware of the pain and suffering that accompanied the highest hopes. The scratchboard drawings are both somber and beautiful, perfect visual accompaniments to the poetry. **NF • HR**

288. RADUNSKY, VLADIMIR. *Manneken Pis: A Simple Story of a Boy Who Peed on a War*. Illustrated by the author. Atheneum, 2002. Cloth 0-689-83193-5. Grades 3 to 5.

In Brussels, Belgium, there is a statue of a little naked boy who is peeing. Radunsky tells a story that may—or may not—explain how this statue came to be. Very long ago there was a peaceful, happy town. Unfortunately, war came to the town; no one knows why. After many days of fighting, a little boy grew sad. His mother and father were gone. When he went to look for them, all he could find were soldiers fighting. He was frightened, but he had to pee. So he stood on the wall of the town and peed right into the warring armies. Suddenly the fighting stopped while everybody looked at the little boy, and then everybody began to laugh. They laughed until they were so tired they fell asleep. When they woke up the next morning, the war was over, and the little boy found his parents again. In honor of the little boy who had helped people see how absurd the war was, they made a bronze statue, and it is there to this day. **F • R**

289. RAPPAPORT, DOREEN. *Martin's Big Words: The Life of Dr. Martin Luther King, Jr.* Illustrated by Bryan Collier. Jump at the Sun/Hyperion, 2001. Cloth 0-7868-0714-8; LB 0-7868-2591-X. Grades All ages.

This eloquent picture-book biography focuses on Dr. Martin Luther King, Jr.'s use of nonviolence as a strategy for achieving social change and social justice. The author explains that he won the Nobel Peace Price in 1964 "because he taught others to fight with words, not fists." The collage and watercolor paintings echo and extend the message of the text. All children should be exposed to this book with its message about the power of big words like love, peace, and freedom. **NF • HR**

290. REES, DOUGLAS. *Lightning Time*. DK Ink/A Richard Jackson Book, 1997. Cloth 0-7894-2458-4. Grades 6 to 8.

Theodore is a young Quaker boy in Boston when he first meets the fiery abolitionist John Brown. The man poses a conflict in values: is slavery or violence the greater evil? Theodore finally decides that John Brown is right when he claims that slavery must be eradicated by any means necessary. He runs away to join the man on his Maryland farm where he is planning his ill-fated raid on Harpers Ferry. Theodore is ultimately spared from participating in the raid itself. Instead, he uses his telegraphic skills to try to mislead the authorities about Brown's plans and about the strength of his forces. Based on sound historical research, this is one of the few novels for young readers to address the moral dilemmas that underlie all war: When is violence justified? Does the end justify the means? What is a just fight? **F • R**

291. RYLANT, CYNTHIA. *I Had Seen Castles*. Harcourt, 1995. Pap. 0-15-205312-3. Grades 7 to 9.

An elderly man remembers the love affair he had when he was 18, just before he enlisted to fight in World War II. Ginny, his sweetheart, was opposed to the war; and their differing positions led to a bitter separation. His experiences as a soldier led him to respect her point of view and to believe as she did that war is a horror. His repugnance for war was strengthened when he learned that his physicist father had participated in the development of the atom bomb that was dropped on Hiroshima. This beautifully written novel about war is ultimately a moving testament to pacifism. **F • R**

292. SCHROEDER, PETER W., AND DAGMAR SCHROEDER-HILDEBRAND. *Six Million Paper Clips: The Making of a Children's Holocaust Memorial*. Kar-Ben, 2004. Cloth 1-58013-169-7; pap. 1-58013-176-X. Grades 5 to 8.

The Schroeders are the German journalists who helped the middle school students of Whitwell, Tennessee, achieve their goal of collecting 6 million paper clips. They also organized the transfer of a World War II-era rail car from Germany to the school site in order to create a Children's Holocaust Memorial. The story that is documented here and in the DVD *Paper Clips* is a remarkable testimony to dedicated educators and empowered students and the possibility of teaching tolerance and peace. **NF • HR**

293. SEEGER, PETE. *Turn! Turn! Turn!* Illustrated by Wendy Anderson Halperin. Simon & Schuster, 2003. Cloth 0-689-85235-5. Grades All ages.

Pete Seeger's music turned these classic words from Ecclesiastes into a stirring song of hope for many protest movements. People who have rallied for peace, in particular, have found inspiration in the words that assure that there is a time for peace, as well as a time for war. Wendy Halperin's illustrations in a circular frame capture both the everyday as well as the overarching meanings of the words. A CD, with performances of the song by both Pete Seeger and The Byrds, is included. **F • R**

294. SHERLOCK, PATTI. *Letters from Wolfie*. Viking, 2004. Cloth 0-670-03694-3. Grades 6 to 8.

When his older brother Danny volunteers to fight in Vietnam, 13-year-old Mark decides to do his part by donating his German Shepherd, Wolfie, to be trained as a scout dog. His conviction that he has done the right thing is shaken, however, when he begins a correspondence with Wolfie's army trainer and learns that his dog isn't as aggressive as he should be. He tries to have his dog returned, but the army says that Wolfie is now official army "equipment." Mark is even more confused when he begins dating a girl whose brother has gone to Canada to avoid the draft and who is opposed to the war. When an activist teacher convinces Mark to stage a protest in an effort to have Wolfie returned to him after one year of service, his own family becomes divided. His father staunchly supports the war, and his mother is increasingly convinced that her older son has been put in harm's way for the wrong reasons. Danny returns from Vietnam with one leg amputated at the knee. Embittered by his experiences, he joins the anti-war cause. Wolfie does not return at all. He dies heroically in a scouting expedition. Young readers may empathize more with the death of this dog than they do with the faceless casualties from Iraq and other war zones today. They may also acquire a historical framework for understanding that opposition to war can be as patriotic as support of it. **F • R**

295. TSUCHIYA, YUKIO. *Faithful Elephants: A True Story of Animals, People and War*. Illustrated by Ted Lewin. Houghton Mifflin, 1988. Cloth 0-395-46555-9; pap. 0-395-86137-3. Grades 4 to 8.

Towards the end of World War II, Tokyo was subjected to frequent bombing. The authorities there became concerned that the zoo animals might be freed in a bombing raid and be a danger to the public. Therefore, they ordered that all of the large animals be killed. All of the big cats, bears, and snakes were poisoned. There were three elephants, however, who could not be poisoned. They cleverly rejected poisoned food, and their skin was too thick to be punctured by a needle. Their keepers reluctantly decided to starve them to death. The account of this starvation is almost too painful to bear. Tenderhearted children will grieve for the animals. Some of them—and most adults—will also feel the agony of the zookeepers who had to watch their beloved elephants suffer.

While this is a true story that might be classified with others about the horrors or the consequences of war, it is best understood as a powerful antiwar story. **NF • HR**

296. WEIL, SYLVIE. *My Guardian Angel*. Arthur A. Levine/Scholastic, 2004. Cloth 0-439-57681-2. Grades 5 to 8.

Elvina is 12 years old, the granddaughter of a great rabbi who has taught her how to read and write, an unusual accomplishment for a girl living in Troyes, France, in 1096. The Jewish community is threatened by the imminent arrival of a band of Crusaders led by Peter the Hermit. The Crusaders have been known to terrorize Jews as they marched to the Holy Land. Elvina's father and grandfather are among the leaders who are determined to keep the peace by offering food and assistance to the Christian Crusaders. Elvina, in her turn, secretly helps a young wounded Christian who doesn't want to go on the Crusade or to fight anyone; he just wants to join a monastery where he can be a scholar. For a time it appears that Elvina may have put her community at risk by sheltering a deserter from the Crusade; but in the end, her brave and compassionate act is rewarded.

The novel presents an unusual perspective on the Crusades and a wealth of detail about life in a Jewish community in 11th-century France. It is also a celebration of a peaceful act in a time of war. **F • R**

WEB SITES

297. *The Nobel Peace Prize*.
http://nobelprize.org/nobel_prizes/peace/
Nobel Foundation, 2006. Grades 5 to 8.

This official site of the Nobel Foundation gives information about all of the Nobel Peace Prize Laureates and provides articles by the Laureates and other peace activists. The Educational link has many features that will be interesting to children and relevant to teachers, including a "peace doves" interactive game. **NF • R**

DVDs

298. *Paper Clips*. Ergo Entertainment. 2004. 84 minutes. Grades 6 to 8.

This inspiring documentary is the story of how the students and teachers in a middle school in rural Tennessee set out to learn about tolerance and diversity by studying the Holocaust. When the students had difficulty comprehending the number of 6 million Jews who had been killed, they decided to collect 6 million paper clips. They were helped in their effort by two German journalists stationed in Washington, D.C. When their story was picked up by the *Washington Post* and the national news media, they were flooded with paper clips from all over the world—ending up with 30 million! The next step was to create a Children's Holocaust Memorial. They were able to bring from Germany one of the rail cars used to transport Jews to the concentration camps. The whole town helped to turn this into a memorial containing not just 6 million paper clips, but 11 million, to memorialize the Gypsies, homosexuals, and other "undesirables" murdered by the Nazis.

This DVD, and its companion book *Six Million Paper Clips* by Peter Schroeder and Dagmar Schroeder-Hildebrand, could be classified as dealing with the horrors of war. I believe, however, that the most important message of the paper clips project is peace, tolerance, and the empowerment of children through information. It belongs in this section as a testament to finding alternatives to war. **NF • HR**

CDs

---

299. *Ceasefire*. Riverboat Records/World Music Network, 2005. Grades 6 to 8.

This remarkable music CD is a collaboration between Emmanuel Jal, a Christian rapper from the south of Sudan, and Abdel Gadir Salim, a Muslim and venerated master of the music of northern Sudan. As a child, Jal was forced to serve as a soldier in the civil war that has ravaged Sudan for more than 22 years. The coming together of these two musicians from former enemy factions is a celebration of the fragile peace accord of 2005. The music is exciting, even if you don't understand Arabic, Kiswahili, or Nuer, the languages in which it is sung. English translations convey the message of peace and hope that imbues every track. **HR**

BRINGING IT
ALL TOGETHER:
TWO CASE STUDIES

I N THE PREVIOUS SIX RESOURCE SECTIONS, we have looked at enduring themes: war as history, the hope and glory of war, the consequences of war, the horrors of war, life on the home front, and peace and alternatives to war. Now, in this final section, we take a different approach, bringing together several themes to shed light on two events. One, the Trojan War, has some basis in history but lives on primarily because of the epic poems of Homer and their mythic legacy. The second event is the attack on the World Trade Center and the Pentagon on September 11, 2001, and its aftermath. As we examine the resources for young people that inform them about the Trojan War and 9/11, we will look for instances in which larger themes emerge and connections are made. How can reading and learning about these two events, separated by centuries, help children understand important issues about war and peace?

THE TROJAN WAR

THE STORY OF THE TROJAN WAR SPEAKS TO US across time and place, as compelling today as it was 3,000 years ago. We know it primarily from retellings of the Homeric epic poems *The Iliad* and *The Odyssey*; and its aftermath from Virgil's *Aeneid*. The Trojan War was also the setting for some of the great Greek tragedies: *Agamemnon* by Aeschylus and *Helen* and *The Trojan Women* by Euripedes. Its persistent relevance is telling evidence of the centrality of war in western civilization. The story has also been a kind of Rorschach test for its audience, allowing people to interpret its meaning and significance in a wide variety of ways. This makes it a particularly good vehicle for exploring and bringing together the various themes highlighted in this book.

Historians and archaeologists have been preoccupied with determining the historical origins of the story. Was there a real Trojan War? Can the site of Priam's Troy be identified? Children who are interested in the Trojan War as history can find resources in the list that follows: The Web site "Was there a Trojan War?" and the DVD *The True Story of Troy* are good updates on what scholars agree and disagree about today. An account of Heinrich Schliemann's fascination with *The Iliad* and his subsequent archaeological exploits is found in Giovanni Caselli's *In Search of Troy: One Man's Quest for Homer's Fabled City.*

We have seen in earlier segments of this book that men have often gone to war with dreams of hope and glory. Certainly this theme can be found in the *Iliad*. One can focus on Achilles, with his dream of immortality through military feats, or on Hector, the noble defender of his homeland. Both are heroes in the classic model. Both are exemplars of a kind of honor that exists primarily in wartime. Leo Braudy (2003) writes that war gives shape and justification to physical violence through a soldier's code of honor. Achilles is a particularly interesting example of this. Initially, with his warrior furor, he represents the nostalgic ideal of single hand-to-hand combat. When he kills Hector to avenge the death of his comrade Patroclus, his furor almost turns to merciless madness. He has violated the code. Then, when he accedes to Priam's plea to return his son Hector's body, his honor is at least partially restored and modified, according to Braudy, to a "more just, and even more tender, kind of heroism" (p. 46).

Rachel Bespaloff (2005), writing in France at the start of World War II, found Hector to be the more resonant hero of the story. For her, he represented the resistance to force and the defense of homeland that her own country was mounting against its Nazi invaders and occupiers. She describes him as he faces Achilles: "Hector has nothing, courage, nobility, or reason, that is not bent and sullied by war, nothing except that self-respect that makes him human, comes to his rescue at the end, steadies him before the inevitable, and brings him his clearest vision in the instant of death" (p. 48). Bespaloff appreciated the ambiguity of Homer's treatment of war and war's use of force. She saw this ambiguity in Homer's depiction of the beauty of warriors, made glorious by their wielding of force even in the face of their own death and destruction (p. 47).

Writing at the same time and place as Bespaloff, but apparently without any knowledge of her efforts, Simone Weil (2005) also found relevance in *The Iliad*. However, for this committed pacifist (who later, however, came to see some justification for the Second World War), it was a story that dramatized the horrors of war and its use of force. She opens her essay: "The true hero, the true subject, the center of the *Iliad* is force. Force employed by man, force that enslaves man, force before which man's flesh shrinks away" (p. 3). Although she sometimes edited the epic poem to suit her arguments, Weil nevertheless writes an eloquent anti-war essay in which the dehumanizing force, crushing pity, and uselessness of war are denounced over and over again.

Perhaps the power of *The Iliad* lies in just this elusive ambiguity. Both Bespaloff and Weil are right. This epic story is both a tribute to man's nobility and heroism in battle and a horrific account of the disastrous consequences of war. The retellings for young people, particularly those for older readers, such as *Black Ships Before Troy: The Story of the Iliad* by Rosemary Sutcliff and Padraic Colum's *Children's Homer: The Adventures of Odysseus and the Tale of Troy*, capture this tension between the excitement and drama of military feats and the agony of war's victims.

The Iliad can also be read as a tale of capricious gods who manipulate hapless human beings for their own amusement. After all, the war supposedly began with the famous beauty contest in which the goddesses Aphrodite, Athena, and Hera compete for the golden apple and the title of "the fairest of all." Young readers will find that Doris Orgel's *We Goddesses: Athena, Aphrodite, Hera* is a fine introduction to the worldview that informed the Homeric epic.

CONTEMPORARY CHILDREN AND THE STORY OF TROY

Children are among the most tragic characters in *The Iliad*. Agamemnon must sacrifice his own daughter, Iphigenia, in order to win favorable winds for the Greek ships. Hector's infant son is thrown to his death from the parapets of Troy. The teenage Cassandra is scorned for her prophetic visions of doom for the Trojan people. Do contemporary children recoil from these images? Or do they see Achilles as a larger-than-life superhero, perhaps as personified by the handsomely muscled Brad Pitt in the movie *Troy*. Can they appreciate the subtlety of the conflicting messages of war and peace that the French philosophers Simone Weil and Rachel Bespaloff uncovered? Will they find relevance in this story from so long ago?

A British educator, Bob Lister (2005), wanted to bring the story to life for 9- to 11-year-old schoolchildren. He decided to do this through storytelling since the epic was originally presented in oral form, probably by Greek singers. He commissioned two storytellers to create a CD that he then introduced in 15-minute segments in classrooms in England. The retelling that resulted focused on Achilles but also extended the story beyond the time frame of *The Iliad,* giving the children a contextualizing framework for the narrative. Lister found that the children appreciated the episodic structure of the CD and the vivid language that brings characters and their actions to life. He found that the children used highly descriptive language and dramatic visual recreations in follow-up activities.

If children are unable on their own to see the relevance of the story of the Trojan War to contemporary events, Paul Fleischman has made the connections for them. The revised 2006 edition of *Dateline: Troy* links episodes from the epic poem with events surrounding the September 11, 2001, attacks and the resulting wars in Afghanistan and Iraq. The introduction says it best: "Envy-maddened Ajax, love-struck Paris, crafty Odysseus, and all the others have walked the earth in every age and place. They live among us today. Though their tale comes from the distant Bronze Age, it's as current as this morning's headlines. The Trojan War is still being fought. Simply open a newspaper . . . " (p. 9).

Bibliography

✄

BOOKS

300. CASELLI, GIOVANNI. *In Search of Troy: One Man's Quest for Homer's Fabled City*. Peter Bedrick, 1999. Cloth 0-87226-542-0. Grades 4 to 6.

This brief, heavily illustrated volume tells how as a boy Schliemann became entranced with the stories told in *The Iliad*. Later, he devoted himself to finding the lost city of Troy. He became the first person to excavate an archaeological site in the hope of testing an ancient myth. His success in finding Priam's city and what he thought was his treasure is told here, along with other facts about life in 1800 to 1240 B.C. **NF • R**

301. CLEMENT-DAVIES, DAVID. *Trojan Horse: The World's Greatest Adventure*. DK Publishing, 1999. Cloth 0-7894-4475-5; pap. 0-7894-4474-7. Grades 3 to 5.

This abridged and somewhat fragmented account of the Trojan War contains the usual DK sidebars with snippets of background information that some young readers will find fascinating and others will find distracting. The high points of the narrative are here, but the language lacks the color and excitement of other retellings. **NF • RWR**

302. COLUM, PADRAIC. *The Children's Homer: The Adventures of Odysseus and the Tale of Troy*. Illustrated by Willy Pogany. Aladdin/Simon & Schuster, 2004. Pap. 0-689-86883-9. Grades 6 to 8.

This reprint of the classic 1918 edition is still a good choice for young readers who want all of the detail and formal language that we associate with Homer's epic poem, but prefer it delivered in prose. This retelling covers both *The Iliad* and *The Odyssey* and delivers a first-rate education in the Greek classics. Willy Pogany's line drawings are appropriate to Colum's narrative and make this a handsome package. **F • R**

303. FLEISCHMAN, PAUL. *Dateline: Troy*. Illustrated by Grover Frankfeldt and Glenn Morrow. Hyperion, 1996. Cloth 1-56402-469-5. Grades 6 to 8.

Fleischman demonstrates the timeless relevance of the Trojan War by juxtaposing his retelling with actual newspaper accounts of contemporary incidents that echo and parallel the legendary story. Newborn babies are abandoned today in dumpsters just as Paris was abandoned by his parents. The Greek siege of Troy, like the Soviet war against Afghanistan, went on for years in an apparent stalemate. Agamemnon's claim to the beautiful Chryseis is paired with accounts of Japanese soldiers' use of Korean "comfort women" as sex slaves. The Greek massacre of Trojan citizens when they finally succeed in entering the walled city in their wooden horse is compared with the massacre at My Lai. The last pages focus on the ultimate human cost and waste of the years of battle. **F • HR**

304. HOVEY, KATE. *Voices of the Trojan War*. Illustrated by Leonid Gore. McElderry/Simon & Schuster, 2004. Cloth 0-689-85768-3. Grades 6 to 8.

Hovey's rhymed verse captures some of the feel of Virgil and Homer's epic poetry. She pays homage to other classic writers who have told this story as well—Lucian, Ovid, Aeschylus, and Euripedes—with quotes introducing each of her poems. This retelling focuses on the gods and goddesses who control the destinies of mere humans. One by one, the great heroes—Hector, Achilles, Patroclus, and Paris—die in a futile war whose beginnings and end were caused by the jealousies of the gods.

Gore's acrylic illustrations in shades of gray are as dark and menacing as the winds of war. This book is a fine introduction to classic literature. **F • HR**

305. HUTTON, WARWICK. *The Trojan Horse*. Margaret K. McElderry/Macmillan, 1992. Cloth 0-689-50542-6. Grades 2 to 5.

This picture-book account opens with a summary of the events leading up to the Trojan War and the stalemate that ensued after ten years of battle and siege. The narrative quickly moves to the disappearance of the Greek ships and the appearance of the great wooden horse on the sand outside Troy. Laocoon makes his warning against Greeks bearing gifts, but he is ignored and subsequently killed by the great sea serpents sent by Poseidon to punish him. The fate of the Trojans is thus sealed, and the Greeks win the war with trickery and deception. **NF • R**

306. LIVELY, PENELOPE. *In Search of a Homeland: The Story of the Aeneid.* Illustrated by Ian Andrew. Delacorte, 2001. Cloth 0-385-72937-5. Grades 6 to 8.

We don't hear much about Aeneas, son of Venus and the mortal Anchises, in Homer's story of the Trojan War. He was there, however, fighting on the Trojan side. When Troy is finally defeated, he escapes with his father, his young son, his household gods, and a small band of warriors. The gods have promised that he will find a homeland and a glorious future for his people in Italy, so they set sail to find that haven. On the way, they encounter the horrible Harpies and terrible weather. Aeneas dallies for a while in Carthage with Dido and ventures into the underworld, where he sees the fallen heroes on the Elysian Fields and is shown a glimpse of the future that awaits his ancestors. Finally, he arrives at the site of the promised homeland and defeats the rival Latin armies. Aeneas's son founds a city that will eventually become Rome.

The story of Aeneas, as told by the great Roman author Virgil, ties up some of the ends left hanging in Homer's account of the Trojan War. Most importantly, it traces the history of the Trojan people to their ultimate home in Rome. Of course, here the gods and goddesses go by their Latin names, but children will soon recognize them as they continue to meddle in the lives of mortal men and women. **F • R**

307. LOGUE, CHRISTOPHER. *All Day Permanent Red: The First Battle Scenes of Homer's Iliad Rewritten.* Farrar Straus & Giroux, 2003. Cloth 0-374-10295-3. Grades 7 to 8.

The British poet has been rewriting Homer's *Iliad* in striking, contemporary verse. He uses metaphors much as Homer did, but with contemporary images. Here an arrow makes a tunnel through a man's neck "the width of a lipstick." This slim volume presents only the first battle, in which Hector rallies the Trojans and engages the Greeks at the start of this long and bloody war. Young people enthralled by battle scenes and by strong, vivid language will find this a rewarding read. **F • R**

308. McCARTY, NICK. *The Iliad.* Illustrated by Victor Ambrus. Kingfisher/Houghton Mifflin, 2004. Pap. 0-7534-5722-9. Grades 5 to 8.

This is a fine prose retelling of Homer's poem. The print is large; the language is lively and more contemporary than Colum's retelling. Ambrus's illustrations convey the drama of the narrative. **F • R**

309. McLAREN, CLEMENCE. *Inside the Walls of Troy.* Atheneum, 1996. Cloth 0-689-31820-0; Simon Pulse, 2004, pap. 0-689-87397-2. Grades 6 to 8.

This novel presents the Trojan War from the perspective of two women who experienced the event from within the walls of Troy—Helen and Cassandra. Helen is a sympathetic character here, a victim of her own beauty and of Aphrodite's promise to Paris that he would wed the fairest woman in the world. Cassandra is a more tragic figure, cursed with visions and prophecies that no one would heed. In this telling, both women survive the siege and the follies of war brought about by men, with their lust for revenge and their insatiable greed. **F • R**

310. ORGEL, DORIS. *We Goddesses: Athena, Aphrodite, Hera.* Illustrated by Marilee Heyer. Richard Jackson/DK Ink, 1999. Cloth 0-7894-2586-6. Grades 6 to 8.

Here are the three goddesses whose competition for the golden apple put into motion the events that led to the Trojan War. An introduction sets the context within the worldview of Greek mythology. Orgel makes these women larger than life—as goddesses should be—but also gives them the quirks and foibles that make them so interesting. Each tells her own story and in doing so interweaves her tale with those of the other two. In a creative epilogue, Orgel returns the three goddesses to Mount Olympus for a replay of the contest for the golden apple. This time the ending is surprising; history does not repeat itself. The paintings throughout the book are beautiful, and there are also reproductions of images of the three women from ancient Greece. **F • R**

311. SUTCLIFF, ROSEMARY. *Black Ships Before Troy: The Story of the Iliad.* Illustrated by Alan Lee. Delacorte, 1993. Cloth 0-385-31069-2. Grades 5 to 8.

Sutcliff's clear, dramatic retelling of *The Iliad* resonates with much of the imagery and power of Homer's epic poem. We grieve at the tragic fates of Achilles, Patroclus, Hector, and the other heroes on both sides of the Trojan War and watch with awe the machinations of the gods and goddesses who capriciously intercede in the lives of mere mortals. The values and civic practices depicted here belong to another time and place, but they have clearly influenced how western civilizations think about war and heroism to this day. Alan Lee's color illustrations are a perfect match in this highly accessible introduction to a classic work of literature. **F • HR**

312. WILLIAMS, MARCIA. *The Iliad and the Odyssey*. Candlewick, 1996. Cloth 0-7636-0053-9; 1998, pap. 0-7636-0644-8. Grades 2 to 5.

The author/illustrator enhances a simple, straight-forward retelling of the Homerian epics with comic strip illustrations. This is a raucous, childlike introduction to these classic tales. Many of the most intriguing mythological characters—Cyclops, Circe, Scylla—are found in *The Odyssey*, and this is a great way for children to get to know them. **F • HR**

WEB SITES

---

313. *Images of the Trojan War Myth*.
http://www.temple.edu/classics/troyimages.html
Robin Mitchell-Boyask, Temple University, 2002. Grades 5 to 8.

A classics professor at Temple University has collected many images that illustrate events leading up to the war, the Trojan War itself, the fall of Troy, and the homecoming of Odysseus. These visual representations bring the events to life and also demonstrate how powerfully this legend has resonated throughout time. **NF • R**

314. *Was There a Trojan War?*
http://www.archaeology.org/0405/etc/troy.html
Archaeology Institute of America, 2004. Grades 6 to 8.

The author of this readable article from the online publication *Archaeology* is the lead archaeologist on the current excavations at Hisarlik/Troy in northwestern Turkey. There are many relevant links from this site, including one to an archaeologist's review of the movie *Troy* starring Brad Pitt. There is also a link to the home page of the Troia Project that includes computer models that reconstruct the ancient city of Troy. **NF • R**

DVDs

315. *True Story of Troy*. A & E Television Networks. 2004. 100 minutes. Grades 7 up.

Produced for the History Channel, this documentary is a good introduction to the significance of the ancient story of the Trojan War. Using reenactments, footage from the site of current excavations in Turkey, computer simulations, and commentary by military experts, historians, archaeologists, and classics scholars, this video explores the historical roots of the legend and the story told by Homer five centuries after the supposed historic event. The final conclusion seems to be that there was a historical city of Troy, or Ilium, on the site where the Troia Projekt is conducting its dig. On the whole, scholars seem to agree that there probably was a historical event much like the Trojan War described by Homer in *The Iliad*, although it was much more likely to have been a war over strategic trade routes than over the beautiful Helen. One is also left with a profound admiration for Homer's work, which remains one of the most eloquent works of literature about the glory and the tragedy of war. **NF • R**

SEPTEMBER 11, 2001

MOST AMERICAN ADULTS CAN TELL YOU exactly where they were and what they were doing when they heard about the attacks on the World Trade Center and the Pentagon on September 11, 2001. They can also tell you what their first reactions were: fear, confusion, rage, worry, horror. People all across the country were united, however briefly, in an experience that would change our lives in ways we could only begin to imagine.

For young people who entered college that fall, 9/11, as we soon came to refer to the events of that day, shaped the identity of their cohort and perhaps of their entire generation. A *New York Times* article ("Class of 2005 . . . ," 2005) revisited those students four years later, as many of them prepared to graduate. Many of these young people say the attacks made them question their life goals as they faced a suddenly scarier world. Some changed their academic majors as a result of 9/11; the enrollment in Arabic classes doubled in 2002. Many took an interest in religion and international politics for the first time.

Children were also affected by 9/11, of course. Obviously, the closer a child was to the actual attacks, the more direct the impact. We know that a day care center on the site was successfully evacuated with no physical injuries. Estimates of the number of children who lost a parent in the attacks range from 6,000 ("Children Who Lost . . . ," 2003) to 15,000 (Chen, 2002). Others were relocated from their apartments for days and weeks at a time because of the extreme pollution and disruption from the clean-up efforts. There are 15 public elementary, middle, and high schools in the immediate vicinity of the World Trade Center (Hoven, et al., 2005). Most notably, many students at Stuyvesant High School saw the planes hit the towers, saw the resulting flames, smoke, and falling bodies, and saw the towers collapse. Some of them created a moving dramatic piece out of their experiences, which was published as a book for young people called *With Their Eyes*. Thousands of children in New York and Washington, D.C., experienced the chaos and confusion of that day as family members struggled to make contact.

And of course, children all across the country watched as the images were played and replayed on television sets. Parents and caregivers struggled to explain what had happened and almost certainly communicated their own emotional distress to the children in their lives. Children knew that something very serious and very scary had occurred, something that not even their parents seemed to understand. Adults did not seem to have answers to the children's questions. Why did this happen? What does it mean? Will I be safe? Even the more concrete questions that emerged were new to many of us: Who is Osama Bin Laden? What is Al Qaeda? What does Islam have to do with this? Why do they hate us so much? We did not have ready answers.

It is important to remember that the 10- to 13-year-olds who are the target audience for the books and other information resources listed here may have only the haziest memories of this historic event. In fact, it is history for many of them. I recently asked my two oldest grandchildren—who were 10 and 7 on September 11, 2001—if they could remember what happened that day. The younger child had very little recall. The older girl, a teenager now, said she could remember her teacher crying and her parents talking about it that night at the dinner table. What stayed in her memory was not the event itself, but the reactions of adults. At her request, we recently watched the movie *UA 93* together. At times I had to cover my eyes and consciously keep myself from crying out as we watched the planes fly into the towers.

Again, she watched an adult struggle to keep her emotions in control. And this time she had questions. If we want children to learn from 9/11 and to understand its lasting consequences, they will need to know what happened that day—and why. They have a right to know.

Kay Vandergrift (2002), professor emerita at Rutgers University, maintains a Web site that is rich in its insights and resources about children's literature. I was not surprised to see that she had a page devoted to "9/11 and Children." Here are the questions she poses to educators like herself:

◆ What is the legacy for us and for our children of those relentless images of the WTC, the Pentagon, and that field in Pennsylvania?
◆ Will any of us ever again feel completely safe in an airplane, on a city street, or even in our own homes or schools?
◆ How can we help young people move beyond fear and despair, from grief to consolation, and then to hope and even to celebration?

There are many resources available for adults who need guidance in talking to children about 9/11 and the bigger topics it generates—terrorism, hatred, safety and security, and war. The best of these, written by experts in child development, provide adults with the reassurance that we really have the answers to the important questions Vandergrift poses. Or if not, that we can find a way to communicate our uncertainties without further traumatizing the children we care about. Look to Part III of this book for some helpful books and Web sites.

American publishers, most of which are headquartered in New York City, rushed to bring to press books that would explain this unprecedented event to children, memorialize the losses of that day, and celebrate the heroes who contributed to the massive rescue effort. These books fell into several distinct categories:

◆ Informational books about the September 11 attacks
◆ Books that celebrated the heroes of September 11—firefighters, rescue workers, and the people of New York
◆ Books designed to inspire or rekindle patriotism
◆ Books about Islam and/or the Middle East

Many of the first publishing efforts may have done more to bring comfort to the authors, illustrators, and publishers than to the children for whom they were intended. Few of these books, published in haste, reached levels of distinction in illustrations or text. Many of them—and these are included in the resource list that follows—are useful, however, for creating a frame of reference for adults who want to open up a discussion with today's children about the significance of 9/11.

We have yet to see any longer fiction for children dealing with the events of 9/11, certainly nothing that approaches the eloquence of Jonathan Safran Foer's novel for adults, *Extremely Loud and Incredibly Close* (2005). Art Spiegelman's *In the Shadow of No Towers* (2004) is a brilliant graphic novel, also created for adults. Interestingly, Foer's novel features a precocious child protagonist and many of the graphic elements we associate with some post-modern juvenile literature, including pages at the end that mimic a flip book. Spiegelman's graphic novel is printed on heavy card stock, like a child's board book. Why did these two book creators resort to some of the traditional design elements of children's literature? Was it perhaps to highlight the horror of the content by placing it in a context that evokes childhood innocence?

While the great children's novel about 9/11 has yet to be written, at least two picture books that memorialize the Twin Towers and the attack that destroyed them have some claim to distinction. *The Man Who Walked Between the Towers*, written and illustrated by Mordecai Gerstein, was awarded the Caldecott Medal for the most distinguished illustrations in an American children's book published in 2003. Maira Kalman's *Fireboat: The Heroic Adventures of the John J. Harvey* received the Boston Globe/Horn Book Award for excellence in a picture book. Both of these books could be considered nonfiction picture books, telling true stories in a picture-book format. Both can be appreciated as fine children's literature, apart from their subject matter.

In the resource list that follows, you will find several nonfiction books, Web sites, and DVDs that can inform children about the events of 9/11. There is also one good book about the Iraq War that began in 2003 as at least an indirect consequence of the 2001 attacks on the World Trade Center and the Pentagon—David Downing's *War in Iraq*. There are actually two books about the librarian who saved much of the collection in the Central Library from bombing—*Alia's Mission* by the graphic novelist Mark Alan Stamaty and *The Librarian of Basra* by Jeannette Winter. I have also included books and web sites that give American children some knowledge of Islam, since that religion has been much maligned and misunderstood since the terrorist attacks. One of the many unhappy consequences of 9/11 has been increased prejudice against Muslim Americans; these books may help to counter that unfortunate response.

The information resources about 9/11 bring together many of the themes explored earlier: history, hope and glory, and the consequences and horrors of war. American children on the home front are living in a world that has changed dramatically, especially if their parents are serving in the military. I wish there were books here that made a case for peace or alternatives to war, but they have not been written yet.

Bibliography

❧

BOOKS

316. AL-WINDAWI, THURA. *Thura's Diary: My Life in Wartime Iraq*. Viking, 2004. Cloth 0-670-05886-6. Grades 7 to 8.

The introduction tells us that this diary was kept by a 19-year-old Shia girl living in Baghdad as war threatens Iraq in 2003. Thura is attending college and living a relatively comfortable life in the repressive regime ruled by Saddam Hussein. She describes her daily routine and the changes that happen when Americans attack in March 2003. Her middle-class extended family was better able than some to cope with the shortages and hardships that came as a result of the bombing, but there were still serious difficulties to face. Certainly Thura's words give a human face to the suffering and destruction that have taken place during the years of war there. However, I have two reservations about the book. One is that it appears to be written for foreign eyes to read. There is as much explanation of customs and description of places where action is taking place as there is recording of personal experience and reflection. My second reservation is that both the introduction to the diary and its last entries give the impression that the war ended in two months, with the capture of Saddam Hussein. We know that the war continued long after this event; in early November 2006, U.S. troops were still heavily engaged; and more than 2,800 Americans and unknown thousands of Iraqis had died. **NF • RWR**

317. DEMI. *Muhammad*. Margaret K. McElderry/Simon & Schuster, 2003. Cloth 0-689-85264-9. Grades 2 up.

A simple, easy-to-understand text and gorgeous illustrations in the style of Persian paintings tell how Muhammad, born in what is now Saudi Arabia in the year 570, grew to be the prophet to whom Allah revealed the Koran, the scripture of Islam, thereby founding that religion. As is traditional and in keeping with Islamic law, neither Muhammad nor his family are depicted visually. Rather, they are shown in silhouettes. Well-chosen translations from the Koran and an enumeration of the key observances of the religion, the Five Pillars of Islam, give a good introduction to its basic beliefs. A bibliography and a foreword by a Muslim scholar lend credibility and authenticity to the work. **NF • HR**

318. DOWNING, DAVID. *The War in Iraq.* Heinemann Library, 2004. Pap. 1-4034-6261-5. Grades 6 to 8.

This is a well-balanced, objective overview of the Iraq War that began when the United States and its small coalition of allies invaded Iraq in March 2003. It gives some basic historical background about the nation of Iraq, the neo-conservative foreign relations policies of the George W. Bush administration, and the events after the September 11, 2001, attacks that led to the war. It covers the objections to the war as well as its justifications. The coverage of the war ends with the collapse of Saddam Hussein's regime when he is captured by U.S. forces. The author goes on to discuss the subsequent tensions in the Middle East and within Iraq and to give a fairly gloomy prognosis for peace. **NF • R**

319. FRANK, MITCH. *Understanding September 11: Answering Questions About the Attacks on America.* Viking, 2002. Cloth 0-670-03582-3; pap. 0-670-03587-4. Grades 5 to 8.

Using a question-and-answer format, a *Time* magazine reporter gives background information on a range of issues relating to the attacks on September 11, 2001. He covers terrorism, U.S. interests in the Middle East, Islam, the U.S. invasion of Afghanistan, and other complex topics. Wilborn Hampton's book, *September 11, 2001: Attack on New York City* (see below), tells what happened on that day. This book attempts the much more difficult task of telling *why.* **NF • R**

320. GELLMAN, MARC. *And God Cried, Too: A Kid's Book of Healing and Hope.* HarperCollins, 2002. Cloth 0-06-009887-2; pap. 0-06-009886-4. Grades 4 to 6.

The author is a rabbi who has written other books on religion for children. This volume uses the attacks on September 11, 2001, as an example of a tragic event that can test a person's belief in God. For families who hold a similar humanistic, mainstream Judeo-Christian worldview, this could be a helpful book. Families who follow other belief systems will find less relevance and comfort. In any case, children are most likely to read this book if a caring and trusted adult shares it with them. The approach is relatively child-friendly: Big Angel Gabe, the wise old angel, helps Little Angel Mikey, a guardian angel in training, work through some tough questions in order to understand God's compassion and people's ability to bear terrible burdens. **NF • RWR**

321. GERSTEIN, MORDICAI. *The Man Who Walked Between the Towers*. Illustrated by the author. Roaring Brook, 2003. Cloth 0-7613-1791-0; LB 0-7613-2868-8. Grades 2 to 4.

This picture-book biography celebrates the astonishing feat accomplished by Philippe Petit, who managed to walk a tightrope between the World Trade Center Towers in 1974, just as the two skyscrapers were being completed. The illustrations are particularly successful in communicating awe at the young man's daring, the astonishing view he must have enjoyed from his very high wire, and the beauty of New York City. The book is also a moving testimony to those iconic towers, lost in the attack on September 11, 2001. The penultimate page reads, "Now the towers are gone," and shows the city's skyline without the towers. But the last page shows the towers in shadowy outline, with Petit walking between them. The text: "But in memory, as if imprinted on the sky, the towers are still there. And part of that memory is the joyful morning, August 7, 1974, when Philippe Petit walked between them in the air." There is no further explanation for the Towers' disappearance; children will have to look to other sources for that information. **NF • HR**

322. GHAZI, SUHAIB HAMID. *Ramadan*. Illustrated by Omar Rayyan. Holiday House, 1996. Cloth 0-8234-1254-7; pap. 0-8234-1275-X. Grades 2 to 5.

Hakeem and his family live in what appears to be a middle-class community somewhere in the western world. This picture book tells how and why they observe the important holiday of Ramadan. The simple, direct text and lovely illustrations in which realistic paintings are framed by borders in a traditional Islamic style give a human face to a religion that remains poorly understood in the United States. **NF • R**

323. HAMPTON, WILBORN. *September 11, 2001: Attack on the World Trade Center.* Candlewick, 2003. Cloth 0-7636-1949-3. Grades 5 to 8.

The author, a veteran newspaper reporter, gives a straight-forward, eloquent account of the events precipitated by the terrorist attacks on New York and Washington, D.C., on September 11, 2001. He tells the story through the perspectives of people who lived through it—a man who lost his wife and the mother of his children, a blind man and his dog who managed to escape from the North Tower, a company of firefighters, and a young man who felt compelled to volunteer as a rescue worker. Dramatic black-and-white photos communicate the larger horror. While this is painful reading, it would be a good place for older children to start understanding what happened in the United States on that day. With admirable restraint, Hampton does not try to explain why, just what happened. **NF • HR**

324. HEIDE, FLORENCE PARRY, AND JUDITH HEIDE GILLILAND. *The House of Wisdom.* Illustrated by Mary Grandpré. DK Ink, 1999. Cloth 0-7894-2562-9. Grades 3 to 6.

Children who see only the war-torn streets of Baghdad on the television news might be surprised to learn that in the 9th century, the ruler of Baghdad so valued learning that he constructed a House of Wisdom, a grand library and translation center. Then he sent men throughout the civilized world to bring back books that scholars would translate. This is the fictionalized story of one young man who found his passion translating the complete works of Aristotle, thereby making available classic Greek thought to Europe and stimulating the beginning of the Renaissance. **F • R**

325. KALMAN, MAIRA. *Fireboat: The Heroic Adventures of the John J. Harvey.* Illustrated by the author. Putnam, 2002. Cloth 0-399-23953-7. Grades 3 to 5.

The *John J. Harvey*, the fireboat featured in this book, began life in New York Harbor in 1931. In 1995, it was considered obsolete and was waiting to be sold for scrap. A group of friends decide to save the *Harvey*, just for fun. Then, after the attack on the World Trade Center on September 11, 2001, the boat was pressed into service, its hoses working when the damage to the water pipes on land prevented their use. The story is told with the irrepressible high spirits of Kalman's trademark writing and illustrative style, making this a good choice when an upbeat story highlighting the positive response to the attack is wanted. **NF • R**

326. MACAULAY, DAVID. *Mosque.* Walter Lorraine/Houghton Mifflin, 2003. Cloth 0-618-24034-9. Grades 5 to 8.

Macaulay uses the technique that was so successful in earlier books such as *Cathedral, Castle,* and *Pyramid* to demonstrate how a great Ottoman mosque might have been built. It is a fictional 16th-century mosque, but a typical one. He creates some hypothetical characters. There is the successful Muslim admiral who wants to follow the pillar of his faith that decrees that he practice charity by building the mosque and giving it to his community. Even more important, however, is the architect, Akif Agha, whose advanced technological expertise is required to create the complex building with its massive half dome. Macaulay describes each step of the building process in clear pictures and text; and as he explains the construction of the mosque, he weaves in information about Islamic customs and practices. This is a painless way for non-Muslim children to absorb a little comparative religion, and a positive, affirming book for Muslim children to discover. **NF • HR**

327. MARSTON, ELSA. *Muhammad of Mecca: Prophet of Islam.* Franklin Watts, 2001. LB 0-531-20386-7; pap. 0-531-15554-4. Grades 5 to 8.

Intended as a supplementary text, this book lacks the artistry of Demi's biography of Muhammad. However, it is more detailed and offers more information about the development of the Islamic religion and its subsequent spread throughout the world. While the early conflict over succession and leadership that generated the schism between Sunnis and Shiites is discussed, there is little insight into the virulence that characterizes that split in the Middle East today. A chronology, glossary, and resources for further information are included. The author has credible ties to Islam and the Islamic world. **NF • R**

328. MELTZER, MILTON. *The Day the Sky Fell: A History of Terrorism.* Random House, 2002. LB 0-375-92250-4; pap. 0-375-82250-X. Grades 5 to 8.

In this revised and expanded edition of a 1983 title, Meltzer does a masterful job of focusing on the immediate events of the September 11, 2001, attack on the World Trade Center and presenting an objective, clear account of the history of terrorism and its incidents around the world, from Russia to Ireland to Palestine and Israel, to the Tupamaros in Uruguay and their imitators in Germany and the United States. He writes convincingly about the distinctions between dissent and civil disobedience and terrorism and also documents the rise of terrorist nations. Young people can learn a great deal about the complex forces shaping much of the political violence in our world from this book. **NF • HR**

329. *A Nation Challenged: A Visual History of 9/11 and Its Aftermath: Young Reader's Edition.* Scholastic, 2002. Cloth 0-439-48803-6. Grades 5 to 8.

The contributors to this book are all *New York Times* editors, reporters, and photographers. It is a compendium of information and images about what happened on September 11, 2001, and its aftermath as we attacked Afghanistan for its role in sheltering Osama Bin Laden and Al Qaeda. The visual images are particularly effective in evoking the events of that time. **NF • R**

330. OSBORNE, MARY POPE. *New York's Bravest.* Illustrated by Steve Johnson and Lou Fancher. Knopf, 2002. Cloth 0-375-82196-1; LB 0-375-92196-6. Grades 2 to 4.

In the mid-1800s, legendary tales began to circulate about a real-life New York firefighter named Mose Humphreys. The author describes him as America's first urban folk hero, a man who represents the courage and strength of firefighters throughout history. This picture book retells some of the tall tales associated with Mose. Only a historical note at the beginning of the book and the dedication to the 343 New York City firefighters who died on September 11, 2001, link the story to the contemporary event; but the author's intent is clear. She wants to pay tribute to the modern-day heroes by calling attention to the legend. **F • R**

331. STAMATY, MARK ALAN. *Alia's Mission: Saving the Books of Iraq.* Knopf, 2004. Cloth 0-375-83217-3; LB 0-375-93217-8. Grades 5 to 8.

This graphic novel tells about Alia Muhammad Baker, head of the Central Library of Basra, Iraq. As the 2003 war looms, she fears for the safety of the books in her library. Government officials refuse her pleas to move the books so she takes matters into her own hands. At first, she carries the books to her home, armfuls at a time. Then, as the bombing begins and soldiers occupy the building, she enlists friends to move the books over the wall behind the library to the restaurant next door. The library finally burns, as she had feared, but she and the citizens of Basra had succeeded in saving 30,000 volumes. This is a moving testament to the unforeseen consequences of war, the importance of books as a record of a culture and a society, and the activism of one heroic librarian. See also *The Librarian of Basra: A True Story from Iraq* by Jeannette Winter, a picture book for younger children. **NF • HR**

332. THOMAS, ANNIE, ED. *With Their Eyes: September 11th: The View from a High School at Ground Zero.* HarperCollins, 2002. LB 0-06-051806-5; pap. 0-06-051718-2. Grades 7 to 12.

The students at Stuyvesant High School were four blocks from Ground Zero when the planes hit the World Trade Center. Many saw it happen. A gifted English teacher had the idea of using the theater-making techniques developed by Anna Deavere Smith to create drama out of the students' and other school staff's experiences that day. Students interviewed members of their school community, edited the interviews into coherent monologues, and acted out the narratives, taking on the voices of the interviewees. The script that resulted is presented here, along with photos of the young actors. The project may have initially been intended as a kind of therapy that would help the young people process what they had witnessed, but the result is a moving and coherent work of art that transcends any such functional use. **NF • R**

333. WILKINSON, PHILIP. *Islam.* DK, 2002. Cloth 0-7894-8870-1. Grades 4 to 8.

This overview of the Islamic religion and its practice around the world is presented in the usual Eyewitness Guide format. Many topics are covered—the life of Muhammad, the Five Pillars of Islam, mosques, Islamic scholars and teachers, nomadic and settled lifestyles, the Crusades, practices in specific countries, costumes and jewelry, festivals and ceremonies. The book is lavishly illustrated with colored photographs. There is more breadth than depth, and students will need to do more investigation and analysis to pull together what they learn. However, the child-friendly format may motivate young readers to do just that. **NF • R**

334. WINTER, JEANETTE. *The Librarian of Basra: A True Story from Iraq*. Harcourt, 2004. Cloth 0-15-205445-6. Grades 3 to 4.

This is a picture-book account of the librarian who worked with friends and neighbors to move the books in the Central Library of Basra to safety when they were threatened by the bombing in 2003. Simple words and color illustrations communicate both the consequences of war for ordinary people and the need for unlikely heroes. See also *Alia's Mission: Saving the Books of Iraq*, a graphic novel for older children. **NF • HR**

335. WINTER, JEANETTE. *September Roses*. Frances Foster Books/Farrar Straus & Giroux, 2004. Cloth 0-374-36736-1. Grades 4 to 8.

In this tiny picture book that is simple enough for the youngest children and subtle enough for adults, Jeannette Winter tells of one meaningful act by two individuals immediately after the attack on the World Trade Center. Two sisters from South Africa were flying to New York to participate in a flower show on September 11, 2001. They had with them 2,400 roses that they had planned to exhibit in the show. After the attack, the flower show was canceled, and the women were stranded at the airport. Members of a local church offered them shelter. In gratitude for this offer of help and in support of the tragedy that had befallen the city, the women took their roses to Union Square, where many people had created spontaneous memorials. There they arranged their roses on the grass in the shape of the two fallen towers. **F • R**

WEB SITES

336. *Afghanistan*.
https://www.cia.gov/cia/publications/factbook/geos/af.html
Central Intelligence Agency, 2006. Grades 5 to 8.

The CIA *World Factbook* is a reputable, up-to-date source for basic geographic, political, environmental, economic, and demographic information about countries of the world. Students can also find a map and a picture of the country's flag. **NF • R**

337. *Country Profile: Afghanistan.*
http://news.bbc.co.uk/2/hi/south_asia/country_profiles/1162668.stm
BBC. Grades 6 to 8.

This up-to-date Web site gives recent developments in the country as well as basic facts such as population, languages, life expectancy, etc. The content emphasized is the political situation. There are links to other media sources. **NF • R**

338. *Country Profile: Iraq.*
http://news.bbc.co.uk/2/hi/middle_east/country_profiles/791014.stm
BBC. Grades 6 to 8.

This is a good source for background information as well as updates about the political situation in this turbulent country. There are links to other media sources. **NF • R**

339. *Iraq.*
https://www.cia.gov/cia/publications/factbook/geos/iz.html
Central Intelligence Agency. Grades 5 to 8.

The CIA *World Factbook* is a reputable, up-to-date source for basic geographic, political, environmental, economic, and demographic information about countries of the world. Students can also find a map and a picture of the country's flag. **NF • R**

340. *The September 11 Digital Archive: Saving the Histories of September 11, 2001.*
http://www.911digitalarchive.org
American Social History Project/Center for Media and Learning at the City University of New York Graduate Center, 2002–2005. Grades 6 to 8.

This Web site, in partnership with the Library of Congress, the American Red Cross, and the Smithsonian, uses electronic media to collect, preserve, and present the history of the 9/11 attacks. It contains visual images, audio clips, documents, FAQs, and links to other relevant Web sites and online resources. **NF • R**

341. *September 11 Web Archive.*
http://www.loc.gov/minerva/collect/sept11
Library of Congress, 2004. Grades 6 to 8.

The Library of Congress partnered with the Internet Archive, WebArchivist.org, and the Pew Internet & American Life Project to create this collection of digital materials. It contains more than 30,000 selected Web sites archived between September 11, 2001, and December 1, 2001. What is particularly valuable about these records is that they are international in scope. A student can use this archive to find out what people in Malaysia, France, Mexico, or other parts of the world were saying about the tragic event that happened in the United States. Many of the sites in this collection were "born digital," never printed on paper, and would probably have been lost if they had not been preserved here. **NF • HR**

342. *Understanding Afghanistan: Land in Crisis.*
http://www.nationalgeographic.com/landincrisis/
National Geographic. Grades 6 to 8.

Excellent maps and good photography are hallmarks of National Geographic publications, and this Web site is no exception. There are also excellent links for teachers giving online activities and lesson plans. **NF • HR**

DVDs

343. *In Memoriam: New York City 9/11/01*. HBO Home Video. 2002. 60 minutes. Grades 7and up.

This is recommended with reservations only about its possible emotional impact on young people. This is unquestionably one of the finest films made about 9/11. Intended as a memorial for those who died in the attack on the World Trade Center, it evokes horror, anger, profound sadness, and ultimately pride in the heroism of ordinary people's responses to this dramatic event and hope that life will go on and the city will rebuild. Be warned; the documentary footage is graphic. You see those bodies falling from the tower and hear the screams of those who watched in horror. Interviews with Mayor Giuliani and other New York officials provide some context, but the film does not attempt to explain or interpret—only to present the attacks and their aftermath and the reactions of the New Yorkers who witnessed them. **NF • RWR**

REFERENCES

"ALSC/Robert F. Sibert Informational Book Award Terms and Criteria." (2006). Chicago: Association for Library Service to Children. http://www.ala.org/ala/alsc/awardsscholarships/literaryawds/sibertmedal/Sibert_Medal.htm.

Anderson, Fred, and Andrew Cayton. (2005). *The Dominion of War: Empire and Liberty in North America 1500–2000.* New York: Viking.

Appy, Christian G. (2004). "The Ghosts of War." *Chronicle of Higher Education.* July 9, 2004, Section B, pp. 12–13.

Barnitz, Laura A. (1999). *Child Soldiers: Youth Who Participate in Armed Conflict.* Washington, D.C.: Youth Advocate Program International.

Baruch, Dorothy. (1942). *You, Your Children, and War.* New York: D. Appleton-Century.

Bespaloff, Rachel. (2005). "On the Iliad." In Simone Weil and Rachel Bespaloff, *War and the Iliad.* New York: New York Review of Books, pp. 39–100.

Braudy, Leo. (2003). *From Chivalry to Terrorism: War and the Changing Nature of Masculinity.* New York: Knopf.

Breed, Clara. (1943). "Americans with the Wrong Ancestors." *The Horn Book* (July–Aug. 1943), pp. 253–261.

Ceadel, Martin. (1987). *Thinking About Peace and War.* Oxford and New York: Oxford University Press.

Chen, Victor. (2002). "Weill Cornell Psychiatrists Receive Grant to Study Stress on 9/11 Children." *Cornell Chronicle*, June 6, 2002, p. 1.

Children in Wartime: Parents' Questions. (1943). New York: Child Study Association of America.

"Children Who Lost Parents on 9/11 Still Struggle." (2003). *USA Today*, Feb. 16, 2003, p. 1.

"Class of 2005, Shaped by September 11." (2005). *The New York Times*, May 15, 2005, Section 1, p. 24.

Coates, A. J. (1997). *The Ethics of War*. Manchester and New York: Manchester University Press.

Expectations of Excellence: Curriculum Standards for Social Studies. (1994). Silver Springs, MD: National Council for the Social Studies.

Fleischman, Paul. (2006). *Dateline: Troy*. Revised edition. Cambridge, MA: Candlewick Press.

Flower, Elizabeth. (1973). "Peace, Ethics of." In Philip P. Wiener, editor, *Dictionary of the History of Ideas: Studies of Selected Pivotal Ideas,* Vol. III. New York: Scribner, pp. 440–447.

Foer, Jonathan Safran. (2005). *Extremely Loud and Incredibly Close*. Boston: Houghton Mifflin.

Gillespie, Angus Kress. (1999). *Twin Towers: The Life of New York City's World Trade Center*. New Brunswick, NJ: Rutgers University Press.

Goldson, Edward. (1993). "War Is Not Good for Children." In Lewis A. Leavitt and Nathan A. Fox, editors, *The Psychological Effects of War and Violence on Children*. Mahwah, NJ: Lawrence Erlbaum, pp. 3–22.

Hedges, Chris. (2002). *War Is a Force That Gives Us Meaning*. New York: Anchor/Random House.

"A History of the CND Logo." (n.d.). London: Campaign for Nuclear Disarmament. http://www.cnduk.org/INFORM-1/symbol.htm.

Holm, Tom. (1996). *Strong Hearts, Wounded Souls: The Native American Veterans of the Vietnam War*. Austin, TX: University of Texas Press.

Hoven, Christina W., et al. (2005). "Psychopathology Among New York City Public School Children 6 Months After September 11." *Archives of General Psychiatry* (May 2005), Vol. 62, pp. 545–552.

Kirk, Robert Wm. (1994). *Earning Their Stripes: The Mobilization of American Children in the Second World War*. New York: Peter Lang.

Kuehl, Warren F. (1973). "Peace, International." In Philip P. Wiener, editor, *Dictionary of the History of Ideas: Studies of Selected Pivotal Ideas*, Vol. III. New York: Scribner, pp. 448–457.

Le, Thi Diem Thuy. (2003). *The Gangster We Are All Looking For.* New York: Borzoi/Knopf.

Lister, Bob. (2005). "Hearing Homer's Scream Across Three Thousand Years." *Children's Literature in Education* (Dec. 2005), Vol. 36, No. 4, pp. 395–411.

Machel, Graça. (2001). *The Impact of War on Children: A Review of Progress Since the 1996 United Nations Report on the Impact of Armed Conflict on Children.* London: Hurst & Company.

"On Teaching About Intolerance and Genocide." (1993). Urbana, Illinois: National Council of Teachers of English, 1998–2006. http://www.ncte.org/about/over/positions/category/rights/107439.htm.

Oppenheim, Joanne. (2006). *Dear Miss Breed: True Stories of the Japanese American Incarceration During World War II and a Librarian Who Made a Difference.* New York: Scholastic.

Ozick, Cynthia. (1997). "Who Owns Anne Frank?" *The New Yorker* (Oct. 6, 1997), pp. 76–87.

Protection and Assistance to Unaccompanied and Separated Refugee Children: Report of the Secretary General. (2001). United Nations General Assembly.

Rosen, David M. (2005). *Armies of the Young: Child Soldiers in War and Terrorism.* New Brunswick, NJ: Rutgers University Press.

Rubin, Elizabeth. (1998). "Our Children Are Killing Us." *The New Yorker* (March 23, 1998), pp. 56–64.

Singer, P. W. (2005). *Children at War.* New York: Pantheon Books.

Sontag, Susan. (2003). *Regarding the Pain of Others.* New York: Farrar, Straus & Giroux.

Spiegelman, Art. (2004). *In the Shadow of No Towers.* New York: Pantheon Books.

Stephens, Elaine C., Jean E. Brown, and Janet E. Rubin. (1995). *Learning About the Holocaust: Literature and Other Resources for Young People.* North Haven, CT: Library Professional Publications.

Tuttle, William M., Jr. (1993). *"Daddy's Gone to War": The Second World War in the Lives of America's Children.* New York: Oxford University Press.

"Twentieth Century Warriors: Native American Participation in the United States Military." (1997). Washington, D.C.: Department of the Navy, Naval Historical Center. http://www.history.navy.mil/faqs/faq61-1.htm.

"UN Refugee Agency." (2006). United Nations High Commissioner for Refugees. http://www.unhcr.org/cgi-bin/texis/vtx/home.

Vandergrift, Kay E. (2002). "9/11 and Children." New Jersey, Rutgers University. http://www.scils.rutgers.edu/~kvander/911/index.html.

Walter, Virginia A. (1993). *War and Peace Literature for Children and Young Adults: A Resource Guide to Significant Issues.* Phoenix, AZ: Oryx Press.

Weil, Simone. (2005). "*The Iliad*, or the Poem of Force." In Simone Weil and Rachel Bespaloff, *War and the Iliad.* New York: New York Review of Books, pp. 1–37.

Wolf, Anna W. M. (1942). *Our Children Face War.* Boston: Houghton Mifflin.

"Women in Combat." (2005). Online Newshour (Aug. 3, 2005). Public Broadcasting System. www.pbs.org//newshour/bb/middle_east/july-dec05/women_8-03.html.

"Wounded in War: The Women Serving in Iraq." (2005). All Things Considered (March 14, 2005). National Public Radio. http://www.npr.org/templates/story/story.php?storyId=4534450.

Young, James E. (1988). *Writing and Rewriting the Holocaust: Narrative and the Consequences of Interpretation.* Bloomington and Indianapolis: University of Indiana Press.

PART III

RESOURCES FOR ADULTS

OVERVIEW

THE FINAL SECTION OF THIS BOOK PRESENTS selected resources for adults who want to do more reading on the topics of war and peace and their implications for children and children's literature. I have extended the scope here to include books published through June 2006. The first resource list deals with the consequences of war for children. The resources here include historical and sociological accounts of the lives of children during wartime as well as guides to help adults deal effectively with children's questions and concerns about war and terrorism. The second resource list focuses on children's literature about war and peace. All of the books and Web sites included in these two resource lists are helpful in creating a framework for understanding the complexities of sharing books and other informational resources about war and peace with children.

CHILDREN AND WAR, CHILDREN AND PEACE

Bibliography

BOOKS

344. BARNITZ, LAURA A. *Child Soldiers: Youth Who Participate in Armed Conflict*. Youth Advocate Program International, 1997. Pap. 0-96637-094-5.

This booklet gives a good view of the basic humanitarian perspective on child soldiers. It outlines the conditions that make it more likely that children will be inducted into armed service, describes the typical duties assigned to them, and explains why children are still used as soldiers around the world today. It describes the negative impact on children who become soldiers. It also discusses some possible measures to stop the practice as well as efforts that are being made to integrate child soldiers back into civilian life.

345. GEIST, ANTHONY L., AND PETER N. CARROLL. *They Still Draw Pictures: Children's Art in Wartime from the Spanish Civil War to Kosovo*. University of Illinois Press, 2002. Cloth 0-252-02716-7; pap. 0-252-07026-7.

A collection of drawings created by children living in refugee camps during the Spanish Civil War in 1937 is housed in the University of California at San Diego's special collections library. They were recently made available in a traveling exhibition, and this is the catalog. A fore-word by the psychiatrist Robert Coles and an essay by the curators add significant context to the drawings, which are moving testimonies in themselves of children's experiences during a war.

346. GOODMAN, ROBIN F., AND ANDREA HENDERSON FAHNESTOCK. *The Day Our World Changed: Children's Art of 9/11*. Abrams, 2002. Cloth 0-8109-3544-9.

This book was a project of the New York University Child Study Center and the Museum of the City of New York. The artwork, created by chil-dren from 5 to 18 years of age, was featured in a juried exhibition. It is a stunning testament to children as witnesses to history and to their use of art as a means of expression. The art is beautifully reproduced, but this is much more than a coffee table art book. There are signifi-cant essays representing a number of perspectives on the events of September 11, 2001, and their effects on children in New York and everywhere.

347. HOLLIDAY, LAUREL. *Children in the Holocaust and World War II: Their Secret Diaries*. Pocket Books/Simon & Schuster, 1995. Cloth 0-671-52054-7.

This anthology of children's diaries from World War II is unique in its inclusion of Gentile as well as Jewish children and for the range of cir-cumstances in which the young authors found themselves. There are diarists from the ghettos of Lithuania, Poland, Latvia, and Hungary, from concentration camps and a Nazi prison, and from the bombed-out cities of London and Rotterdam. The editor points out that they write with courage and with humor and often with as much skill as the more well-known diarist, Anne Frank. Holliday believes that writ-ing was for these children an act of resistance. It was often an incredi-ble challenge just to find paper and writing implements, and in many cases, just writing the truth about their situations would have been grounds for death. Their persistence is evidence of children's sense of agency in the most punitive environments.

348. KIRK, ROBERT WILLIAM. *Earning Their Stripes: The Mobilization of American Children in the Second World War.* Peter Lang, 1994. Cloth 0-8204-2408-0.

This readable, scholarly history of American childhood during World War II provides important background for understanding books about the home front. The author also makes the point that the experiences of children during World War II created some shared generational attitudes and values as they became adults. It was a relatively small cohort because the Depression of the 1930s had led to low birthrates. However, 183,000 American children lost their fathers in the war. Others were latchkey kids, as their mothers went to work for the first time. Many grew up in safety and look back on these years with nostalgia. While Kirk does address the topic of ethnic prejudice, including anti-Japanese sentiments, he does not deal specifically with the internment camp experience. Given that limitation, this is an excellent treatment of the general topic of American children and World War II.

349. LEAVITT, LEWIS A., AND NATHAN A. FOX. *The Psychological Effects of War and Violence on Children.* Lawrence Erlbaum, 1993. Cloth 0-8509-1171-0; pap. 0-8058-1172-9.

These scholarly papers were first presented at a conference held during the first Gulf War. Their intent was to assess the state of knowledge about the psychological trauma of children exposed to war and violence and to develop some strategies for mental health intervention. The focus is on the Middle East, but there are also papers dealing with the politicized youth of South Africa, children exposed to the "troubles" in Northern Ireland, and inner-city children who witness violence in a Washington, D.C., neighborhood. It is a sobering volume.

350. MARTEN, JAMES. *Children and War: A Historical Anthology.* New York University Press, 2002. Cloth 0-8147-5666-2; pap. 0-8147-5667-0.

Twenty-one essays by scholars from many disciplines and a foreword by Robert Coles lay out a historical perspective on children and war, from the time of the American Revolution to the Kindertransports of World War II to the fears of American children during the Cuban Missile Crisis.

351. MARTEN, JAMES. *The Children's Civil War*. University of North Carolina Press, 1998. Cloth 0-8078-2425-9; pap. 0-8078-4904-9.

This is a comprehensive examination of the experiences of young people during the American Civil War. Marten, a highly regarded historian, looks at black and white children in the North and in the South and also discusses the ways in which their wartime childhood influenced the kind of adults they became. Chapter 2 is a particularly interesting and relevant look at the way in which the war was reflected in children's literature and textbooks of the time.

352. MOSES, LISA F., ET AL. *Children's Fears of War and Terrorism: A Resource for Teachers and Parents*. Association for Childhood Education International, 2003. Pap. 0-87173-160-6.

This is probably the single best resource for adults wanting guidance on helping children deal with anxieties and fears about war and terrorism. An introduction gives historical background about children's fears during earlier wars. Other chapters focus on the impact of context, the influence of a child's own temperament, and developmental considerations on an individual's emotional responses. The authors share their expertise on using books and art activities to make a difference with children and also discuss the complexities and ambiguities many adults face as they help young people work through their fears.

353. NICHOLAS, LYNN H. *Cruel World: The Children of Europe in the Nazi Web*. Vintage, 2006. Pap. 978-0-679-77663-5.

This is a comprehensive account of the consequences of the Nazi regime for all children in Europe. The author covers the programs of applied eugenics promulgated by the government, the strategies for eliminating Jews and other "undesirables" from German soil, the socialization of German children through programs such as the Hitler Youth, efforts to hide or rescue children in danger, and of course, the unspeakable conditions in the concentration camps. She also covers the chaotic period after World War II when massive efforts to repatriate families were occurring and unaccompanied refugee children roamed Europe.

354. ROSEN, DAVID A. *Armies of the Young: Child Soldiers in War and Terrorism*. Rutgers University Press, 2005. Cloth 0-8135-3567-0; pap. 0-8135-3568-9.

An opening chapter points out that children, young people under the age of 18, have fought in wars throughout history, notably in the American Civil War, in which between 250,000 and 420,000 boys were engaged. Subsequent chapters look at the particular cases of Jewish child resistance fighters during World War II, the child soldiers of Sierra Leone, and the Palestinian children who have resisted Israeli occupation with weapons ranging from stones to suicide bombs. The author's thesis is that the basic humanitarian approach to child soldiers, which sees all of them as victims, oversimplifies the issue. Instead, in many cases the children are not passive victims. Rather, they have made the rational decision that not fighting would be worse than fighting. This is a provocative book that should be read by all child advocates.

355. SINGER, P. W. *Children at War*. Pantheon, 2005. Cloth 0-375-42349-4.

The author takes a wide-ranging look at the contemporary use of child soldiers, individuals under the age of 18, in warfare around the world. Using a policy approach, he examines the reasons for the increased utilization of children in this role, the implications of this phenomenon for the conduct of war, for the children themselves, and the societies in which they live, as well as strategies for rehabilitating children and reintegrating them back into civilian life.

356. TUTTLE, WILLIAM M. *"Daddy's Gone to War": The Second World War in the Lives of America's Children*. Oxford University Press, 1993. Cloth 0-19-504905-5.

This social history of American children during World War II explores one generation's development from childhood to middle age and acknowledges the tremendous influence of the war on their identity. Tuttle drew from 2,500 letters from men and women who were children during the war as well as other primary source documents. The result is a compelling look at children playing war games, contributing to the war effort, taking care of themselves as latchkey kids, worrying about fathers fighting overseas, reading comics, listening to the radio, and going to the movies. Tuttle acknowledges the racial and ethnic conflicts that both reinforced and conflicted with the conformist, patriotic values that were being instilled in the children.

WEB SITES

357. *Talking with Children About War and Violence in the World.*
http://life.familyeducation.com/war/parenting/36559.html
Educators for Social Responsibility, 2003.

A group of educators have updated an earlier Web site that was drafted during the first war in the Persian Gulf in 1991. This is a guide for adults who want to help children understand difficult issues in the world. The question-and-answer format covers most issues that parents care about.

358. *Talking to Children About War and Terrorism: 20 Tips for Parents.*
http://www.aacap.org/
American Academy of Child and Adolescent Psychiatry, 2003.

The author, a practicing child and adolescent psychiatrist, offers guidance for parents who want to open up a helpful dialogue with children about terrorism. The Web page was created to mark the anniversary of the September 11 attack, acknowledging that the need for information continues long after the event itself.

CHILDREN'S LITERATURE ABOUT WAR AND PEACE

Bibliography

BOOKS

359. BOSMAJIAN, HAMIDA. *Sparing the Child: Grief and the Unspeakable in Youth Literature About Nazism and the Holocaust.* Routledge, 2002. Cloth 0-8153-3856-2.

In this scholarly monograph, Bosmajian considers the dilemma of children's literature about the Holocaust and Nazism. The conventions of children's literature require an affirmative, if not a happy ending. Yet affirmative endings in stories about the Holocaust and its parallel event, Nazism, deny the reader the essential truth of those disasters: that they are essentially meaningless. They also require that the young reader understand Nazism without understanding the attraction it had for Aryan youth in Germany and that they empathize with the victim of the Holocaust while acknowledging that they can never really know what the horrors were like. Bosmajian considers a few representative titles, but this is not a comprehensive treatment of Holocaust literature for children.

360. LENZ, MILLICENT. *Nuclear Age Literature for Youth: The Quest for a Life-Affirming Ethic.* American Library Association, 1990. Pap. 0-8389-0535-8.

This scholarly account of nuclear themes in literature for young people focuses on the need to redefine heroism in a post-nuclear age. She advocates a more feminist and holistic approach, exemplified by the Gaia myth. Given the current concerns about emerging nuclear capabilities in North Korea and Iran, these arguments may assume renewed relevance.

361. MACDONALD, MARGARET READ. *Peace Tales: World Folktales to Talk About.* Linnet/Shoestring, 1992. Cloth 0-208-02328-3; pap. 0-208-02329-1.

The noted storyteller and folklorist has gathered tales from around the world that deal with war and peace. There are stories that point out the pathways to war and others that demonstrate the folly of fighting and pathways to peace. There are suggestions for storytellers and discussion leaders, notes about story sources, and a bibliography of recommended books about peace for children and adults.

362. MEDIAVILLA, CINDY. *Arthurian Fiction: An Annotated Bibliography.* Scarecrow, 1999. Pap. 0-8108-3644-0.

A terrific resource for adults looking for background material and recommended reading for young people about King Arthur and the legends surrounding this mythic figure.

363. MICKENBERG, JULIA L. *Learning from the Left: Children's Literature, the Cold War, and Radical Politics in the United States.* Oxford University Press, 2006. Pap. 0-19-515281-6.

The author looks at a little-known phenomenon in children's literature, the influence of a few left-leaning authors, illustrators, and editors during the years immediately preceding and following World War II. During the war, many children's books featured themes of anti-fascism and thus supported the dominant values in the United States. After World War II, however, when the United States continued to fight a Cold War against Communism, trade books tended to subvert the dominant values in school textbooks.

364. STEPHENS, ELAINE C., JEAN E. BROWN, AND JANET E. RUBIN. *Learning About the Holocaust: Literature and Other Resources for Young People*. Library Professional Publications/Shoe String Press, 1995. Cloth 0-208-02398-4; Library Professional Publication/Shoe String Press, 1995, pap. 0-208-02408-5.

The authors have created a useful handbook of Holocaust resources for educators. The extensive bibliography of materials for children from preschool through secondary school is organized by genre. Each entry contains a brief entry that summarizes the book followed by a more extensive discussion, some teaching considerations, and a listing of additional related titles.

365. WEE, PATRICIA HACHTEN, AND ROBERT JAMES WEE. *World War II in Literature for Youth: A Guide and Resource Book*. Scarecrow Press, 2004. Pap. 0-8108-5301-9.

This extensive classified bibliography of resources about World War II focuses on upper elementary and secondary levels. Many of the entries are adult titles appropriate for using with high school students. Annotations are brief but descriptive. While the emphasis is on books, there are also smaller sections listing periodicals, electronic resources, and World War II museums and memorials.

ARTICLES

366. AUSTIN, PATRICIA, AND JAMES A. BRYANT, JR. "Children Caught in War." *Book Links*. March 2004 (Vol. 13, No. 4): 14–18.

The authors list books about children caught in the maelstrom of wars fought during the 20th and 21st centuries. All of the titles present war in a realistic way and offer portraits of children who are empowered by their own actions.

367. CHATTON, BARBARA, AND JENNIFER GERINGER. "World War II on the Home Front." *Book Links*. September 1999 (Vol. 9, No. 1): 30–34.

An extensive bibliography of books for young people in the U.S. who experienced World War II at home.

368. Chatton, Barbara, and Shirley Tastad. "The American Revolution: 1754–1783." *Book Links*. May 1993 (Vol. 2, No. 5): 7–12.

An overview of themes and curriculum connections introduces a bibliography of basic children's books about the American Revolution.

369. Frew, Andrew W. "Park's Quest by Katherine Paterson." *Book Links*. September 1991 (Vol. 1, No. 1): 29–32.

Frew presents strategies for using this powerful story about the lasting impact of the war in Vietnam in a classroom setting. A bibliography suggests links to books about family issues, war, Southeast Asia, and the Vietnam War.

370. Gerson, Lani. "Journey to Topaz by Yoshiko Uchida." *Book Links*. March 1993 (Vol. 2, No. 4): 59–64.

A detailed guide to using *Journey to Topaz* in a 4th-grade literature unit, with suggestions for setting the scene, leading discussions, activities, research, and related books.

371. Ozick, Cynthia. "Who Owns Anne Frank?" *The New Yorker*. Oct. 6, 1997: 76–87.

Ozick argues persuasively that the true message of Anne Frank's diary has been distorted by its champions and by adolescent readers who have identified with its universal teenage angst. The diary is not a "song to life" or a testament to the human spirit, she says. It is rather a very well-written but expurgated and truncated account of a child's life under dehumanizing conditions. There are no diary entries for the days in Auschwitz or Bergen-Belsen, where she died a horrendous death from typhus. Ozick ends her essay with the shocking contention that it might have been better if Miep Gies had indeed burned the diary when she found it. That way it would have been "saved from a world that made of it all things, some of them true, while floating lightly over the heavier truth of named and inhabited evil" (p. 87).

372. Rochman, Hazel. "Bearing Witness to the Holocaust." *Book Links*. January 1998 (Vol. 7, No. 3): 8–14.

Rochman gives invaluable guidance to adults trying to help young people think effectively about the tragedy of the Holocaust, using books to create frames of reference. She draws connections to other forms of racism and persecution and provides a list of recommended books for middle grades.

373. ROCHMAN, HAZEL. "Holocaust Survivors, Rescuers, and Bystanders." *Book Links*. January 1999 (Vol. 8, No. 3): 54–57.

An introduction to books for middle grades and up about the Holocaust. The author has selected books that do not skip over the horrors that the survivors have lived through; her intent is to help young readers consider their own moral choices as they learn more about the history of this horrible event.

374. SAINSBURY, MIKE. "The Theft of Childhood: Depictions of the Second World War in The Dolphin Crossing and Dawn of Fear." *The Looking Glass*. Sept. 2, 2005 (Vol. 9, Issue 3).

The author compares two novels that depict the experiences of children in England during World War II. He makes the point that those that deal with the military aspects of that war are often appealing to boys as they highlight issues that are relevant to them: bullies, bravery, courage, and the prospect of their own future participation in military service.

375. SCHNEIDER, DEAN. "The American Revolution—An Update." *Book Links*. June/July 2002 (Vol. 11, No. 6): 17–22.

A brief overview and a selected annotated bibliography of fiction and nonfiction books for children and young adults about the American Revolution published between 1994 and 2002. This updates the Chatton and Tastad treatment listed above.

376. SCHNEIDER, DEAN. "The Civil War—An Update." *Book Links*. September 2003 (Vol. 13, No. 1): 36–41.

This updates bibliographies on the Civil War published in *Book Links* in 1991 and 1995. Writing on this topic for young people is prolific; these annotated compilations are invaluable for keeping librarians and teachers up to date.

377. SCHOMBERG, JANIE. "Messages of Peace." *Book Links*. September 1993 (Vol. 3, No. 1): 9–17.

In addition to an annotated bibliography of books for lower elementary and middle grades, the author provides strategies and resources for classroom explorations of peace.

378. STAN, SUSAN. "Rose Blanche in Translation." *Children's Literature in Education*. March 2004 (Vol. 5, No. 1): 21–33.

A scholarly examination of three different translated editions of the classic picture book about a young German girl who discovers a Nazi concentration camp outside her city.

APPENDIX AND INDEXES

NCSS THEMATIC STRANDS

THIS APPENDIX CATEGORIZES THE RESOURCES for children found in Part II under the ten thematic strands defined by the National Council for the Social Studies in *Expectations of Excellence: Curriculum Standards for Social Studies* (1994). References are to entry numbers, not page numbers.

CIVIC IDEALS AND PRACTICES

Allen, Thomas B. *Remember Pearl Harbor*, 3

Almond, David. *The Fire-Eaters*, 141

Avi. *Don't You Know There's a War On?* 249

Ayer, Eleanor. *Parallel Journeys*, 208

Banks, Sara Harrell. *Abraham's Battle*, 72

Beller, Susan Provost. *To Hold This Ground*, 7

Besson, Jean-Louis. *October 45*, 8

Bolden, Tonya. *The Champ*, 277

Borden, Louise. *The Little Ships*, 75

Burchard, Peter. *Frederick Douglass*, 11

Cheney, Lynne. *When Washington Crossed the Delaware*, 13

The Civil War, 65, 69

Cooper, Michael L. *Fighting for Honor*, 16

Hell Fighters, 81

Remembering Manzanar, 254

Cox, Clinton. *Come All You Brave Soldiers*, 83

Crossley-Holland, Kevin. *At the Crossing Places*, 84

King of the Middle March, 85

The Seeing Stone, 86

Dear Miss Breed, 275

Deedy, Carmen Agra. *The Yellow Star*, 279

Demi. *Gandhi*, 280

Dolan, Edward F. *The Spanish-American War*, 22

Farmer, Nancy. *The Sea of Trolls*, 92

Fradin, Dennis Brindell. *Samuel Adams*, 23

Frank, Mitch. *Understanding September 11*, 319

Freedman, Russell. *Give Me Liberty! The Story of the Declaration of Independence*, 25

Lincoln, 26

Garland, Sherry. *A Line in the Sand*, 97

Hahn, Mary Downing. *Promises to the Dead*, 163

INDIVIDUALS, GROUPS, AND INSTITUTIONS

RESOURCES FOR CHILDREN: AUTHOR INDEX

THIS INDEX COVERS RESOURCES LISTED IN PART II. References are to entry numbers, not page numbers.

TITLE INDEX

SUBJECT INDEX

T HIS INDEX COVERS RESOURCES LISTED IN PART II.
The format follows the title in parentheses. References are to entry numbers, not page numbers.

Fisher, Leonard Everett. *Gandhi* [Book], 281

GEORGE III, KING OF GREAT BRITAIN, 1738–1820

Schanzer, Rosalyn. *George vs. George* [Book], 50

GREECE — CIVILIZATION — TO 146 B.C.

Califf, David J. *Marathon* [Book], 12

GUATEMALA

Mikaelsen, Ben. *Red Midnight* [Book], 180

HANUKKAH

Adler, David A. *One Yellow Daffodil* [Book], 206

HASTINGS, BATTLE OF

Denny, Norman, and Josephine Filmer-Sankey. *The Bayeux Tapestry* [Book], 20

HIROSHIMA (JAPAN) — BOMBARDMENT

Maruki, Toshi. *Hiroshima No Pika* [Book], 222

HISTORICAL REENACTMENTS

Lewin, Ted. *Red Legs* [Book], 35
Lyon, George Ella. *Here and Then* [Book], 36

HITLER, ADOLF, 1889–1945

French, Jackie. *Hitler's Daughter* [Book], 159
Giblin, James Cross. *The Life and Death of Adolf Hitler* [Book], 28

HMONG (ASIAN PEOPLE)

Shea, Pegi Deitz. *The Whispering Cloth* [Book], 193

HMONG AMERICANS

Tangled Threads [Book], 192

HOLOCAUST (JEWISH)

Adler, David A. *A Hero and the Holocaust* [Book], 203
Hiding from the Nazis [Book], 204
Hilde and Eli [Book], 205
One Yellow Daffodil [Book], 206
The Anne Frank Guide [Web site], 56
Anne Frank in the World [Book], 207
Ayer, Eleanor. *Parallel Journeys* [Book], 208
Bitton-Jackson, Livia. *I Have Lived a Thousand Years* [Book], 209
Chotjewitz, David. *Daniel Half Human and the Good Nazi* [Book], 210
The Devil's Arithmetic [DVD], 248
Frank, Anne. *The Diary of a Young Girl* [Book], 211
Greenfeld, Howard. *After the Holocaust* [Book], 162
The Hidden Children [Book], 212
Hesse, Karen. *The Cats in Krasinski Square* [Book], 213
Innocenti, Roberto, and Christophe Gallaz. *Rose Blanche* [Book], 214
Johnston, Tony. *The Harmonica* [Book], 215
Kushner, Tony. *Brundibar* [Book], 216
Lawton, Clive A. *Auschwitz* [Book], 217
Lobel, Anita. *No Pretty Pictures* [Book], 219
Lowry, Lois. *Number the Stars* [Book], 173
McCann, Michelle R. *Luba* [Book], 220
McDonough, Yona Zeldis. *Anne Frank* [Book], 221
Matas, Carol. *After the War* [Book], 177
In My Enemy's House [Book], 223
Mazer, Norma Fox. *Good Night, Maman* [Book], 224
Mochizuki, Ken. *Passage to Freedom* [Book], 225
Nieuwsma, Milton J. *Kinderlager* [Book], 227
Orlev, Uri. *Run, Boy, Run* [Book], 228
Paper Clips [DVD], 298
Perl, Lila, and Marion Blumenthal Lazan. *Four Perfect Pebbles* [Book], 229

RESOURCES FOR ADULTS: AUTHOR INDEX

THIS INDEX COVERS RESOURCES LISTED IN PART III. References are to entry numbers, not page numbers.

TITLE INDEX

THIS INDEX COVERS RESOURCES LISTED IN PART III. References are to entry numbers, not page numbers.

ABOUT THE AUTHOR

V IRGINIA A. WALTER is Professor and Chair, Department of Information Studies, Graduate School of Education and Information Studies, University of California, Los Angeles. She is also the author of a number of books on children's literature and services.